Neolithic Enclosures
in Atlantic Northwest Europe

Neolithic Studies Group Seminar Papers 6

Edited by
Timothy Darvill and Julian Thomas

Oxbow Books

Published by
Oxbow Books, Park End Place, Oxford OX1 1HN

ISBN 1 84217 045 7

This book is available direct from
Oxbow Books, Park End Place, Oxford OX1 1HN
(Phone: 01865-241249; Fax: 01865-794449)

and

The David Brown Book Company
PO Box 511, Oakville, CT06779
(Phone: 860-945-9329; Fax: 860-945-9468)

or

from our website
www.oxbowbooks.com

Cover: Reconstruction view of the screened entrance to Sarup I, Denmark.
(Drawing by Phil Marter, based on Neils Andersen *Sarup*)

Printed in Great Britain by
The Information Press
Eynsham, Oxford

This volume of papers is the sixth set of proceedings from a meeting of the Neolithic Studies Group to be published. Like its predecessors it reports the presentations made at a meeting of the Group, complemented by some additional material and reflections by the authors on their original submissions.

The Neolithic Studies Group is a loose-knit collectivity of archaeologists, mainly from Britain and the Atlantic seaboard countries of the European Union, with an interest in the Neolithic period. It was formed in the Spring of 1984, the first meeting being held in Cheltenham, Gloucestershire, UK. Since then, the Group has generally met twice a year: Spring and Autumn. The Autumn meetings are held in London and address a specific topical theme. Spring meetings are held outside London to examine at first hand the Neolithic remains of a defined area and consider recent research relevant to the region. Spring field meetings have included: western Ireland, southeast Scotland, eastern Scotland, north Wales, North Yorkshire and Humberside, Northumberland, Wessex, the Channel Islands, Sussex, Cambridge and Grimes Graves, Normandy, and the Isle of Man.

All the meetings depend for their success upon the efforts and enthusiasm of local organizers. The occasion of publishing this volume provides an appropriate opportunity to thank all those who have helped organize and host the Group's meetings over recent years.

Membership of the Neolithic Studies Group is open to anyone active in studying any aspect of the Neolithic period in Europe. The present membership list, which stands at about 250 individuals, includes: academic staff, researchers and students from universities and colleges in several European countries; museum curators and museum-based research and field staff; and field archaeologists from national and local government institutions, and from archaeological trusts and units. There is no application procedure or subscription to join the Group; members are simply those currently on the mailing list. Anyone can ask to be added to the mailing list at any time, the only rule of the Group is that names are deleted from the list if the individual concerned misses four meetings in a row (*i.e.* two years) and has not contacted the Group Co-ordinators asking to be kept on the list during that time.

Further information about the history of the Group, and details of forthcoming events and publications can be found on the Group's internet pages at:

http://csweb.bournemouth.ac.uk/consci/text/nsghome.htm

As already mentioned, the Group relies on its members to organize meetings so that this responsibility is shared round. There are two co-ordinators who look after the mailing list and finances, and who juggle offers to arrange meetings so that there is a fair spread of venues and themes.

We hope that you will find this volume of papers published by the Neolithic Studies Group useful, and we look forward to seeing you at one of our future meeting.

Timothy Darvill and Gordon Barclay
(Neolithic Studies Group Co-ordinators)

The following volumes are published by Oxbow Book of Oxford and, while stocks last, are available from: Oxbow Books, Park End Place, Oxford, OX1 1HN. Phone: +(0)1865 241249. Fax.: +(0)1865 794449

1   ***Neolithic Houses in Northwest Europe and Beyond***. Edited by Timothy Darvill and Julian Thomas. 1996. Oxbow Monograph 57

2   ***Neolithic Landscapes***. Edited by Peter Topping. 1997. Oxbow Monograph 86

3   ***Grooved Ware in Britain and Ireland***. Edited by Ann McSween and Ros Cleal. 1999

4   ***Pathways and Ceremonies. The Cursus Monuments of Britain and Ireland***. Edited by Alistair Barclay and Jan Harding. 1999

5   ***Plants in Neolithic Britain and beyond***. Edited by Andrew S Fairbairn. 2000

6   ***Neolithic Enclosures in Atlantic Northwest Europe***. Edited by Timothy Darvill and Julian Thomas. 2001

Contents

This volume of papers relating to Neolithic enclosures of various kinds in Atlantic northwest Europe represents the proceedings of a meeting of the Neolithic Studies Group held in the rooms of the Society of Antiquaries of London on 6th November 1998. The seminar had the same title as this book and was organized by the present editors. Not all of the fourteen papers presented on that occasion are included here because some have been, or are about to be, published in other places. In this connection special mention may be made of the proceedings of a complementary conference entitled "Neolithic Causewayed Enclosures in Europe" that was held in London on 23 October 1999 to provide a European context for an extensive survey and mapping programme of causewayed enclosures in England by the then Royal Commission on the Historical Monuments of England (now English Heritage). These proceedings, edited by Peter Topping, are being published separately.

The contributions from the Neolithic Studies Group Meeting included here incorporate relevant elements of the discussion on the day, and accordingly no attempt has been made to summarize the discussion separately. Three papers not given at the meeting have been introduced to provide a more wide-ranging review of the evidence.

We have arranged the papers in a rough geographical order. Our basic theme is the fact that recent work in many parts of the Atlantic coastlands and offshore islands has revealed a growing diversity of enclosures relating to all the main phases of the Neolithic, but especially the earlier Neolithic in each respective region. At one level these can be set alongside the more familiar causewayed enclosures, henges, and palisaded enclosures of various kinds in southeastern England, eastern France, Germany, and the Low Countries, and serve to extend known distributions. At another level the new discoveries illustrate a degree of diversity and variation in form, use, purpose, organization, and positioning that calls for a major re-think of this aspect of the European Neolithic.

In the first Chapter we address some of these implications by way of a general introduction to set the scene. The following chapters comprise a range of regional reviews and site-specific discussions broadly arranged to work from southwest to northeast; from Brittany and the seaboard of western France to Scandinavia.

The idea of Atlantic northwest Europe is liberally interpreted. What we mean by this rather general geographical region is that part of northwestern Europe that is directly or indirectly influenced by, and united through, the waters of the Atlantic Ocean and its connected seaways; in other words the coastlands, peninsulas, and large and small islands from Brittany in the south to Norway in the north. A perspective based on these western seaways has a long history in archaeological thought, and with reference to the Neolithic period provides an alternative and potentially powerful approach that contrasts with the more traditional land-based definitions of territories and regions.

We have also take a broad view of what represents an enclosure. Terms such as "causewayed enclosure", "interrupted ditch system", or "causewayed camp" are restrictive in their application or pejorative by their implicit interpretation. They are used in a number of chapters in this volume because they have a currency in the archaeological literature and represent familiar concepts, especially what many authors now refer to as the "classic" causewayed enclosure. It is now clear, however, that the whole idea of Neolithic enclosures needs re-thinking and a number of contributors take tentative steps towards beginning that process. Throughout the papers in this volume we take a Neolithic enclosure to be any substantial space that is wholly or partly defined and/or delimited in some way by constructions of some kind, typically ditches, banks, walls, or palisades. Elements of what we would today regard as natural topography or land-form may also be used in the definition of enclosure boundaries, for example rivers, streams, cliffs, and rock outcrops. What such features may have meant to Neolithic populations is of course a subject for investigation and interpretation. In general, the emphasis here is placed on earlier and middle Neolithic enclosures; structures such as henges, cursuses, enclosed cremation cemeteries, and other similar things are not discussed in detail although a number of authors refer to them and it is recognized that these too need to be brought into general discussions of the enclosure phenomenon, especially for the later Neolithic.

In preparing this volume for the printers it has been editorial policy to tamper as little as possible with the papers as presented. We have not tried to standardize terminology, nor to reconcile differences of interpretation or perspective between contributions.

The editors would like to thank the Society of Antiquaries of London, and in particular Dai Morgan Evans and Richard Mager for arranging use of the Society's rooms and for coping so courageously with what turned out to be a capacity audience. Thanks are also extended to various staff in the School of Conservation Sciences at Bournemouth University and the Department of Archaeology at Southampton University, in particular Louise Pearson, Miles Russell, Jeff Chartrand, and Eileen Wilkes for translating computer files from one format to another, tracking down references, and answering endless queries and questions.

Timothy Darvill and Julian Thomas
August 2000

List of Contributors

Gordon Barclay
Department of Environmental Science
University of Stirling
Stirling
FK9 4LA
Scotland
United Kingdom

John Barnatt
Archaeology Service
Peak District National Park
Aldern House
Baslow Road
Bakewell
Derbyshire
DE45 1AE
England
United Kingdom

Helmut Becker
Bayerisches Landesamt für
        Denkmalpflege
Hofgraben 4
Munich
Germany

Bill Bevan
Archaeology Service
Peak District National Park
Aldern House
Baslow Road
Bakewell
Derbyshire
DE45 1AE
England
United Kingdom

Steve Burrow
Curator of Early Prehistory
Department of Archaeology
        and Numismatics
National Museums and galleries of Wales
Cathays Park
Cardiff
CF10 3NP
Wales
United Kingdom

Timothy Darvill
Professor of Archaeology
School of Conservation Sciences
Bournemouth University
Fern Barrow
Poole
Dorset
BH12 5BB
England
United Kingdom

Toby Driver
Air Survey Officer
Royal Commission on the Ancient and
        Historical Monuments of Wales
Crown Building
Plas Crug
Aberystwyth
SY23 1NJ
Wales
United Kingdom

Mark Edmonds
Senior Lecturer in Archaeology
Department of prehistory and
        Archaeology
University of Sheffield
Northgate House
West Street
Sheffield
S1 4ET
England
United Kingdom

Alex Gibson
Lecturer in Archaeology
Department of Archaeological Sciences
University of Bradford
BD7 1DP
England
United Kingdom

Eoin Grogan
Director of the North Munster Project
The Discovery Programme
13–15 Lower Hatch Street
Dublin 2
Ireland

F M Griffith
County Archaeological Officer
Archaeology Group
Devon County Council
Matford Offices
County Hall
Topsham Road
Exeter
Devon
EX2 4QW
England
United Kingdom

Nigel Jones
Contracts Manager
Clwyd-Powys Archaeological Trust
20 High Street
Welshpool
Powys
SY21 7JP
Wales
United Kingdom

Barry Masterson
The Discovery Programme
13–15 Lower Hatch Street
Dublin 2
Ireland

R J Mercer
The Secretary
Royal Commission on the Ancient and
        Historical Monuments of Scotland
John Sinclair House
Bernard Terrace
Edinburgh
EH8 9NX
Scotland
United Kingdom

Keith Ray
County Archaeologist
Herefordshire Archaeology
Planning HQ
PO Box 3
Leominster
Herefordshire
HR6 8LU
England
United Kingdom

Chris Scarre
The McDonald Institute for
       Archaeological Research
University of Cambridge
Downing Street
Cambridge
Cambridgeshire
CB2 3ER
England
United Kingdom

Alison Sheridan
Department of Archaeology
National Museums of Scotland
Chambers Street
Edinburgh
EH1 1JF
Scotland
United Kingdom

David Thomas
Air Photo Mapping Officer
Royal Commission on the Ancient and
       Historical Monuments of Wales
Crown Building
Plas Crug
Aberystwyth
SY23 1NJ
Wales
United Kingdom.

Julian Thomas
Professor of Archaeology
Department of Archaeology
University of Manchester
Oxford Road
Manchester
M13 9PL
England
United Kingdom

I J N Thorpe
Lecturer in Archaeology
Department of Archaeology
School of Humanities and Social Sciences
King Alfred's College
Sparkford Road
Winchester
Hampshire
SO22 4NR
England
United Kingdom

Blaise Vyner
Archaeological Consultant
69 The Village
Hartburn
Stockton-on-Tees
Cleveland
TS18 5DY
England
United Kingdom

AARG	Aerial Archaeology Research Group
AMS	Accelerator Mass Spectrometry (for radiocarbon dating)
ASL	Above Sea Level
BC	calendar years Before Christ. Unless otherwise stated, specific radiocarbon dates cited in the text are expressed as age-spans at the *c.* 95% probability range (2σ), the laboratory determinations (RCYBP) having been calibrated using OxCal 3.5 (Bronk Ramsey 2000).
BP	calendar years Before Present (*i.e.* AD 1950)
CAU	Cornwall Archaeology Unit
CBA	Council for British Archaeology
CNRS	Centre National de la Recherche Scientifique
CPAT	Clwyd-Powys Archaeological Trust
CUCAP	Cambridge University Committee for Aerial Photography
DOENI	Department of the Environment Northern Ireland
EN	Early Neolithic
GGK	*Großgartach*
GIS	Geographical Information System
HMSO	Her Majesty's Stationery Office
MN	Middle Neolithic
MNI	Minimum Number of Individuals
NGR	National Grid Reference
NMGW	National Museums and Galleries of Wales
NMR	National Monuments Record
NPRN	National Primary Record Number
NS	New series
LBK	*Linearbandkeramic*
LN	Late Neolithic
OD	Ordnance Datum
PPJPB	Peak Park Joint Planning Board
PRN	Primary Record Number
RCAHMS	Royal Commission on the Ancient and Historical Monuments of Scotland
RCAHMW	Royal Commission on the Ancient and Historical Monuments of Wales
RCHME	Royal Commission on the Historical Monuments of England
RCYBP	Radiocarbon Years Before Present. These refer to uncalibrated radiocarbon determinations and are accompanied by the laboratory-determined standard deviation shown at 1σ.
SMR	Sites and Monuments Record
TRB	*Trichterbeckerkultur*
UCL	University College London
UIPPS	Union Internationale de Sciences Préhistoriques et Protohistoriques
UK	United Kingdom
USA	United States of America

Chapter 1

Neolithic enclosures in Atlantic northwest Europe: some recent trends

Timothy Darvill and Julian Thomas

INTRODUCTION

In January 1984 an international conference was held in Newcastle upon Tyne University on the theme of "Enclosures and defences in the Neolithic of western Europe". Subsequently published (Burgess *et al.* 1988), the papers resulting from the conference include general discussions about the nature of enclosure as a process and a phenomenon, reports about specific sites, and surveys of enclosures in particular regions including northeastern France, western France, southern Scandinavia, and Germany. Together, these papers allowed a timely reflection on the way enclosures were understood and studied across a broad compass. As a result, two trends developed in the way that Neolithic enclosures were perceived in the archaeological record.

First, it was becoming clear that Neolithic enclosures were an extremely widespread phenomenon across Europe. Second, in the words of the editors of the printed papers:

> "one of the most interesting aspects of the conference was to discover how repetitive certain features were throughout all the regions discussed. ... nowhere were these sites merely simple settlements; always there were ambiguities which made it difficult to pin down specific roles." (Burgess *et al.* 1988, iii)

Thus although the Newcastle enclosures conference represents a watershed in the study of these structures, much previous work in terms of trying to classify and categorize sites and their functions was called into question and in some cases demolished. At the very moment that something of the pan-European distribution of enclosures was recognized their inherent heterogeneity appeared too; just as with chambered tombs before them, one of the themes that potentially links together in space and time many of the communities occupying northern Europe between the sixth and third millennia BC also serves to divide them and emphasize the essentially local character and regional geographies of these early farming groups.

Since 1984 much has happened in terms of the way that enclosures are known about and understood. This introductory Chapter highlights some of the developments that seem to us especially relevant to the situation in northwestern Europe, and as such provides a broader context for the papers that follow. Paramount in this is the recognition that the overall distribution and variety of enclosures exceeds even the expectations expressed in 1984. This is particularly so in respect of the Atlantic fringe of Europe where recent work now shows that enclosures occur in considerable numbers right up to the edge of the continental land-mass and across the archipelago of smaller islands beyond. We conclude with some suggestions as to elements that might in future be incorporated into evolving research agendas for the Neolithic of northwest Europe.

FILLING UP THE MAP

Looking back at the closing decades of the 20th century it is possible to recognize two broadly parallel trends in the way in which archaeological research has elaborated our understandings of the distribution and nature of Neolithic enclosures in northern Europe. First is the enrichment of cores areas of enclosure distribution through the discovery of previously unrecorded sites and the investigation of recorded examples. Second is the expansion of the territory over which enclosures are known to have been built.

Alasdair Whittle's review of early Neolithic enclosures in northwest Europe (Whittle 1977) provides a useful starting point for reviewing these achievements. He identified a broad, if in places thinly populated, core area of early Neolithic enclosure building stretching from the Jura of southern France and the Black Forest of Germany along the major river valleys of the north European Plain and across into southern England. Within this broad spread of sites it was possible to detect four main areas with respectable distributions of enclosures of the Linear Pottery culture (LBK), Michelsberg, and Chasséen: the Rhine Valley and its tributaries between the Switzerland/German border through to the Netherlands; the upper Rhone valley of southern France; the Paris Basin of northern France; and southeastern England. In a wider Europe mention might also be made of the ditched enclosures on the Tavoliere plain of southeastern Italy (Jones 1987; Brown 1997), and the Los Millares culture walled enclosures in the Almería and Tagus regions of southeastern Spain and central-southern Portugal (Whittle 1996, 334–8 for summary) but these fall outside the area of immediate interest here.

Enriching established distribution patterns
Within the distribution of Neolithic enclosures in northwest Europe known by the mid 1970s, the group in southeastern England was amongst the largest and in many quarters perhaps the best known and most widely discussed (Smith 1966; 1971; Whittle 1977). Having been first recognized in the very early years of the 20th century, by 1976 some 43 certain and fairly certain interrupted ditch enclosures had been recorded (Palmer 1976, 184–6) all within an area to the south and east of a notional line drawn between the Severn Estuary and the Humber.[1]

Intensive aerial reconnaissance and the interpretation of earlier aerial photographs together played the single most significant role in documenting the nature and distribution of English sites, and continues to do so. Although it was the Cunnington's excavations at Knap Hill, Wiltshire, in 1908–9 (Cunnington 1912), and H G O Kendall's small-scale diggings at Windmill Hill, Wiltshire, in the early 1920s (Crawford 1960, 133) that represent the first formal recognition of what we now know as Neolithic enclosures, it was aerial photography that really established the class (Curwen 1930; Palmer 1976; Darvill 1996, 28–34). In 1924 Alexander Keiller observed Windmill Hill from the air and decided to buy it in order to save it from destruction. His extensive campaigns of excavations at the site in 1925–39, together with the various analyses of the finds at the time (Keiller 1932) and subsequently (Smith 1965; 1966; 1971) represent the engine that drove forward the interpretation of Neolithic enclosures, and has both prompted and mirrored changing thinking about the purpose and role of enclosures. More importantly, Windmill Hill set the archetype for the recognition of similar sites elsewhere in Britain. But Windmill Hill was not the only example considered by O G S Crawford and A Keiller during their sorties over Wessex in 1924 (Crawford and Keiller 1928), they also studied Hambledon Hill, Dorset, and photographed but did not report on Knap Hill, Wiltshire, and Rybury, Wiltshire.

The subsequent pattern of discovery of enclosure sites in England has been well documented through regular reviews (Piggott 1954, 18–32; Smith 1971; Wilson 1975; Palmer 1976). Aerial photography continued to play a major role in this work throughout the late 20th century, even in areas such as the midlands and Thames Valley where substantial distributions of sites had been well established (*cf.* Benson and Miles 1974; Barclay *et al.* 1996). Until recently, however, there have been two rather glaring gaps in the distribution of enclosures in England: Kent and the north Midlands of Leicestershire and Nottingham. Recent discoveries in both areas have fleshed out the picture. Two definite and two probable Neolithic enclosures are now known in Kent, Chalk Hill, Ramsgate (Shand 1998; Dyson *et al.* 2000, 470–1) and Kingsborough Farm, Eastchurch (Dyson *et al.* 2000, 471–2) have been fairly extensively excavated, while the possible sites at Burham and Tilmanstone have been identified through survey work (Dyson *et al.* 2000, 472). Meanwhile, in Leicestershire, geophysical surveys over a flint scatter at Husbands Bosworth in the south of the county identified an enclosure with two closely spaced concentric boundary ditches defining an area of about 1.5ha (Clay 1999).

What is perhaps especially significant about these recent finds that enrich the established general distribution by filling previously intractable gaps is the proportion brought to light through development-prompted excavation. The two certain sites in Kent were found during excavations for a road-scheme (Ramsgate) and a housing scheme (Kingsborough Farm), while at Husbands Bosworth in Leicestershire it was the potential for mineral extraction that prompted interest. The quality of evidence recovered in all cases is remarkable, and collectively these examples alone should put the lie to those sceptics who consider developer-prompted excavation strategies to be of little archaeological value. As archaeological curators develop greater familiarity with the use of planning-based approaches to the fulfilment of coherent research strategies we can confidently expect further such discoveries in future.[2]

Research-prompted work of course continues to play an important role, and in the midst of the Avebury World Heritage Site, one of the most studied landscapes in England, investigations aimed at identifying the route of the lost Beckhampton Avenue also revealed an oval ditched enclosure 140m by 100m pre-dating the Avenue and yet seemingly of later Neolithic date (Gillings *et al.* 2000). The form of this enclosure is superficially quite different from that of the more usual causewayed enclosures or interrupted ditch systems found in central southern England (the site is overlooked by Windmill Hill) and opens up yet another dimension: increasing site diversity (see below).

If the old adage that a site is not discovered until it is published holds true, then the period between 1984 and 2000 must also be seen as a significant one for the enrichment of distributional data through the publication of earlier investigations. Among the more important sites for which detailed reports are now available are: Briar Hill, Northamptonshire (Bamford 1985); Staines, Surrey (Robertson-MacKay 1987); the 1985–6 excavations at Maiden Castle (Sharples 1991); Combe Hill, Sussex (Drewett 1994); Crofton, Wiltshire (Lobb 1995); the 1991–93 excavations at Whitehawk, East Sussex (Russell and Rudling 1996); Etton, Cambridgeshire (Pryor 1998); and the 1988 excavations and re-evaluation of Windmill Hill, Wiltshire (Whittle *et al.* 1999). However, other substantial excavations at important sites still remain unpublished, notably Hambledon Hill, Dorset (expected in 2001), Crickley Hill, Gloucestershire, and Haddenham, Cambridgeshire.

Although the English enclosures are generally well known in the archaeological literature, important discoveries and very similar trends can be seen within other areas included in Whittle's general distribution of known enclosure sites. Andersen (1997, 133) conveniently summarizes the research history and the state of knowledge in the later 1990s for all these areas, and provides a valuable selection of plans and illustrations. Ahead of discoveries in England, Neolithic enclosures within the Rhine – Rhone – Saine corridor have been known through excavation since the later 19th century: Peu-Richard near Thénac, Charente-Maritime in France, for example, excavated in 1882 (see Joussaume 1986, 64); Michelsberg near Urmitz, Germany in 1884 (Lehner 1910, 6–7); Urmitz in Germany in 1898 (Lehner 1910, 8–14); Lengyel, Hungary, between 1888 and 1891 (Lehner 1910, 14–16); and Boitsfort, Belgium, in 1888 (Hubert 1971, 214–8). Building on this foundation, the number and range of Neolithic enclosures within the area has expanded considerably during the middle and later 20th century, again through the impact of aerial photography and development-prompted excavation and survey. In the Rhine valley through western Germany and eastern France more than 60 LBK enclosure sites have been recorded (Höckmann 1990) and a selection excavated (see Andersen 1997, 172–214 for summary). In Bavaria, three sites were recognized before 1970, 17 enclosures were identified between 1970 and 1980, but by the turn of the century some 3000 had been identified (Petrasch 1990). This is enrichment on a grand scale and much the same can be seen happening in the Paris Basin (Andersen 1997, 217–233). In many parts of the Rhine-Rhone-Saine new discoveries of Neolithic enclosures sites have served to link together some of the widely scattered population of sites known by the early 1970s so that now there are much broader and more or less continuous distributions along most of the major river systems.

Extending distributions

Filling out distributions is one thing, extending them significantly is another and represents the second major achievement of enclosure studies during the last quarter of the 20th century. Along the Atlantic fringe, the focus of this volume of papers, the hints of widely scattered sites that were beginning to emerge by 1988 are now clearly visible and it can confidently be asserted that the practices of building and using large enclosures of various sorts extends to the Atlantic façade of the continental land-mass and across many of the islands beyond.

As Scarre shows (Chapter 2), although there are early excursions into enclosure sites in Brittany and the Loire region recorded, it is only since the 1980s that the distribution and density of these sites from the Armorican massif to the Gironde has come to be recognized. More than 100 sites are now known and many more may be suspected.

Across the English Channel/la Manche the picture is more or less the same. As Roger Mercer shows (Chapter 3), clues as to the existence of Carn Brea, Cornwall, have been on the ground and sitting in museum stores since the 19th century, but it is only since his excavations in 1970–73 that the nature of the site has been properly recognized (Mercer 1981) and still more recently that comparable sites have been identified in the far southwest as at Helman Tor (Mercer 1986; forthcoming), and perhaps Trencrom Hill south of St Ives (Johnson and Rose 1994, 48). Elsewhere in the southwest peninsular a combination of aerial survey and ground survey has recognized other potential sites at Roughtor and Stowe's Pound on Bodmin Moor, Cornwall (Johnson and Rose 1994, 46–8), while aerial survey and development-prompted evaluation has contributed to a greater understanding of sites in Devon (Chapters 4 and 5).

Wales and the land west of the Severn has traditionally been a difficult area for recognizing Neolithic enclosures. Like Cornwall, however, there are clues to be found and as far back as 1983 two possible sites west of the Severn were proposed at Dinedor Hill, Herefordshire and Sharpstones, Shropshire on the basis of recorded finds and results from small-scale excavations (Darvill 1983, 190). What have long been regarded as unenclosed Neolithic settlements at Clegyr Boia, Pembrokeshire, (Williams 1953) and Fridd Faldwyn, Montgomery (O'Neil 1942) are now to be regarded as possible enclosures too (Chapter 6; Arnold 1987 respectively). Clearly, the possibility that other supposedly Iron Age sites, especially in the southwest of Wales, are Neolithic in origin now needs urgent attention. And new discoveries have been made in recent years as well. In the Vale of Glamorgan there are two probable sites (Chapter 7), the one at Norton looking very like the kind of monument that might be expected east of the Severn (and see Driver 1997a; 1997b), while, if provisional interpretations prove correct, the example at Corntown yet again serves to expand the range of enclosure forms. Other possible sites at Ewenny in the same region have tentatively been proposed by Graves-Brown (1998). On Anglesey excavations at Bryn Celli Wen, east of the henge and developed passage grave of Bryn Celli Ddu, revealed a segmented ditch, showing typical evidence of recutting and refilling (Edmonds and Thomas 1990; Chapter 10). The potential complexity of what might be expected in Wales is perhaps best illustrated by the discoveries made in the Walton Basin on the Powys/Herefordshire border (Gibson 1999) where two large palisaded enclosures are associated with two cursus monuments, a mound, hengi-form monument, and about 40 round barrows and ring-ditches. The Hindwell Enclosure, roughly oval in plan, covering about 34ha, has a palisaded boundary involving posts set in a continuous slot as at Greyhound Yard, Dorchester, Dorset (Chapter 8; and see Gibson 1998 for general discussion of the class). It dates to the mid third millennium BC. The Walton Enclosure, about 1km to the south-southwest is also oval in plan, covers an estimated 7.6ha, and has a palisaded boundary comprising separate uprights. It is probably early third millennium BC in date and comparable to examples at Meldon Bridge, Peebleshire, and Forteviot, Perthshire.

New discoveries of previously unsuspected Neolithic enclosures have become frequent in central and northern England too. At Gardom's Edge, Derbyshire, the discovery of an enclosure high on the Eastern Moors associated with rock art and other structures (Chapter 9) shows that, contrary to conventional wisdom, some upland areas were well used in the early and middle Neolithic. Mention may also be made of the substantial, although strictly undated, enclosure partly overlain by the massive stone circle at Long Meg and Her Daughters (Soffe and Clare 1988). This is another site discovered by aerial photography, although here in quite a different environment to that usually found in southern England. It again raises the question of whether other enclosures in the region may be of Neolithic origin. The site at Long Meg, which is 220m by 190m in extent, can only be assigned to the period because the stone circle effectively seals the ditch of the earlier enclosure in a manner highly reminiscent of the arrangements found at the Beckhampton Avenue near Avebury, Wiltshire, referred to above. Across the country in the east Riding of Yorkshire, the interrupted ditch encircling the great round barrow of Duggleby Howe provides another example of a potentially Neolithic enclosure recently discovered in association with a familiar monument that has been known for centuries (Kinnes *et al.* 1983; Stoertz 1997, 30–2). Elsewhere in northern England a small D-shaped enclosure near the coast at Plasketlands, Cumbria, is dated to the mid fourth millennium BC. It was identified from aerial photographs and then sampled by excavation (Bewley 1993). Other possible sites are known at Carrock Fell, Cumbria (Collingwood 1938; Edmonds 1999, 84), and Harehaugh, Northumbria (Waddington 1998).

Scotland, like Wales, contains a number of sites which have at one time or another been suggested as possible early or middle Neolithic enclosures, but, as Barclay explains (Chapter 11), the cases for most sites remain unproven no matter how tantalizing the evidence looks. Excavations at Meldon Bridge, Peeblesshire (Burgess 1976) and Dunragit, Galloway (RCAHMS 1993, 10; Thomas 1999a; 2000a) have demonstrated the existence of a later Neolithic enclosure tradition in Scotland other than henges. At Dunragit at least there are hints of an origin for these structures early in the third millennium BC.

Westwards, the Isle of Man has recently begun to reveal the presence of Neolithic enclosures on a scale comparable with many in southern Britain (Darvill 2000; Chapter 12), a phenomenon that might be explained by the geographical position of the Island at a pivotal node in the western seaways. Ireland too is beginning to reveal a tradition of Neolithic enclosures, especially in the north of the Island (Chapter 13; Cooney 2000, 14–17). Lyles Hill, County Antrim, was the first to be suggested (Evans 1953) and has more recently been the subject of further investigations (Gibson and Simpson 1987; Simpson and Gibson 1989). The single earthwork defining an area about 380m by 210m (*c.* 6.2ha) is now known to be of post-Neolithic date, but a pair of broadly concentric stone-packed palisade slots show that the hilltop was enclosed in the third millennium BC. By contrast, Donegore Hill, County Antrim, encloses an area about 150m in diameter within three rings of broadly concentric boundaries resembling the causewayed enclosures of England (Mallory and Hartwell 1984; Mallory 1993). Palisaded enclosures are known in eastern Ireland at Knowth, County Meath (Eogan 1984) and Tara (Newman 1997). In the west, exciting new discoveries at Knocknarea suggest that hilltop enclosures associated with large passage graves exist here too (Bergh 2000), again perhaps just the first traces of a tradition that will prove widespread along the west coast of Ireland.

While these Irish enclosures currently represent the most westerly Neolithic enclosures in northwest Europe, the Danish examples are the most northerly. Sarup was the first to be recognized for what it was, in 1972, since when more than a dozen examples have been identified both through new investigations and the reinterpretation of earlier work (Chapter 14). Whether examples remain to be discovered still further north along the Atlantic fringe of Sweden or Norway only time will tell.

Although outside the scope of the papers included here, it may be noted that the distribution of known Neolithic enclosures has gradually been expanding eastwards from the Rhine-Rhone-Saine corridor too, especially into central and eastern Europe. In large measure this is again attributable to results from aerial photography, and with the opening up of eastern Europe in particular the possibility of carrying out archaeological aerial reconnaissance and, for the first time, having access to the accumulated wealth of information on existing aerial photographs (Behrens 1981; Gojda 1997). Andersen again provides a usefully summary of available work in the Balkans, Romania, and the lower Danube through to the River Bug, the western Ukraine, Caucasus, Carpathian Basin, Slovakia, Czech Republic, and Poland (1997, 146–172). There is certainly much more to be found in these regions. How far into the forest zone of eastern Europe Neolithic enclosures will be found remains an open question and a potentially important theme for future research.

The big picture

As a result of work both to enrich established distributions and expand the known spread of enclosure sites a new map of fifth to third millennia BC enclosures can be built up (Figure 1.1). It is very different from that published in 1977 by Alsadair Whittle (*cf.* Whittle 1977, fig 1) and more than anything else serves to emphasize the huge amount of research carried out and published right across Europe over the last three decades or so. The overall spread can now be seen as ranging across most of the lower-lying plains and river systems from the Black Sea in the east to Portugal in the west, and from Scilly in the south to Scotland in the north. Beyond this spread are occasional outliers in the Caucasus and Dnieper Valley, prompting the speculation that these regions too will one day be drawn into the distribution as research proceeds.

Developing the big picture has, however, involved a number of fundamental shifts in archaeological thinking. At a simple level this has meant increasing the physical scale at which archaeological materials are viewed. Small holes and limited surveys do not usually find large enclosures unless the investigator is very lucky. Extensive geophysical survey, aerial photography, large-scale field-survey, extensive field evaluation, widespread test-pitting, and massive open-area excavation are the techniques that have allowed the majority of Neolithic enclosures to be discovered, mapped, and investigated. In a sense, the map of Neolithic enclosures remains a map of the distribution of such techniques routinely applied.

A more significant shift in thinking that has accompanied, perhaps even allowed, the expansion of horizons has been the abandonment of type-site categories and the expectation that well-known sites will provide the blue-print to finding other contemporary examples. Nowhere is this more painfully evident than in the extreme northwest of Europe, especially in the British Isles. The idea that "classic" sites such as Windmill Hill, Wiltshire, will be found in other parts of the British Isles has, it can be argued, blinkered approaches

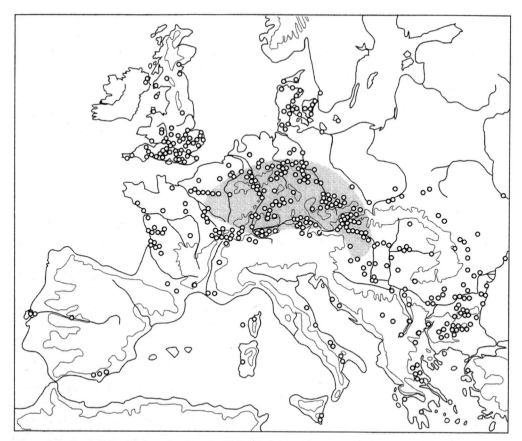

Figure 1.1: General distribution of early and middle Neolithic enclosures in north-west Europe (after Andersen 1997 with additions)

to the remains out in the field. And while it is certainly true that the distribution of classic sites is far wider than once imagined, it is also the case that much greater variety must now be recognized. It is not only a matter of expectation, but also issues of visibility and scale. It is now clear that most of the Neolithic enclosures in the north and west of Britain are small compared with most contemporary sites in southeastern England. The enclosure boundaries are not necessarily complete circuits; cliffs and natural rock outcrops may also form part of the circuit. Once such adjustments in thinking are taken into account, the potential for identifying sites increases dramatically.

Alongside our expectations of site morphology must be placed our assumptions regarding the place that enclosures might occupy in site hierarchies. It has been conventional to see Neolithic enclosures as "central places", associated with the activities of a large community, while barrows and chambered tombs are to be connected with a smaller and subordinate grouping (Renfrew 1973; Barker and Webley 1978). However, it is increasingly clear that enclosures can be more densely distributed than this model would predict. In the upper reaches of the Thames valley, for instance, a dense cluster of interrupted-ditched enclosures has been identified (Barclay *et al.* 1996).

The abandonment of fixed notions of typology and the translation of type-site principles to the field-study of sites also allows presumptions about the date of monuments based on morphology to be broken down. As later papers show, a number of sites in the west of Britain were assumed to be Iron Age on the basis of morphology but are now known to be Neolithic. Even within the Neolithic, however, there are patterns and sequences of changing traditions over time both at the grand scale of the European distribution as a whole and the events and actions represented at individual sites.

NARRATIVES AND BIOGRAPHIES

On the grand scale, the chronological development of enclosures in Europe is moderately well understood, with a general drift progressively northwestwards from the earliest examples at around 5500 BC in the lower Danube and Carpathian Basin through to about 3800 BC in the British Isles (well illustrated in a series of maps in Andersen 1997, fig 289). The culture-history of this process was summarized by Whittle (1977, 329) and more recently elaborated by Andersen (1997, 133–300). The earliest examples can be attributed to the LBK cultures, perpetuated by Lengyel culture communities, and continued in the Rhineland by the Großgartach and Rössen culture groups. Enclosures were proliferated by Michelsberg, Chasséen, and most other post-Rössen culture groups on the north European plain. But these general patterns mask much local detail, and for some parts of Europe, the Atlantic fringe in particular, it may be inappropriate to think in terms of what are essentially diffusionist models or transmission processes. Already there are hints from marker dates taken through the sequence of monument building at Billown, Isle of Man, that here some of the early structures may relate to the mid fifth millennium BC, a full thousand years before most of the enclosures so far dated in southern England get going (Chapter 12). A more complete picture must await the results of a detailed dating programme, but there is a tantalizing scatter of early dates for traditionally Neolithic activities around the Irish Sea (*cf.* Monk 1993) and these may presage a rethinking of models of social process in the area.

Local sequences and the narratives offered by groups of sites are important as indicators of the actions and events behind the formal remains that archaeologists uncover and describe. Richard Bradley (1996; 1998a, 200) has argued that the roles of enclosures were transformed from one area and cultural context to the next and that while the form of enclosures was dictated by traditional norms, the activities that took place within them were less stable.

Where large-scale excavations have been undertaken at enclosure sites there is usually evidence for pre-enclosure features and structures of various sorts. This is well-known in southern England, where, to return to the archetype site at Windmill Hill, for example, some kind of post-built structure, pits, and a grave all pre-date the construction of the monument (Whittle *et al.* 1999, 350–353). Further west, at Crickley Hill, Gloucestershire, there were again post-built structures (three investigated), groups of postholes, pits, and a small oval mound sealed by the earliest enclosure ditches (Dixon 1988, 78). At Billown, Isle of Man, the enclosures are pre-dated by pits and shafts that on present evidence show an uninterrupted sequence from the early fifth millennium BC. Similar structures continue to be made and used after the enclosures are built (Chapter 12). Three pits dating to the Maglemose Culture were found on the southeastern slope of the site occupied by the Sarup enclosures, Denmark, but seemingly little of the intervening Ertebølle culture that might connect these with the communities responsible for building the enclosures around 3800 BC (Andersen 1997, 23).

Closely associated with the narratives that individual sites and groups of sites within a region might tell, are the biographies of those sites and the highly individualized patterns and arrangements that they represent. General disenchantment with the available and commonly used terminology such as "causewayed camp", "causewayed enclosure", "interrupted ditch system" and so on has frequently been voiced (Palmer 1976; Whittle 1977, 329; Evans 1988, 14; Edmonds 1993) not so much because of the language itself and its appropriateness to specific cases but because of the categories and classifications that the terms are trying to reflect. Certainly it is true that particular sites share traits of construction and use with other sites, but the body of archaeological data that can be considered as Neolithic enclosures is extraordinarily heterogeneous. As we have already emphasized, the concern for classification and tight definition in the past has probably had the effect of restricting research in northern and western parts of the British Isles at least, and probably in many other parts of Europe too. In western Europe, the techniques have been available, but the will to use them has been lacking; the opposite seems to apply to eastern Europe where advances are being made as the opportunities for aerial reconnaissance and development-prompted excavation become practical realities.

Leaving aside what may be considered the archetypal "causewayed" Neolithic enclosure so typical of southeastern England, and known in lesser numbers across western Britain and through into western France (Joussaume 1988; Chapter 2) and Scandinavia (Madsen 1988; Chapter 14), attention may be drawn to half a dozen or so other kinds of enclosure all of which are generally large and mainly of early to middle Neolithic date.

Perhaps most numerous are what might pragmatically be described as the "non-causewayed" enclosures. These are generally only known where they have a stratigraphic relationship with reasonably well-dated structures or where they have been excavated. Their distribution is extremely widespread. Bury Hill, West Sussex (Bedwin 1981), showed clearly that such enclosures existed within well-established groups of classic causewayed enclosures. The recently discovered Beckhampton enclosure, Wiltshire, appears to show the same situation for the very heartland of the causewayed enclosure distribution. Crickley Hill, Gloucestershire, (Dixon 1988) demonstrated a stratigraphic sequence in which an enclosure with a non-causewayed ditch succeeded a fairly conventional causewayed structure. In the north and west of Britain, sites such as Corntown, Glamorgan (Chapter 7) and Plasketlands, Cumbria (Bewley 1993) illustrate something of the spread. Such enclosures are not easily distinguishable from similarly shaped and positioned examples of later date when revealed by aerial photographs or surface survey. Yet simple ditched enclosures probably represent the single biggest group of major recorded archaeological features in northwest Europe. A study of 3000 square kilometres of the central Welsh Marches revealed 449 crop-mark enclosures of various kinds but only ten of these had been subject to any kind of investigation and only one to extensive excavation (Whimster 1989, 35). If, nationwide, even a small percentage of known examples turned out to be

Neolithic the scale of the enclosure distribution for the period would increase by several orders of magnitude. In some cases the evidence is probably already extant to link artefact scatters with spatially coincident crop-mark or surface-relief enclosures. Roger Mercer notes for example that:

> "hints of Neolithic presence on hilltop locations are common in the South West [of England] but later and recurring occupation on these sites has rendered the information retrieved of low value, and often little appreciated as the evidence has only marginal significance within the research designs of the projects leading to their recovery." (Mercer 1981, 189)

He goes on to list nearly a dozen sites including: South Cadbury, Somerset, where the possible corner of an enclosure was found, Cadbury-Congresbury, Somerset, Milverton, Somerset, and Ham Hill, Somerset, to which might be added many others including Uleybury, Gloucestershire (Saville and Ellison 1983, 1), Dinedor Hill, Herefordshire, and Sharpstones Hill, Shropshire (Darvill 1983, 190). All have yielded substantial assemblages of Neolithic material culture either from excavations too small to stand much hope of locating enclosure boundaries, or from sites where non-causewayed boundaries have been found but generally assigned a later date on topological grounds.

Somewhere between the enclosures with causewayed ditches and those with uninterrupted ditches is a small but important group of circular sites with very regular circular boundary earthworks and partially segmented ditches. Sometimes considered as enclosed cemeteries within the broad tradition of Neolithic ring-ditches (Kinnes 1979, 67), their size (generally over 80m across), construction, and associations suggests that they should be seen as part of the emergent range of middle to late Neolithic enclosures. The two most well-known examples are in Wessex: Stonehenge I, Wiltshire, dated to the very beginning of the third millennium BC (Cleal *et al.* 1995, 63–114); and Flagstones, Dorset, tentatively dated to the same general period (Woodward 1988). Both are defined regular circular ditches, 110m and 100m in diameter respectively, with internal banks. Flagstones had rock art applied to the ditch walls in a way that raises questions as to whether Stonehenge did as well given the decoration applied to selected stones there in later phases (Cleal *et al.* 1995, 30–3). It is these sites, and no doubt others that await discovery or recognition, that perhaps provide the oft discussed but rarely substantiated link between the early and middle Neolithic enclosures and the later Neolithic henges (Smith 1966; Harding and Lee 1987, 58–9).

Timber stockaded or palisaded enclosures with post-built boundaries are also relatively new additions the range of structures recorded. Meldon Bridge, Peebleshire, opened up the possibilities here in the early 1970s (Burgess 1976), and since that time nearly a dozen examples have been identified through aerial photography and, in the case of the Dorchester, Dorset, example, the cumulative results of several relatively small but nonetheless important pieces of development-prompted excavation. An initial review of examples in England (Darvill 1989) has now been superseded by a more wide-ranging review for the British Isles as a whole (Gibson 1998). This recognizes three main styles which show some evidence to suggest a progressive chronological development headed by post-defined sites with widely spaced uprights (*e.g.* Walton, Radnorshire; Dunragit, Galloway, and Newgrange, Co. Meath) of the late fourth and early-mid third millennium

BC. Post-defined sites with close-set posts (*e.g.* Hindwell, Radnorshire; Dorchester, Dorset) are dated to the mid third millennium BC. And continuous palisaded sites (*e.g.* Mount Pleasant, Dorset; West Kennet 1 and 2, Wiltshire; and Knowth, Co. Meath) date to the mid-late third and early second millennium BC (Gibson 1998). The essentially northern and western distribution of these palisaded enclosures is especially notable, with the examples at Newgrange and Knowth, Co. Meath, Ireland (Sweetman 1987; Eogan 1984, 219), showing the need to look widely along the Atlantic coastlands for further discoveries. At Dunragit, Galloway, excavations in summer 2000 demonstrated that the post-defined enclosure had three distinct phases of construction (Thomas 2000a). The two latest of these are securely associated with Grooved Ware and coarse Beaker pottery respectively, whilst the only pottery recovered from the first phase appears to be Impressed Ware. This could suggest a span of dates across the early-to-mid third millennium BC. Much of the enclosure remains to be investigated, but it presently seems possible that each phase of construction consisted of two concentric rings of uprights. In the earliest phase at least, the inner ring was made up of free-standing timbers, while the large posts of the outer ring were interspersed with smaller uprights, creating a more continuous boundary (see Chapter 10).

Stone walled enclosures must now also be seen as an established part of the picture. Carn Brea, Cornwall, led the way in showing how such enclosures may have been constructed and what they were like (Mercer 1981). Other examples are now known in Cornwall, and there are good grounds for thinking that at least some of the smaller so-called hillforts in Wales might also be Neolithic in origin. Clegyr Boia, Pembrokeshire, provides one possible model (Chapter 6). For central and northern England the enclosure at Gardom's Edge, Derbyshire, provides clear evidence of what might be expected elsewhere in this region. As with the simple ditched enclosures discussed above, it may be noted that the number of small (and not so small) stone walled enclosures recorded in the west of Britain is very considerable. Not all are Neolithic, but again, if a small percentage are then the picture of Neolithic settlement patterns changes drastically. As an example, Hogg (1972) shows about 500 small "hillforts" under about 2ha in extent in Wales and the Welsh Marches, broadly clustered into eleven spatial groups. Many of these coincide with distributions of chambered tombs (*cf.* Daniel 1950, fig 2) and focus around areas in which Neolithic enclosures are already known or strongly suspected.

That not all Neolithic enclosures were completely enclosed is another dimension of variability that deserves attention and has a major influence on recognition rates. The late Neolithic enclosure at Broome Heath, Norfolk, has long been recognized as having a D-shaped form with an open side to the east (Wainwright 1972). The outer ditches at Combe Hill, East Sussex, were probably not complete circuits (Drewett 1994) as they seem to end on a steep escarpment slope. Likewise at Gardom's Edge, Derbyshire, the enclosure wall forms only part of a circuit that defines an area whose other edges are delimited (at least to the modern eye) by a precipitous slope (Ainsworth and Barnatt 1998). Elsewhere, rivers and natural outcrops of rock form what might be regarded as the enclosure boundary. The great henge monument at Marden in Wiltshire has a southern boundary formed by the River Avon (Wainwright 1971,181), while the large enclosure at Waulud's Bank, near Leagrave in Bedfordshire is D-shaped, with its western side constituted by the River Lea (Dyer 1964; Wainwright 1979, 235–6). While this latter site has generally been discussed in the context of the henge tradition, it may be that it has a rather earlier origin (C Richards and I J Thorpe pers. comm.). Similar patterns involving the incorporation of topographic features into enclosures, particularly Michelsberg sites (see Andersen 1997, fig 223), those in western France (Chapter 2), and Scandinavian examples (Andersen 1997, fig 284; Chapter 14). Whether, in this light, such structures should properly be called "enclosures" at all is a moot point and perhaps deserves further consideration. Richards (1996) has recently suggested that the ditches and banks of henge monuments may refer to, or represent, aspects of the local landscape, notably hills and watercourses. Some late Neolithic enclosures may symbolically represent wider worlds in microcosm (Darvill 1997, 181). This being the case, the polarity between culturally-constructed boundaries and "natural" features may not have been absolute in the Neolithic.

Yet another variation which follows on from the definition of partial enclosures may be represented by cross-ridge dykes. Vyner (1994) has argued that for the Cleveland Hills of northeast England such earthworks serve to define and enclose promontories and areas of upland plateaux that often contain burial mounds of various kinds. In some cases, for example Horness Rigg, the boundary appears to be causewayed in form, and overall Vyner argues for a late/final Neolithic or early Bronze Age date for these structures, while hinting that some might be earlier. Indeed, the apparent poverty of early and middle Neolithic enclosures of familiar form in the region might be explained if their roles prove to have been taken by cross-ridge dykes and the land they define. It may also be remembered that cross-ridge dykes are by no means confined to the northeast of England. More than a dozen are known on the Cotswolds, for example, and while some might be later Bronze Age or Iron Age in date (Darvill 1987, 121 and 127) and relate to the hilltop enclosures in the area, a number, for example at Randwick, Gloucestershire, do cut off promontories containing substantial middle Neolithic burial monuments. Much the same applies in Dorset where 26 are recorded in the central part of the county (RCHME 1970, xl) and a further 17 in the north (RCHME 1972, xxvii). At Hambledon Hill the cross-dykes are demonstrably of Neolithic date and are intimately associated with enclosures and boundaries more immediately recognizable from surface evidence as Neolithic structures (Mercer 1980; 1988, 98).

We are not here trying to set out a new typology of Neolithic enclosures for such a task would, given the current state of knowledge, be futile and anyway of doubtful value except as an *aide-mémoire* to those sifting through surveys and accounts of archaeological materials. The point here is that, throughout northwest Europe, Neolithic enclosures are a major element of the archaeology of the period, but that they are extremely diverse in their archaeological manifestation. Such diversity may also be argued to relate to the range of actions and events that took place at and around these sites.

ENCLOSURES, PEOPLE, AND NATURE

The idea that all Neolithic enclosures had a similar role or function within the societies that created and used them is as laughable as the idea that some kind of universal classification can be applied to all sites. Even a cursory examination of the material culture revealed at excavated sites in the British Isles, taking into account differences in preservation, survival, and recovery, shows tremendous diversity in terms of the nature, range, and quantity of different kinds of materials and objects represented. Where adjacent enclosures within a single complex have been investigated, as at Hambledon Hill, Dorset, there is immense scope for exploring such variability. Interim conclusions relating to the Hambledon Hill landscape suggest differences, for example, between the use of the Main Enclosure and the Stepleton Enclosure (Mercer 1988). At a wider scale differences can also be seen between sites in relation to cattle husbandry (Legge 1981). Context is important here, not just archaeological context, but also social context in terms of the action sets represented and the ways in which architecture and structure mediate action and events.

At a superficial level there is the likelihood, still to be demonstrated however, that there are regional differences to the way that enclosures were used. The recurrence of large projectile point components in the lithic assemblages of some enclosures in the southwest of England together with evidence of warfare at these sites (see Mercer 1989a and 1989b for review) may suggest that in this region enclosures had a special role. Indeed, at some stages in their histories (if not continuously) they may have constituted important residential locations. That need not imply, of course, that broadly similar enclosures in, say, the east midlands held the same place in the lives of their local communities (*cf*. Pryor 1998). If the constructional devices that made up the enclosure traditions were used to provide a spatial context for social action, that activity would often have had the effect of transforming the organization and significance of each individual site. Each enclosure was the product of a particular group (or set of groups) of people, who used established methods to create a structure for their own purposes. In subsequently using the enclosure for significant social transactions, people would have transformed both the monument and their own social relationships.

Despite this, enclosures should not be viewed in isolation. Well established in the archaeological literature, the category of enclosure remains useful up to a point but they must be seen in the context of much broader sets of relationships, not only with activities at other places but also in terms of their place in the natural world. Stuart Piggott rather perceptively began to explore this line of thinking when discussing the evidence from the West Kennet long barrow (Piggott 1962, 68). Following suggestions from Isobel Smith, the link was made between the body parts represented in the tomb and those present at the Windmill Hill enclosure. This has, of course been developed since (*e.g.* Edmonds 1993, 116–8; 1999; Thomas 2000b), and a close relationship between enclosures and tombs is generally accepted. Indeed here it is interesting to note that most recorded enclosures have a long barrow or chambered tomb within 1–2km, often intervisible, and thus to pose the question that naturally follows: whether all recorded long barrows and chambered tombs should have an associated enclosure. If that is the case then there are a lot more enclosures out there to find!

It is now possible to go beyond the simple recognition of connections between tombs and enclosures. Patterns in the treatment of artefacts and body parts, and sequences of access and reuse need to be explored too. The connection between different classes might actually have taken a number of different forms. For instance, Thorpe (1984) suggested that the bodies represented at enclosure sites in Wessex contained a higher proportion of females and children, while the skeletal assemblages from earthen long barrows were often dominated by the remains of males. This could be taken to suggest that some form of selection had taken place, with bodies or body-parts being abstracted from enclosures prior to being deposited in barrows and chambered tombs. But alternatively, it is possible to imagine a more generalized pattern in the **circulation** of human remains, within which enclosures, tombs, and other kinds of sites represented the locations for significant transactions (Thomas 2000b). This would help to explain why human (and indeed animal) bones had often been curated for considerable periods of time before their final deposition. Under these circumstances the presence of bones in a particular location might have been considerably less important than the cycle of movement between places in which they had been involved. The same applies, of course, to artefacts. The circulation of goods as gifts, and the alliances, affinities, and debts that they engender is often as important as their ownership in pre-modern societies (Sahlins 1974). These considerations would encourage us to think of enclosures less as "containers" within which restricted items were concentrated, and more as significant foci through which multiple circuits of movement and exchange passed. While these may seem to be somewhat abstract arguments, it is important to point out that they are not beyond the scope of what might be definitively demonstrated using the existing evidence.

Patterns of structured relationship between persons and social groups could arguably be extrapolated from the physical relations of structure and form in the enclosures and tombs. One possibility is that while the tombs may be allegorically structured to reflect familial and gender order of the kind that might elsewhere be found in the organization of a house or tent, enclosures may be arranged at a quite different level to reflect power, status, and organizational structuring at a community scale. Indeed, Bradley (1998b, 68– 82) has argued that the origin of Neolithic enclosures in Europe lay in the abstraction and monumentalization of aspects of the village settlement, while tombs elaborated on the theme of the house.

We still know perilously little about Neolithic belief systems and the concomitant cosmological/ideological ordering and structuring of actions and material culture. However, it is reasonable to suppose that sets of relations with the natural world were embedded in beliefs and that these will find expression through patterns of material culture and the structuration of action. The place of the natural world in the construction and use of enclosures has only recently begun to come to the fore (*e.g.* Tilley 1996; Bradley 1998c; 2000) and remains an important field for further research. We have already argued that topographical features may have been understood as being an integral part of some enclosures, and it is now widely recognized that elements of the natural world, for example rivers, escarpments, cliffs, and outcrops of living bedrock are incorporated in the lay-out and construction of enclosure boundary systems. Examples include Carn Brea, Cornwall (Mercer 1981), Gardom's Edge, Derbyshire (Ainsworth and Barnatt 1998), and Stowe's Pound and Roughtor, Bodmin Moor, Cornwall (Johnson and Rose 1994, 46–8). Natural features may also be related to events inside enclosures, and perhaps provided the reason for blocks of land being defined as they are in the first place. It may be that particular rocks and watercourses were perceived as being inherently powerful or auspicious, and that this power was appropriated through the act of enclosure (*cf.* Mulk 1994). At Eastleach, Gloucestershire, a spring rises within the enclosure to feed a small stream that flows directly into the River Leach, a major north-bank tributary of the Thames (Darvill and

Locke 1988, 196–8). Similarly at Crofton, Wiltshire, the River Dunn originally flowed
more or less through the middle of the enclosure from its source nearby (Lobb 1995, 18).
At Stowe's Pound, Bodmin Moor, Cornwall, a massive granite tor known as The
Cheesewring stands closeby the enclosure within its own bounded space (Johnson and
Rose 1994, 46 and fig 6; and see Tilley 1996, 167). Some low-lying enclosures, like Etton
(Pryor 1998) may actually have been seasonally inundated, and such happening would at
once have connected the monument with powerful elemental forces and tied it in to the
seasonal cycles of the cosmos. At Billown, Isle of Man, it is possible that natural collapse
structures in the underlying limestone caused surface depressions that were a source of
interest to those who first dug pits and shafts here and who later built the enclosures
nearby (Darvill 2000, 68; Chapter 12). Similar possibilities have been explored for the
development of later Neolithic ceremonial monuments around a collapse feature next to
the Dorset Cursus at Down Farm, Dorset (Allen and Green 1998). In a few cases it may
be the hill itself which is of sufficient significance to warrant the construction of an
enclosure or the definition, through the process of enclosure, of a special place. The very
elaboration of a place through the construction of an enclosure would, of course have
fundamentally changed its character.

It is worth remembering that the construction of enclosures involved the opening up
of the earth, through the digging of ditches or postholes. This could itself be understood
as an interaction with significant materials and substances: earth, chalk, clay, sand, wood,
and stone (Thomas 1999b). Rather than simply deploying a series of constructional
techniques, the building of enclosures can be understood as a means by which the elements
of the material world (and their symbolic significance) were mobilized and incorporated
into human projects. Conversely, the deposition of artefacts (principally pottery and stone
tools) and the bones of humans and animals within ditch deposits or inside postholes can
be seen as incorporating a human presence, or even the events of human life-histories into
a significant location.   * Here

In future, excavations at enclosure sites need to pay special attention to the recognition
of archaeological traces of natural features that might have had special significance, for
example the position of ancient trees, boulders, standing stones, "totem poles", and so on.
The wider physical context is important too. It has long been recognized that some of the
Sussex enclosures were constructed within a wooded environment (Thomas 1982), while
at Maiden Castle there was small-scale clearance associated with the building of the
enclosure (Evans *et al.* 1988, 79). Other enclosures, for example Windmill Hill, Wiltshire,
stood in more open environments (Fishpool in Whittle *et al.* 1999, 131). How this relates
to the patterns of deposition and use of material culture has yet to be explored, but is
potentially a critical dimension of the relationships between people and their world.

CONCLUSION

The enrichment of existing distributions of known enclosure sites and the expansion of
these distributions into new territories is opening up many new and fruitful lines of
inquiry, some of which have been touched on here. Fundamental is the need to get to grips
with the overall distribution patterns, if only at a crude level, and the range of enclosures

represented within each. In this there is a need to avoid the pitfalls that have ensnared such studies in the past: the blinkered application of a single archetype and over-reliance on a limited range of discovery techniques. The implications of the work presented in the papers that follow is that there is much more still to find, and that the leads presented here now urgently need to be followed up. Three research objectives might be identified in this connection:

1.   Implement an extensive sampling programme to establish the nature of date of a selection of the numerous single and multi ditched enclosures known from aerial photography, especially focusing on those that can be spatially associated with flint scatters or known finds of Neolithic material.

2.   Implement an intensive sampling programme to establish the nature and date of a selection of small walled enclosures and "hillforts" in western parts of the British Isles known from field survey, especially focusing on those that can be spatially associated with known finds of Neolithic material

3.   Systematically review the evidence from multi-period sites, especially those in hilltop locations, that have yielded substantial assemblages of Neolithic material through fieldwalking or earlier excavations and supplement existing work with geophysical surveys and, where appropriate, field evaluation.

Limited but evolving knowledge of the enclosure sites along the Atlantic fringe of northwest Europe is currently full of as many questions as answers. Some are rather basic and refer to distribution, chronology, sequence, associations, and so on. Others are more complicated and focus on the intricacies of the actions and events that took place at particular sites and what linked the site itself inter wider patterns of social relations. What the essays that follow emphasize is the diversity and complexity of Neolithic enclosures as part of the archaeology of the fifth to second millennia BC. Where extensive work has already been carried out elements of the picture can already be glimpsed. But enclosures are not only a big question and a big problem. They are also physically big in archaeological terms and sorting them out calls for big scales of study. With the results of large-scale excavations of enclosure sites in southern Britain and elsewhere to hand, a fourth research priority is now:

4.   The extensive examination through excavation of a selection of enclosure sites in western of Britain, reflecting the main regional geographies of the distributions that can be glimpsed. In designing the excavation strategy, attention needs to be given to the interior of the enclosure as well as its boundary works.

NOTES

1   Palmer's definition was slightly restrictive in the sense that Carn Brea, Cornwall, had already been discovered and established as Neolithic by this time (*cf.* Mercer 1981) but was not included in Palmer's analysis.

2.   The annual *Gazetteer of Archaeological Investigations in England* published by the Council for British Archaeology in tandem with the *British and Irish Archaeological Bibliography* provides an invaluable

reference source to what is being brought to light by all kinds of archaeological work. The CBA Regional Groups in Scotland and Wales provide comparable listings of recent work in their respective territories.

BIBLIOGRAPHY

Ainsworth, S, and Barnatt, J, 1998, A scarp edge enclosure at Gardom's Edge, Baslow, Derbyshire. *Derbyshire Archaeological Journal*, 118, 5–23

Allen, M, and Green, M, 1998, The Fir Tree Field Shaft; the date and archaeological palaeo-environmental potential of a chalk swallowhole feature. *Proceedings of the Dorset Natural History and Archaeological Society*, 120, 25–38

Andersen, N H, 1977, *Sarup vol. 1. The Sarup enclosures* (= Jutland Archaeological Society Publications 33:1). Moesgaard. Jysk Arkæologisk Selskab

Arnold, C, 1987, Fridd Faldwyn, Montgomery: the Neolithic phase. *Archaeologia Cambrensis*, 136, 39–42

Bamford, H M, 1985, *Briar Hill. Excavation 1974–1978*. Northampton. Northampton Development Corporation

Barclay, A, Bradley, R J, Hey, G, and Lambrick, G, 1996, The earlier prehistory of the Oxford region in the light of recent research. *Oxoniensia*, 61, 1–20

Barker, G W W, and Webley, D, 1978, Causewayed camps and early Neolithic economies in central southern England. *Proceedings of the Prehistoric Society*, 44, 161–186

Bedwin, O, 1981, Excavations at the Neolithic enclosure on Bury Hill, Houghton, West Sussex. *Proceedings of the Prehistoric Society*, 47, 69–86

Behrens, H, 1981, The first "Woodhenge" in middle Europe. *Antiquity*, 55, 172–8

Benson, D, and Miles, T, 1974, *The Upper Thames Valley: an archaeological survey of the river gravels*. Oxford. Oxford Archaeological Unit

Bergh, S, 2000, Transforming Knocknarea – the archaeology of a mountain. *Archaeology Ireland*, 14.2 (number 52), 14–18

Bewley, R H, 1993, Survey and excavation at a cropmark enclosure, Plasketlands, Cumbria. *Transactions of the Cumberland and Westmorland Antiquarian and Archaeological Society*, 93, 1–18

Bradley, R, 1996, Long houses, long mounds, and Neolithic enclosures. *Journal of Material Culture*, 1, 239–56

Bradley, R, 1998a, Interpreting enclosures. In M Edmunds and C Richards (eds), *Understanding the Neolithic of north-west Europe*. Glasgow. Cruithne Press

Bradley, R, 1998b, *The significance of monuments.* London. Routledge

Bradley, R, 1998c, Ruined buildings, ruined stones: enclosures, tombs and natural places in the Neolithic of south-west England. *World Archaeology*, 30.1, 13–22

Bradley, R, 2000, *An archaeology of natural places*. London. Routledge

Brown, K, 1997, Domestic settlement and the landscape during the Neolithic of the Tavoliere. In P Topping (ed), *Neolithic landscapes* (= Neolithic Studies Group Seminar Papers 2). Oxford. Oxbow Books. 125–138

Burgess, C, 1976, Meldon Bridge: a Neolithic defended promontory complex near Peebles. In C Burgess, and R Miket (eds), *Settlement and economy in the third and second millennia BC* (= British Archaeological Reports British Series 33). Oxford. British Archaeological Reports. 151–180

Burgess, C, Topping, P, Mordant, C, and Maddison, M (eds), 1988, *Enclosures and defences in the Neolithic of western Europe* (= British Archaeological Reports International Series 403). Oxford. British Archaeological Reports

Clay, P, 1999, A first causewayed enclosure for Leicestershire. *Past*, 32, 3–4

Cleal, R M J, Walker, K E, and Montague, R, 1995, *Stonehenge in its landscape. Twentieth-century excavations* (= English Heritage Archaeological Report 10). London. English Heritage

Collingwood, R G, 1938, The hillfort on Carrock Fell. *Transactions of the Cumberland and Westmorland Antiquarian and Archaeological Society*, 38, 32–41

Cooney, G, 2000, *Landscapes of Neolithic Ireland*. London. Routledge

Crawford, O G S, 1960, *Archaeology in the field*. London. Phoenix

Crawford, O G S, and Keiller, A, 1928, *Wessex from the air*. Oxford. Clarendon Press

Cunnington, M E, 1912, Knap Hill Camp. *Wiltshire Archaeological and Natural History Magazine*, 37, 42–65

Curwen, E, 1930, Neolithic camps. *Antiquity*, 4, 22–54

Daniel, G E, 1950, *The prehistoric chamber tombs of England and Wales*. Cambridge. Cambridge University Press

Darvill, T, 1983, *The Neolithic of Wales and the mid-west of England: a systemic analysis of social change through the application of action theory*. [Unpublished PhD dissertation. University of Southampton]

Darvill, T, 1987, *Prehistoric Gloucestershire*. Gloucester. Alan Sutton and Gloucestershire County Library

Darvill, T, 1989, *Monuments Protection Programme Single Monument Class Description: Stockaded enclosures*. London. English Heritage. [Limited circulation printed report]

Darvill, T, 1996, *Prehistoric Britain from the air. A study of space, time and society*. Cambridge. Cambridge University Press

Darvill, T, 1997, Ever increasing circles: the sacred geographies of Stonehenge and its landscape. *Proceedings of the British Academy*, 92, 167–202

Darvill, T, 2000, *Billown Neolithic Landscape Project, Isle of Man. Fifth report: 1999* (= School of Conservation Sciences Research Reports 7). Bournemouth and Douglas. Bournemouth University and Manx National Heritage

Darvill, T and Locke, R, 1988, Aerial photography in the upper Thames Valley and eastern Cotswolds in 1986. *Transactions of the Bristol and Gloucestershire Archaeological Society*, 106, 192–98

Dixon, P, 1988, The Neolithic settlements on Crickley Hill. In C Burgess, P Topping, C Mordant, and M Maddison (eds), *Enclosures and defences in the Neolithic of western Europe* (= British Archaeological Reports International Series 403). Oxford. British Archaeological Reports. 75–88

Drewett, P, 1994, Dr V Seton Williams' excavations at Combe Hill, 1962, and the role of Neolithic causewayed enclosures in Sussex. *Sussex Archaeological Collections*, 132, 7–24

Driver, T, 1997a, Norton: the first interrupted ditch enclosure in Wales? *AARGnews*, 15, 17–19

Driver, T, 1997b, Norton, Ogmore by Sea. *Archaeology in Wales*, 37, 66–7

Dyer, J, 1964, A secondary Neolithic camp at Waulud's Bank, Leagrave. *Bedfordshire Archaeological Journal*, 2, 1–12

Dyson, L, Shand, G, and Stevens, S, 2000, Causewayed enclosures. *Current Archaeology*, 14.12 (Number 168), 470–2

Edmonds, M, 1993, Interpreting causewayed enclosures in the past and present. In C Tilley (ed), *Interpretative archaeology*. Oxford. Berg. 99–142

Edmonds, M, 1999, *Ancestral geographies of the Neolithic: landscapes, monuments and memory*. London. Routledge

Edmonds, M, and Thomas, J, 1990, *Anglesey Archaeological Landscape Project 1990* (= Department of Archaeology, St David's College, Lampeter, Occasional Paper 16). Lampeter. St David's College

Eogan, G, 1984, *Excavations at Knowth 1*. Dublin. Royal Irish Academy

Evans, C, 1988, Monuments and analogy: the interpretation of causewayed enclosures. In C Burgess, P Topping, C Mordant, and M Maddison (eds) *Enclosures and defences in the Neolithic of western Europe* (= British Archaeological Reports International Series 403). Oxford. British Archaeological Reports. 47–74

Evans, E E, 1953, *Lyles Hill: a late Neolithic site in County Antrim* (Archaeological Research Publications (Northern Ireland) 2). Belfast. HMSO

Evans, J G, Rouse, A J, and Sharples, N M, 1988, The landscape setting of causewayed camps: recent work on the Maiden castle enclosure. In J C Barrett and I A Kinnes (eds), *The archaeology of context in the Neolithic and Bronze Age: recent trends*. Sheffield. University of Sheffield Department of Archaeology and Prehistory. 97–103

Gibson, A, 1998, Hindwell and the Neolithic palisaded sites of Britain and Ireland. In A Gibson and D Simpson (eds), *Prehistoric ritual and religion. Essays in honour of Aubrey Burl*. Stroud. Sutton Publishing. 68–79

Gibson, A, 1999, *The Walton Basin Project: excavation and survey in a prehistoric landscape 1993–7* (= Council for British Archaeology Research Report 118). York. Council for British Archaeology

Gibson, A, and Simpson, D D A, 1987, Lyles Hill, Co. Antrim. *Archaeology Ireland*, 2, 72–5

Gillings, M, Pollard, J, and Wheatley, D, 2000, The Rev. William Stukeley's lost megalithic avenue. *Past*, 34, 8–9

Gojda, M, 1997, The contribution of aerial archaeology to European landscape studies: past achievements, recent developments and future perspectives. *Journal of European Archaeology*, 5.2, 91–104

Graves-Brown, P, 1998, Ewenny, Beech Court Farm prehistoric enclosure. *Archaeology in Wales*, 38, 111–112

Harding, A F, and Lee, G E, 1987, *Henge monuments and related sites of Great Britain. Air photographic evidence and catalogue* (= British Archaeological Reports British Series 175). Oxford. British Archaeological Reports

Höckmann, O, 1990, Frühneolithischen Einhegungen in Europa. *Jahresschrift für Mitteldeutsche Vorgeschichte*, 73, 57–86

Hogg, A H A, 1972, The size-distribution of hill-forts in Wales and the Marches. In F Lynch and C Burgess (eds), *Prehistoric Man in Wales and the west. Essays in honour of Lily F Chitty*. Bath. Adams and Dart. 293–306

Hubert, F, 1971, Neue Ausgrabungen im Michelsberger Erdwerk in Boitsfort (Belgien). *Germania*, 49, 214–18

Johnson, N, and Rose, P, 1994, *Bodmin Moor: an archaeological survey*. Volume 1: the human landscape to c1800 (= Historic Buildings and Monuments Commission for England Archaeological Report 24 and RCHME Supplementary Series 11). London and Truro. English Heritage, RCHME and Cornwall Archaeological Unit

Jones, G D B, 1987, *Apulia. Volume I: Neolithic settlement in the Tavoliere* (= Reports of the Research Committee of the Society of Antiquaries of London 44). London. Society of Antiquaries and Thames and Hudson

Joussaume, R, 1986, Les sépulture du site triple enceinte de fossés interompus de Champ – Durand a Nieul – sur – L'Autize (Vendée). *III Congrès national des Sociétée Savantes, Poitiers, Pré- et Protohistoire*. 271–288

Joussaume, R, 1988, Analyse structurale de la triple enceinte de fossés interrompus à Machecoul, Loire-Atlantique. In C Burgess, P Topping, C Mordant, and M Maddison (eds) *Enclosures and defences in the Neolithic of western Europe* (= British Archaeological Reports International Series 403). Oxford. British Archaeological Reports. 275–300

Keiller, A, 1932, Excavation at Windmill Hill. In *Proceedings of the first International Congress of Prehistoric and Protohistoric Sciences. London. August 1–6 1932*. Oxford. Oxford University Press. 135–8

Kinnes, I, 1979, *Round barrows and ring-ditches in the British Neolithic* (= British Museum Occasional Paper 7). London. British Museum

Kinnes, I, Schadla-Hall, T, Chadwick, P, and Dean, P, 1983, Duggleby Howe reconsidered. *Archaeological Journal*, 140, 83–108

Legge, A J, 1981, Aspects of cattle husbandry. In R J Mercer (ed), *Farming practice in British prehistory*. Edinburgh. Edinbugh University Press. 169–181

Lehner, H, 1910, Der festungbau der Jüngeren Steinzeit. *Prähistorische Zeitschrift*, 2, 1–23

Lobb, S, 1995, Excavation at Crofton causewayed enclosure. *Wiltshire Archaeological and Natural History Magazine*, 88, 18–25

Madsen, T, 1988, Causewayed enclosures in southern Scandinavia. In C Burgess, P Topping, C Mordant, and M Maddison (eds) *Enclosures and defences in the Neolithic of western Europe* (= British Archaeological Reports International Series 403). Oxford. British Archaeological Reports. 301–336

Mallory, J P, 1993, A Neolithic ditched enclosure in Northern Ireland. In J Pavúk (ed), *Actes de XII Congrès International des Sciences Préhistoriques et Protohistoriques*. Nitra. UIPPS. 415–18

Mallory, J P, and Hartwell, B, 1984, Donegore Hill. *Current Archaeology*, 8.9 (Number 92), 271–4

Mercer, R J, 1980, *Hambledon Hill. A Neolithic landscape*. Edinburgh. Edinburgh University Press

Mercer, R J, 1981, Excavations at Carn Brea, Illogan, Cornwall, 1970–73. A Neolithic fortified complex of the third millennium bc. *Cornish Archaeology*, 20, 1–204

Mercer, R J, 1986, *Excavation of a Neolithic enclosure at Helman Tor, Lanlivery, Cornwall, 1986: interim report* (= Department of Archaeology, University of Edinburgh, Project Paper 4). Edinburgh. University of Edinburgh

Mercer, R J, 1988, Hambledon Hill, Dorset, England. In C Burgess, P Topping, C Mordant, and M Maddison (eds) *Enclosures and defences in the Neolithic of western Europe* (= British Archaeological Reports International Series 403). Oxford. British Archaeological Reports. 89–106

Mercer, R J, 1989a, The earliest defences in western Europe: part 1: warfare in the Neolithic. *Fortress*, 2, 16–22

Mercer, R J, 1989b, The earliest defences in western Europe: part 2: the archaeological evidence. *Fortress*, 3, 2–11

Mercer, R J, forthcoming, The excavation of a Neolithic enclosure complex at Helman Tor, Lostwithiel, Cornwall. *Cornish Archaeology*

Monk, M, 1993, People and environment: in search of the farmers. In E S Twohig and M Ronayne (eds), *Past perceptions. The prehistoric archaeology of south-west Ireland*. Cork. University College Cork. 35–52

Mulk, I M, 1994, Sacrificial places and their meaning in Saami society. In D L Carmichael, J Hubert, B Reeves and A Schanche (eds), *Sacred Sites, Sacred Places*. London. Routledge. 121–31

Newman, C, 1997, *Tara: an archaeological survey* (= Discovery Programme Monograph 2). Dublin. Discovery Programme and the Royal Irish Academy

O'Neil, B H St J, 1942, Excavations at Ffridd Faldwyn Camp, Montgomery, 1937–39. *Archaeologia Cambrensis*, 97, 1–57

Palmer, R, 1976, Interrupted ditch enclosures in Britain: the use of aerial photography for comparative studies. *Proceedings of the Prehistoric Society*, 42, 161–86

Petrasch, J, 1990, Mittelneolithische kreisgrabenanlagen in mitteleuropa. *Bericht der Römisch-Germanischen Kommission*, 71, 407–564

Piggott, S, 1954, *The Neolithic cultures of the British Isles*. Cambridge. Cambridge University Press

Piggott, S, 1962, *The West Kennet long barrow: excavations 1955–56*. (= Ministry of Works Archaeological Report 4). London. HMSO

Pryor, F, 1998, *Etton: excavations at a Neolithic causewayed enclosure near Maxey, Cambridge, 1982–7* (= English Heritage Archaeological Report 18). London. English Heritage

RCHME, 1970, *An inventory of historical monuments in the county of Dorset. Volume three. Central Dorset*. London. HMSO. (3 parts)

RCHME, 1972, *An inventory of historical monuments in the county of Dorset. Volume four. North Dorset*. London. HMSO.

RCAHMS, 1993, *Monuments on record. Annual Review 1992–3*. Edinburgh. RCAHMS

Renfrew, C, 1973, Monuments, mobilisation and social organisation in Neolithic Wessex. In C Renfrew (ed), *The explanation of culture change*. London. Duckworth. 539–558

Richards, C C, 1996, Henges and water: towards an elemental understanding of monumentality and landscape in late Neolithic Britain. *Journal of Material Culture*, 1, 313–36

Robertson-MacKay, R, 1987, The Neolithic causewayed enclosure at Staines, Surrey: excavations 1961–63. *Proceedings of the Prehistoric Society*, 53, 23–128

Russell, M, and Rudling, D, 1996, Excavations at Whitehawk Neolithic enclosure, Brighton, East Sussex: 1991–93. *Sussex Archaeological Collections*, 134, 39–61

Sahlins, M, 1974, *Stone age economics*. London. Tavistock

Saville, A, and Ellison, A, 1983, Excavations at Uleybury Hillfort Gloucestershire 1976. In A Saville (ed), *Uleybury and Norbury hillforts* (= Western Archaeological Trust Excavation Monograph 5). Bristol. Western Archaeological Trust. 1–24

Shand, G, 1998, A Neolithic causewayed enclosure in Kent. *Past*, 29, 1

Sharples, N M, 1991, *Maiden Castle. Excavations and field survey 1985–6* (= Historic Buildings and Monuments Commission for England Archaeological Report 19). London. English Heritage

Simpson D D A, and Gibson, A, 1989, Lyles Hill. *Current Archaeology*, 10.7 (Number 114), 214–15

Smith, I F, 1965, *Windmill Hill and Avebury. Excavations by Alexander Keiller 1925–1939*. Oxford. Clarendon Press

Smith, I F, 1966, Windmill Hill and its implications. *Palaeohistoria*, 12, 469–81

Smith, I F, 1971, Causewayed enclosures. In D D A Simpson (ed), *Economy and settlement in Neolithic and early Bronze Age Britain and Europe*. Leicester. Leicester University Press. 89–112

Soffe, G and Clare, T, 1988, New evidence of ritual monuments at Long Meg and Her Daughters, Cumbria. *Antiquity*, 62, 552–557

Stoertz, C, 1997, *Ancient landscapes of the Yorkshire Wolds. Aerial photographic transcription and analysis*. London. Royal Commission on the Historical Monuments of England

Sweetman, D, 1987, Excavation of a late Neolithic / early Bronze Age site at Newgrange, Co. Meath. *Proceedings of the Royal Irish Academy*, 87C, 283–98

Thomas, J S, 1999a, Excavations at Dunragit, Dumfries and Galloway, 1999. *http://www.arch. soton.ac.uk/Research/Dunragit/index.htm?blank.html*

Thomas, J S, 1999b, An economy of substances in earlier Neolithic Britain. In J Robb (ed), *Material symbols: culture and economy in prehistory*. Carbondale. Southern Illinois University Press. 70–89

Thomas, J S, 2000a, Excavations at Dunragit, Dumfries and Galloway, 2000. *http://www. arch.soton.ac.uk/Research/Dunragit /index.htm?blank.html*

Thomas, J S, 2000b, Death, identity and the body in Neolithic Britain. *Journal of the Royal Anthropological Institute*, 6, 603–17

Thomas, K, 1982, Neolithic enclosures and woodland habitats on the South Downs in Sussex, England. In M Bell and S Limbrey (eds), *Archaeological aspects of woodland ecology* (= British Archaeological Reports International Series 146). Oxford. British Archaeological Reports. 147–70

Thorpe, I J, 1984, Ritual, power and ideology: a reconsideration of earlier Neolithic rituals in Wessex. In R J Bradley and J Gardiner (eds), *Neolithic Studies* (= British Archaeological Reports British Series 133). Oxford. British Archaeological Reports. 41–60

Tilley, C, 1996, The power of rocks: topography and monument construction on Bodmin Moor. *World Archaeology*, 28.2, 161–176

Vyner, B, 1994, The territory of ritual: cross-ridge boundaries and the prehistoric landscapes of the Cleveland Hills, northeast England. *Antiquity*, 68, 27–38

Waddington, C, 1998, Survey and excavation at Harehaugh hillfort and possible Neolithic enclosure. *Northern Archaeology*, 15/16, 87–108

Wainwright, G J, 1971, The excavation of a late Neolithic enclosure at Marden, Wiltshire. *Antiquaries Journal*, 51, 177–239

Wainwright, G J, 1972, Excavation of a Neolithic settlement on Broome Heath, Ditchingham, Norfolk. *Proceedings of the Prehistoric Society*, 38, 1–97

Wainwright, G J, 1979, *Mount Pleasant, Dorset: excavations 1970–1971* (= Reports of the Research Committee of the Society of Antiquaries of London 37). London. Society of Antiquaries

Whimster, R, 1989, *The emerging past. Air photography and the buried landscape*. London. RCHME

Whittle, A, 1977, Earlier Neolithic enclosures in north-west Europe. *Proceedings of the Prehistoric Society*, 43, 329–348

Whittle, A, 1996, *Europe in the Neolithic. The creation of new worlds*. Cambridge. Cambridge University Press

Whittle, A, Pollard, J, and Grigson, C, 1999, *The harmony of symbols. The Windmill Hill causewayed enclosure*. Oxford. Oxbow Books

Williams, A, 1953, Clegyr Boia, St Davids (Pemb.): excavation in 1943. *Archaeologia Cambrensis*, 102, 20–47

Wilson, D R, 1975, "Causewayed enclosures" and interrupted ditch systems". *Antiquity*, 49, 178–86

Woodward, P J, 1988, Neolithic pictures from Dorchester. *Antiquity*, 62, 266–74

Chapter 2

Enclosures and related structures in Brittany and western France

Chris Scarre

THE GENEALOGY OF THE WEST FRENCH ENCLOSURES

Enclosures are one of the recurrent features of the Neolithic of northern and western Europe. The basic concept is simple: a circuit of ditch, bank and/or palisade, defining an area which may contain evidence of houses but is more usually devoid of significant structural remains. The earliest such enclosures in western Europe appear to be associated with the Bandkeramik phenomenon (Lüning 1988; Petrasch 1990). Bandkeramik enclosures are particularly well known in the Rhineland from the examples excavated on the Aldenhovener Platte, notably those at Langweiler (Boelicke *et al.* 1988; Kuper *et al.* 1977), though research on the Rhineland enclosures has a much longer history, beginning with Buttler's excavations between 1929 and 1934 at the site of Köln-Lindenthal (Buttler and Haberey 1936).

The relevance of the Bandkeramik enclosures to the enclosure tradition of Brittany and western France resides in the chronological patterning. This patterning suggests that the Bandkeramik enclosures represent the earliest stage, followed by a successive spread (in chronological terms) of the "enclosure idea" towards the west, so that it can be argued that the latter are derived from the former. Indeed, the possibility that the Neolithic enclosures of Germany, France, Britain, and Scandinavia all owe their origin to Bandkeramik inspiration has frequently been considered (*e.g.* recently by Bradley 1998, 48–49, 68*ff*, though Whittle 1996, 266*ff* is less sure). Such studies invariably conclude that even if there is some single primordial idea behind these various regional manifestations, we must nonetheless recognize that enclosures vary widely in morphology, extent, and location and in the evidence for activity that they may reveal. Thus whatever the origin of the idea, it was one which was reinterpreted in diverse ways by different communities at different times and places.

Most of the early enclosures of western Europe consist of a ditch, or sometimes ditch and bank, or ditch and palisade; occasionally palisade alone. The French enclosures share this general configuration (Figure 2.1 for distribution of sites mentioned in the text). The enclosure at Menneville, for example, the earliest in northern France, and associated with late Bandkeramik material, consists of an interrupted ditch with a palisade and probably a gravel bank on its inner edge (Coudart and Demoule 1982). There is no direct date for the Menneville enclosure, but in chronological terms the Paris Basin Bandkeramik falls within the bracket 5000–4700 BC. Enclosures proliferate in northern France during the

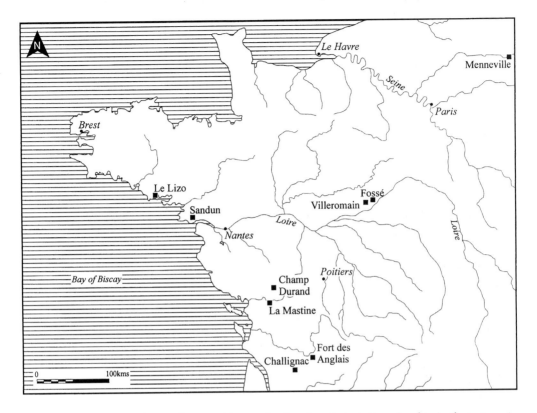

Figure 2.1: Northern and western France, showing the principal sites referred to in the text

succeeding middle Neolithic, with well-known examples such as L'Etoile and Noyen-sur-Seine (Bréart 1984; Dubouloz *et al.* 1991; Mordant and Mordant 1988). It is during this period that the first enclosures appear in the middle Loire region, west of the Paris Basin. The earliest example here is that at Villeromain, closely followed by Fossé; these are assigned to the transition between early Neolithic (Villeneuve-Saint-Germain) and middle Neolithic (Cerny and Chambon) (Despriée 1986; Irribarria 1998). That would place these early Loire Valley enclosures in the second quarter of the fifth millennium BC in calendar years (Constantin *et al.* 1997; Figure 2.2).

The enclosures of Fossé and Villeromain stand at the head of a series of Loire Valley middle Neolithic enclosures. The association of these earliest examples with Villeneuve-Saint-Germain, Cerny, and Chambon material highlights their link with the Paris Basin; Villeneuve-Saint-Germain is a direct descendant of the Paris Basin Bandkeramik tradition, and Cerny and Chambon show many derivative features (Constantin *et al.* 1997). This underlines the impression of a westward expansion which the distribution and chronology of Neolithic enclosures in northern France combine to give.

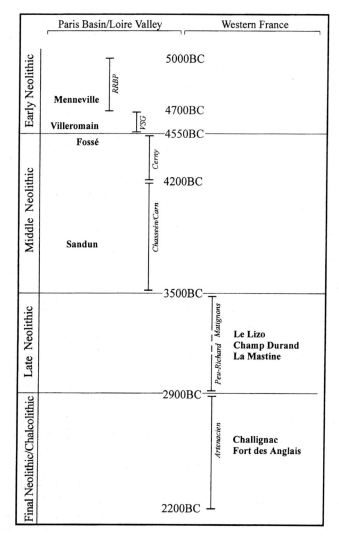

Figure 2.2: Phasing and chronology of the Neolithic of northern France: the principal cultural groupings and their dates

ENCLOSURES IN BRITTANY

There has been much discussion in recent years about the origins of the Neolithic in northwest France, and in particular about the impact on that region of developments taking place further to the east (Scarre 1992; Boujot and Cassen 1992). The recent discovery of a trapezoidal house with Villeneuve-Saint-Germain material at Le Haut Mée, on the borders of Brittany, has lent new weight to the significance of these eastern influences (Cassen *et al.* 1998). Neolithic enclosures, however, which might provide another element of comparison, are remarkable in Brittany chiefly by reason of their rarity. Indeed, only two adequately-documented examples are known: at Sandun on the Loire estuary, and Le Lizo in the southern Morbihan.

The Sandun enclosure stands on a low rise on the edge of the estuarine marshland known as the marais de Grande-Brière. There are two middle Neolithic phases, the earlier of them represented by a trench or gully 25m long, containing remains of 20 pottery vessels which had been broken *in situ*. These vessels have been attributed by the excavator to an early phase of the middle Neolithic, contemporary with (and closely related to) Cerny (Letterlé 1997). The nature of the gully, however, is not explained, and the first enclosure phase belongs to the later part of the middle Neolithic, associated with radiocarbon dates of the early fourth millennium BC (3950–3350 BC: 4890±100 BP, Gif-7701; 4050–3700 BC: 5120±70 BP, Gif-7702) (Letterlé *et al.* 1990). The enclosure takes the form of a ditch some 4.5m wide and 1.5m deep backed by a palisade trench. In the interior, to the northwest, were a series of contemporary pits which may have lain adjacent to houses, though no definite traces of the latter were identified. Topography and the surface distribution of material enabled the excavators to sketch a hypothetical plan for the eastern half of the enclosure; if it continued symmetrically on the west it would have encircled an area of some 6ha.

The Sandun enclosure would not be out of place in the Loire Valley or the Paris Basin; it cannot be said to constitute a regionally specific Breton type. Until further middle Neolithic enclosures are discovered, however, it is difficult to say more about the pattern and plan of early enclosures in this region, or the activities associated with them. New enclosures have been detected by aerial reconnaissance in the basin of the River Vilaine to the east of Rennes: at Boistrudan (La Trappe) and Saint-Aubin des Landes (La Charronnière), for example, with double circuits of interrupted ditch (Leroux 1992). Surface evidence suggests, however, that these are of late Neolithic date.

For the late Neolithic period first mention must go to the Camp du Lizo, near Carnac in the Morbihan. This two hectare settlement on a granite promontory overlooking the Crac'h Valley is enclosed by a rampart of earth and stones still standing 3m high in places. When Le Rouzic excavated the site in 1922 he also traced a second, outer circuit on the north and west, and this has recently been shown to extend around the whole of the enclosure. Within were stone footings of square and circular dwellings, as well as a number of cist burials beneath small mounds (Le Rouzic 1933; Lecerf 1986; Figure 2.3).

Other enclosed settlements of late Neolithic date are known in southern Brittany. At Croh Collé on the Quiberon peninsula, a promontory fort has traces of hut bases in its interior. The small island of Er-Yoh near the Ile de Houat has sections of dry-stone walling up to 4m long blocking the gaps between natural rock formations and creating an enclosure; within were hearths and paved areas (Giot *et al.* 1998, 459). Sherratt has recently added a series of further examples to this list of enclosed sites in southern Morbihan, though the identification is not in all cases sure (Sherratt 1998). In considering these Breton sites, analogy may tentatively be drawn with Carn Brea in Cornwall where excavations showed a suspected Iron Age enclosure to be Neolithic (Mercer 1981). A further parallel is offered by the promontory fort of Castel Coz at Beuzec-Cap-Sizun, on the southwestern peninsula of Finistère, where Mortimer Wheeler excavated in 1938. Beyond the limits of the Iron Age fort are two outer ramparts, still standing to over a

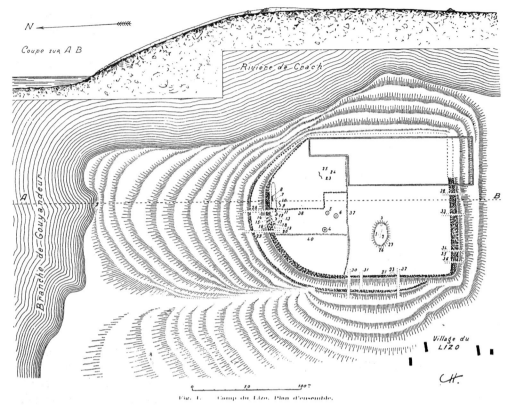

Figure 2.3: The late Neolithic enclosure of Le Lizo near Carnac in southern Brittany. (After Le Rouzic 1933)

metre in height, which Wheeler assigned to the Neolithic. It is likely that further research in Brittany will lead to the identification of other Neolithic enclosures marked by ramparts or upstanding walls of dry-stone construction. The neighbouring promontory fort of Castel-Meur at Cleden-Cap-Sizun has also yielded Neolithic material, though the ramparts here appear to belong to the Iron Age (Maguer 1996).

The nature of these Morbihan enclosures has yet to be properly explored. Le Rouzic interpreted the Camp du Lizo as a fortified settlement protecting the Neolithic inhabitants of southern Morbihan and their sacred landscape around Carnac from the incursion of bronze-wielding enemies from the interior (Le Rouzic 1933). More recently, Sherratt too has favoured a defensive interpretation, seeing Le Lizo and other enclosures as strong-points controlling the waterways of coastal Morbihan, in this case as trade routes rather than invasion avenues (Sherratt 1998). Whether or not the defence hypothesis will stand up to closer scrutiny remains to be seen. What is very evident is that Le Lizo is much more than a mere strong-point or refuge. In the lee of the western rampart, pottery production appears to have been a major activity. In the centre of the site there stands an angled passage grave (*allée coudée*), which may pre-date the enclosure. Indeed, close reading of Le Rouzic's 1933 report suggests that the houses in some cases continued beneath the rampart, and thus the settlement too may (in part at least) have pre-dated the enclosure. In addition to the angled passage grave there were a number of cist burials, one with a cover-stone decorated by cup marks. A menhir fragment decorated with cup-marks and a *crosse* or "crook" was found close to a second cist grave (Le Rouzic 1933). In two cases, cist burials with their associated small tumuli were built directly on top of earlier houses, raising the possibility that there was a direct connection between the occupants of the graves and the inhabitants of the dwellings. The cultural material from Le Lizo was predominantly of late Neolithic date. The angled passage grave may be slightly earlier (late fourth millennium BC on the evidence of a single radiocarbon date from the angled passage grave of Goërem: L'Helgouach 1970). The menhir fragment with crook motif, on the other hand, can be assigned to the late fifth or early fourth millennium BC by analogy with other monuments with similar motifs (Cassen and L'Helgouach 1992); hence this was already a place of special significance long before the rampart was built. To describe the Camp du Lizo simply as a late Neolithic fortified enclosure commanding a strategic waterway would be greatly to understate the complexity of this important site.

ENCLOSURES SOUTH OF THE LOIRE

In sharp contrast to the scarcity of examples in Brittany, the region of France lying south of the Loire is replete with Neolithic enclosures. There are indeed more enclosures here than in any other part of France, and perhaps of western Europe. Claude Burnez has remarked that some 100 enclosures are known in the region, which may suggest an original total (allowing for sites destroyed or yet to be discovered) of around 250 sites (Burnez 1996b). The great majority of these are found in an area 100km by 150km, which (to give a British parallel) is approximately the size of East Anglia.

The first of the West French enclosures to be discovered was found near Saintes in 1882, but intensive research on these structures began only in the 1950s, when Claude Burnez conducted a series of excavations at sites in the region around Cognac. In 1960 he was joined by Humphrey Case of the Ashmolean Museum, Oxford, in joint excavations at Les Matignons, an overlapping pair of enclosures on a chalk hill to the south of the River Charente (Burnez and Case 1966). Within the last 30 years, knowledge of the west French enclosures has been greatly enhanced both by extensive aerial photography and by a series of major excavations at Champ Durand (Joussaume 1981; 1987; Joussaume and Pautreau 1990, 253–75), Semussac (Mohen and Bergougnan 1984), Echiré (Burnez 1996a), Diconche (Burnez and Fouéré 1993), and La Mastine (Cassen and Scarre 1997; Scarre 1998).

The distribution of these enclosures extends across the chalk and limestone terrain from the southern limit of the Armorican massif to the Gironde. They are characterized by rock-cut ditches, sometimes arranged concentrically one within the other, and up to 7m across and 2.5m deep, though most are somewhat less substantial than this. The dimensions of the ditches, and the evidence of dry-stone tumble from a wall or rampart in the ditch fills, led most earlier commentators to interpret them as defensive in function. The interpretation was reinforced by the *pince de crabe* or "crab's pincers" entrances which characterize many of these sites (Figure 2.4). Such complex entrances were taken to represent a strengthening of what is always the weakest point in any defensive perimeter. The defensive interpretation has, however, been thrown into question by recent excavations showing that the *pince de crabe* entrances were not constructed to a single co-ordinated plan but were multi-phase structures. The curving outworks were usually later additions, and may have been created only after the inner ditch stubs had been filled in (Scarre 1998).

Understanding of the west French enclosures has also been broadened by considering the other activities represented at these sites. Almost without exception, the interiors of these enclosures (which are located generally on good agricultural land) have been ploughed out, and preserved occupation surfaces are exceedingly rare. There is, however, evidence for ritual activity in the form of human burials, often on the ditch floor and sometimes accompanied by pottery. At Champ Durand, a series of burials was discovered, some apparently *in situ*, others mixed in among rampart collapse; the excavator concluded that the latter were bodies buried within the rampart itself which subsequently collapsed into the ditch (Joussaume 1981; 1987). Most excavated enclosures have also yielded less formal deposits of human remains scattered within the ditch fills (Boujot *et al.* 1996).

Figure 2.4: The late Neolithic enclosure of La Mastine on the southern edge of the Marais poitevin in Charente-Maritime, western France, showing the "pince de crabe" entrance. (Photo: Maurice Marsac)

In terms of chronology, the west French enclosures just described belong primarily to the late Neolithic period (*c.* 3500–2900 BC); claims for an origin in the later part of the middle Neolithic have been made (Cassen 1993; Boujot *et al.* 1996) but are not yet confirmed. These late Neolithic enclosures are not, however, the only Neolithic examples known from the region south of the Loire.

On the one hand are enclosures which may pre-date the late Neolithic series. A distinct group of enclosures has been discovered by aerial photography in the area north of Poitiers during the last 10 years. They are defined by ditch and palisade, and are located on river terraces, or sometimes valley floors. By their location and morphology, these enclosures can be considered an extension of the Loire Valley tradition of middle Neolithic enclosures referred to earlier. Though a number of them have been shown by excavation to date to the late Neolithic (Ollivier *et al.* 1997), others may be middle Neolithic in origin (Joussaume and Pautreau 1990, 159–161). Whether they provide a direct cultural link between the Loire Valley middle Neolithic enclosures and the late Neolithic enclosures of western France – an intermediate stage in the transmission and translation of a tradition – remains unclear.

On the other hand, there is a second group of enclosures which in chronological terms follow directly on from the late Neolithic series. These later enclosures, distributed throughout the whole of the region from the Marais Poitevin to the Gironde, are dated to the period known alternatively as the Chalcolithic or final Neolithic (*c.* 2900–2300 BC).

THE CHALCOLITHIC ENCLOSURES OF WESTERN FRANCE

The Chalcolithic enclosures of western France differ from the late Neolithic enclosures of the region in a number of respects. Perhaps most conspicuous is the fact that several still survive as upstanding circuits of banks, often on a very substantial scale. One such is the Fort des Anglais near Angoulême, where a large rampart crosses a neck of land between two deeply incised valleys to form a promontory fort. Excavation of this rampart has revealed a whole sequence of barriers, the earliest of them dated to the Chalcolithic period. This first phase took the form of a dry-stone rampart, associated with an occupation layer on its inner side. The remains of the early rampart, incorporated within a later and more massive middle Bronze Age structure, still survive in section to a height of almost 2m (Diot *et al.* 1987; Figure 2.5).

A second and still more impressive Chalcolithic enclosure is that at Challignac, a few kilometres to the south of Barbézieux (Burnez *et al.* 1995). There are in fact two enclosures on this site, succeeding one another in time. The first is a double-ditched circuit revealed by aerial photography. This survives only as a crop-mark, and may probably be assigned to the late Neolithic. The second Challignac enclosure presents an altogether different appearance: a complete circuit formed by a massive upstanding rampart, 3m tall and 10m wide at the base, cutting across the landscape of low rolling hills, incorporating a shallow dry valley within its 18ha area. In one corner it dips down to a natural pond, lying outside the perimeter but accessible through an entrance gap which may be the only original break in the perimeter. It is perhaps not surprising that an enclosure on this scale was initially thought to be of Iron Age date. A section cut across the rampart in 1994–95, however,

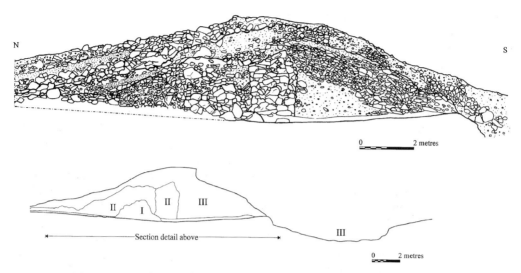

N   S

0   2 metres

II   II   III
     I
III
Section detail above
III

0   2 metres

Figure 2.5: The rampart of the Fort des Anglais, near Angoulême. Note the Chalcolithic core, enlarged and heightened in stages during the middle Bronze Age, with Iron Age additions. Key: I Artenacien (Chalcolithic); II middle Bronze Age (phase 1); middle Bronze Age (phase 2). The second middle Bronze Age phase is radiocarbon dated to the 14th century BC, and includes a shallow ditch. (After Diot et al. *1987)*

showed several constructional phases, all within the Chalcolithic period (radiocarbon dates 2900–2350 BC: 4030±60 BP, Gif-10113; 2580–2300 BC: 3950±40 BP, Gif-10036; cultural material is Artenacien: Burnez *et al.* 1995). Excavations elsewhere along the course of the rampart have discovered lines of postholes at both front and rear of the structure.

It is difficult to believe that such an enormous perimeter could have had a defensive function. One powerful counter-argument is the number of defenders it would have required in order to be effective. Yet the construction of such a rampart would have been a truly massive undertaking, and the social and cultural significance of this and similar sites has yet to be fully assessed.

The site of Challignac raises a number of other issues. One is the contrast between this relatively well-preserved Chalcolithic rampart and the earlier double-ditched enclosure within it, which has been entirely ploughed out. The difference may result from the relative durability of the two enclosures; but as we have seen, late Neolithic enclosures elsewhere in this region have generally given evidence of substantial dry-stone walls or ramparts, and there is no reason to suppose that that was not the case at Challignac. It is possible, nonetheless, that the structures of the double-ditched enclosure have been destroyed by agriculture in recent centuries. More plausible, however, is the possibility that the walls or ramparts were intentionally levelled and the ditches intentionally infilled at the end of the occupation or use. It is this which would most convincingly explain the contrast between the double-ditched enclosure at Challignac, surviving only as a crop-mark, and the Chalcolithic enclosure with rampart still standing up to 3m high. Intentional destruction may have been a practice which affected most or all of the late Neolithic enclosures throughout the region.

A second point to note is the presence of a long house within the Chalcolithic enclosure at Challignac, measuring some 10m wide and 50–60m in length. This is the subject of current excavations. One end lies across the ditch of the double-ditched enclosure, which clearly predates the house, and the house may perhaps be associated with the later (Chalcolithic) enclosure. It takes its place among a group of Chalcolithic long houses in western France, from Pléchâtel near Rennes in the north (Tinevez 1995), down to Douchapt in the Dordogne to the south (Fouéré 1998). Superficially, they resemble the long-houses of the Bandkeramik tradition, but there is a clear chronological separation between them. Indeed, in western France (which lies outside the Bandkeramik area) there is virtually a complete absence of Neolithic house plans until the Chalcolithic period. The most notable exceptions are the structures within the Lizo enclosure in southern Brittany referred to above (Le Rouzic 1933). South of the Loire, remains of a possible dry-stone house were discovered at Saint-Laurent-de-la-Prée in the Charente marshes, and at Ors on the beach of the Ile d'Oléron (Cassen 1987; 37–47; 99–104; 236–8); these serve to remind us that if the ramparts of the late Neolithic enclosures have been destroyed down to ground level, whether by ploughing or intentional destruction, it is probable that any dry-stone structures within them will also have been removed without trace. Yet, taking account of these factors, it is still the case that house plans are exceedingly rare in the west French Neolithic.

The absence of Neolithic house plans parallels the pattern found in southern Britain on which several recent authors have commented (Bradley 1997; Thomas 1991; Whittle 1997). It suggests that the late Neolithic enclosures of western France – and in particular that distinctive group found to the south of the Loire – should perhaps be viewed in the context of mobile or partly mobile economies. The absence of house structures within these enclosures may be taken to indicate that they were places of assembly rather than places of residence. This interpretation can be taken further by considering the landscape setting and the associated faunal assemblages, which together suggest that the late Neolithic enclosures may have played a role for communities which placed particular emphasis on the rearing and herding of cattle.

THE ENVIRONMENTAL SETTING

A major aim of the excavations conducted at La Mastine in the 1980s was to situate the enclosure in its original landscape setting on the edge of the extensive marshland known as the Marais poitevin. At the time when this fieldwork was undertaken, some 15 to 20 late Neolithic enclosures had been found around the margins of the marshland, many of them close to its edge or on one of the arms of marsh formed by the valleys of the rivers which flow into it (Marsac and Scarre 1979). This suggested that the marshland itself may have been a valued resource, but when fieldwork began there was insufficient palaeo-environmental evidence to determine with confidence whether the marshland had been wet or dry during the late Neolithic. On the one hand, a number of authors favoured the hypothesis that the Marais poitevin in the fourth millennium BC was a huge marine inlet, with the enclosures situated on its edge. On the other were those who preferred a landscape with areas of wet lowland grazing fringed by coastal mudflats and backed by the surrounding higher ground (Scarre 1982).

The choice of La Mastine was dictated by the fact that it lay directly on the edge of the marsh (Figure 2.6); indeed, the crop-marks of the Neolithic ditches appeared to pass beneath the marsh clays. Excavation of a section across one of these ditches near the marsh edge revealed a sequence of marine clays in the fill, with late Neolithic pottery near the base of the sequence. This contrasted with the position encountered in another ditch section only 12m to the north, where the original stony fill (usually interpreted as rampart collapse) remained intact (Cassen and Scarre 1997). What seemed to have happened at La Mastine was that the ditch had initially filled (or had been infilled) with the rubble of the dry-stone rampart, but that shortly afterwards the sea had invaded the southern terminals of the ditch, washing away most of the rampart collapse and depositing marine clays in its place. At the same time, wave action had smoothed and rounded the contours of the rock-cut ditch which made a contrast with the appearance of the ditch in cuttings further to the

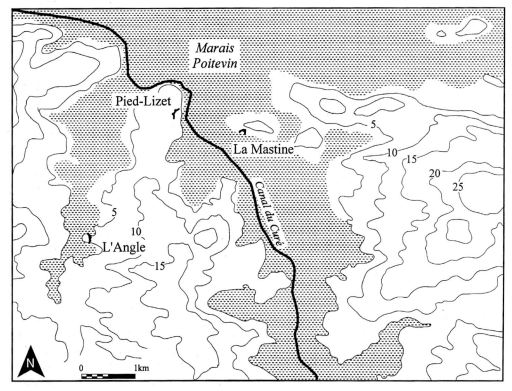

Figure 2.6: La Mastine and adjacent late Neolithic enclosures on the southern edge of the Marais poitevin. The area of marshland is shaded

north, beyond the reach of the flooding, where the ditch edges remained sharp and angular.

This evidence from La Mastine suggested that the sea had flooded the enclosure ditch only after the collapse or demolition of the rampart. Hence when the enclosure was constructed and in use, the sea must have been further away, and there may have been an area of lowland marsh or grassland stretching towards a beach or mudflat. This confirmed an earlier hypothesis (Scarre 1982). Such terrain might have provided suitable grazing for cattle; and cattle were certainly dominant in the (admittedly small) faunal assemblage from La Mastine (188 of 312 identifiable Neolithic fragments: Boujot *et al.* 1997). The high proportion of cattle in the La Mastine assemblage (66%) is indeed typical of faunal assemblages from late Neolithic enclosures in this region of France (Figure 2.7): *e.g.* Semussac 53%; Les Matignons 58%; L'Angle 63%; Echiré 68%; note that while the La Mastine faunal sample is small, the assemblages from Semussac, Les Matignons and Echiré are considerably larger: Semussac 8806 identifiable fragments (Poulain-Josien 1984); Les Matignons 3923 identifiable fragments (Poulain-Josien 1966); Echiré 6712 identifiable fragments (Bökönyi 1996).[1]

To balance the picture we must consider the evidence for crop cultivation in this region during the late Neolithic. Recent studies of the British Neolithic have demonstrated that the dominant role once accorded to plant cultivation in Neolithic lifestyles may have been overestimated (*e.g.* Whittle 1997; Thomas 1991). In the case of the west French enclosures we have the evidence of pollen cores taken from wetlands adjacent to the sites, and samples of charred grain from the enclosures them-selves. A pollen core from Saint-Sorlin, in the marshy floor of the Charente Valley just to the south of

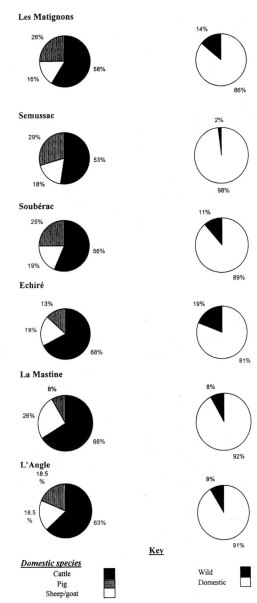

Figure 2.7: Species composition of faunal assemblages from late Neolithic enclosures in western France, illustrating the predominance of cattle among domestic livestock. Information from Poulain-Josien 1965, 1966, 1984 (Soubérac, Les Matignons, Semussac); Poulain-Josien in Joussaume 1981 (L'Angle); Bökönyi 1996 (Echiré); and Boujot et al. *1997 (La Mastine)*

Saintes, gave no evidence of significant woodland clearance and cereal cultivation until the Subatlantic. The pattern was confirmed by another core from Les Breuilhs a little to the south. Here again the major change in forest cover came in the Subatlantic. Laurence Marambat, the specialist who worked on these cores, relates the change in forest cover in the Subatlantic stage to cultivation during the Roman period (Marambat 1995). Marambat was also struck by the absence of cereal pollen in the core taken from the valley floor adjacent to the Echiré enclosure, and concluded that the activities at this late Neolithic enclosure were focused more on livestock rearing than crop cultivation (Marambat 1996).

Are we then to conclude that the cultivation of cereals played only a minor part in the prehistoric economy of this region of France until the Roman period? The pollen core evidence may certainly be taken to suggest that the valley floors were not cultivated – they were probably too wet in any case – and may indicate that such cultivation as was practised was centred some distance away from the valley floors. But that cereal cultivation was indeed practised in the late Neolithic period is amply demonstrated by the discovery of a substantial deposit of cereal grains in the ditch of the enclosure of Réjolles. This quadruple-ditched enclosure on a small side-valley of the River Seugne is only 10km from the pollen core of Les Breuilhs. The cereal deposit consisted of some 9600 carbonized grains, almost exclusively of six-row naked barley (Rowley-Conwy 1990). The predominance of barley was repeated in a sample of 587 carbonized grains from the Echiré enclosure, of which 454 were naked barley, and only 32 wheat (Gyulai *et al.* 1996). The pattern can be amplified by the study of cereal impressions on pottery from late Neolithic sites in the region (Figure 2.8); among 21 sites (predominantly but not exclusively enclosures), naked barley predominates, a fact which may relate to the suitability of winter or spring-sown barley for drier habitats and light, thin, free-draining soils (Cassen 1987, 249–53).

Hence we have a picture of cereal cultivation (demonstrated most graphically by cereal remains from the enclosures themselves) contrasted with pollen core evidence for a wooded environment during the period of the enclosures. Whether these differences are to be explained purely by local effects is unclear. One possible interpretation is that cereal cultivation was small-scale and limited to relatively restricted areas during this period. Support for such an interpretation might be sought in the relatively high proportion of wild animal remains in the faunal assemblages from certain enclosures; up to 19% at Echiré (Bökönyi 1996) and 14% at Les Matignons (Poulain-Josien 1966), and over 10% at Soubérac (Poulain-Josien 1965), though admittedly much lower at other sites such as Semussac (2%; Poulain-Josien 1984). The relative abundance of remains of wild species certainly suggests that substantial parts of the landscape were uncultivated and remained under forest.[2]

There is reason, then, to argue for a mosaic of vegetation during the late Neolithic, with woodland on valley floors and slopes, and perhaps even across parts of the chalk and limestone plateaux. Cereal cultivation, though present, does not seem to have led to large-scale clearance during the Neolithic period. The predominance of cattle, and the importance of pig at certain sites (Boujot *et al.* 1997), may be related to a relatively mobile economy using forest resources and perhaps more open areas of wetland grazing for the pasturing of herds of cattle, with pig and ovicaprids locally important.

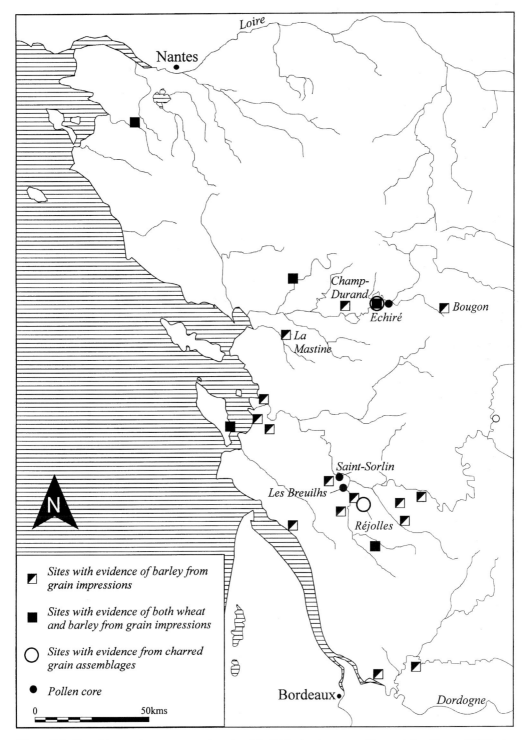

Figure 2.8: Cereal impressions on pottery from late Neolithic sites in western France (after Cassen 1987); the location of the pollen cores referred to in the text is also indicated, along with the enclosures of Réjolles and Echiré which have yielded carbonized cereal assemblages

CONCLUSION

The importance of cattle in the faunal assemblages from west French enclosures suggests that cattle herding was a major element in the daily lives and aspirations of the people who built and used these sites. To draw an analogy with cattle-herding peoples of East Africa such as the Masai or the Nuer (Evans-Pritchard 1940) may be somewhat superficial, given the very different traditions and landscapes involved, but these societies do provide insights into the role which cattle herds may have had as repositories of wealth and status in Neolithic France, and into their symbolic importance. There is abundant evidence for the symbolic role of cattle in the French Neolithic: the cattle burials preceding and subsequently sealed beneath the long mound at Er Grah in Brittany (Le Roux 1998); the long horned cattle depicted on the broken menhir reused at Gavrinis and Locmariaquer (Le Roux 1984); and the cattle skeletons deposited in the inner ditch of the late Neolithic enclosure at Champ Durand, which were dislocated but bore no trace of butchery marks (Cassen 1987, 324–6; figs 34–36).

Thus the late Neolithic enclosures of western France may have been the setting for rituals or ceremonies involving cattle, and the disposal of their remains, just as they were for human remains (Boujot *et al.* 1996; Joussaume 1987). Yet the complexity of activities at these sites goes far beyond this. The rich deposits of decorated pottery found at many of the enclosures – and perhaps especially closely associated with them – suggest that they were also places where group identity was forged and reinforced (Scarre 1998). Furthermore, the large number of known enclosures in such a restricted geographical region poses questions of exclusivity and contemporaneity. The coarseness of the radiocarbon chronology makes it difficult to determine how long the enclosure ditches remained open, and whether adjacent enclosures were in contemporary (and possibly confrontational) use. Some element of competition or rivalry between communities forms a plausible scenario, and one which might best explain the apparent frenzy of activity which led to the creation and elaboration of some 250 enclosures within the space of a few centuries. It is hoped that recent large-scale excavations, soon to be published or still in progress, will provide significant further evidence on the social, cultural, and political phenomenon which these sites represent.

NOTES

1   The percentages cited here and illustrated in Figure 2.7 are for domestic species (cattle, pig, sheep/goat), excluding dog. The figures are based on number of identifiable fragments rather than MNI, and this for two reasons: a) the La Mastine and L'Angle assemblages are too small and the Echiré assemblage too fragmentary for meaningful MNI analysis; inter-site comparisons can therefore only be made on the basis of numbers of fragments; b) at Soubérac, Les Matignons and Semussac, MNI was independently calculated for each stratigraphic unit (as many as eight layers of ditch fill at Les Matignons), without adequate allowance being made for the likely movement of material between layers; hence MNI figures for these sites are probably distorted and must be judged unreliable.

2 These figures once again are based on numbers of identifiable fragments rather than MNI; see
   Note 1. The MNI statistics for the wild component in the three larger assemblages are: Les
   Matignons 27.6%; Soubérac 24.3%; Semussac 7.4%.

BIBLIOGRAPHY

Boelicke, U, von Brandt, D, Lüning, J, Stehli, P, and Zimmerman, A, 1988, **Der bandkeramische Siedlungsplatz Langweiler 8, Gemeinde Aldenhoven, Kreis Düren**. Köln. Rheinland Verlag

Bökönyi, S, 1996, La faune. In C Burnez, **Le Site des Loups à Echiré, Deux-Sèvres**. Bougon. Musée des Tumulus de Bougon. 147–52

Boujot, C, and Cassen, S, 1992, Le développement des premières architectures funéraires monumentales en France occidentale. In C-T Le Roux (ed), **Paysans et Batisseurs. Actes du 17e Colloque Interrégional sur le Néolithique, Vannes, 1990** (= Revue Archéologique de l'Ouest, Supplément 5). 195–211

Boujot, C, Cassen, S, Chambon, P, and Gruet Y, 1996, Matignons et Moulin-de-Vent à Montagant/ Le Brandard (Mainxe, Charente). **Bulletin de la Société Préhistorique Française**, 93, 63–83

Boujot, C, and L'Helgouach, J, 1987, Le site néolithique à fossés interrompus des Prises à Machecoul (Loire-Atlantique). Etudes sur le secteur oriental. **Préhistoire de Poitou-Charentes. Problèmes actuels**. Paris. Editions du Comité des Travaux historiques et scientifiques. 255–69

Boujot, C, Hoad, I, and Serjeantson, D, 1997, Les vestiges osseux des enceintes néolithiques de La Mastine et Pied-Lizet. In S Cassen and C Scarre (eds), 1997, **Les Enceintes Néolithiques de La Mastine et Pied-Lizet (Charente-Maritime). Fouilles archéologiques et études paléo-environnementales dans le Marais Poitevin (1984–1988)**. Chauvigny. Association de Publications Chauvinoises. 111–122

Bradley, R, 1997, **Rock art and the prehistory of Atlantic Europe**. London. Routledge

Bradley, R, 1998, **The significance of monuments.** London. Routledge

Bréart, B, 1984, Le site néolithique du "Champ de Bataille" à l'Etoile (Somme): une enceinte à fossé interrompu. In M Durand (ed), **Le Néolithique dans le Nord de la France et le Bassin Parisien. Actes du 9e colloque interrégional sur le Néolithique (Compiègne 1982)** (= Revue Archéologique de Picardie). 293–310

Burnez, C, 1996a, **Le Site des Loups à Echiré, Deux-Sèvres**. Bougon. Musée des Tumulus de Bougon

Burnez, C, 1996b, Reply to Boujot *et al.* 1996. **Bulletin de la Société Préhistorique Française**, 93, 268–75

Burnez, C, and Case, H, 1966, Les camps néolithiques des Matignons à Juillac-le-Coq (Charente). **Gallia Préhistoire**, 9, 131–245

Burnez, C, Dassié, J, and Sicaud, F, 1995, L'enceinte artenacienne du "Camp" à Challignac (Charente). **Bulletin de la Société Préhistorique Française**, 92, 463–78

Burnez, C, and Fouéré, P, 1993, Les enceintes du Néolithique récent et final de Diconche à Saintes (Charente-Maritime). In J-C Blanchet, A Bulard, C Constantin, D Mordant, and J Tarrête (eds), **Le Néolithique au Quotidien. Actes du XVIe colloque interrégional sur le Néolithique** Paris. Documents d'Archéologie Française. 106–119

Buttler, W, and Haberey, W, 1936, **Die bandkeramische Ansiedlung bei Köln-Lindenthal**. Berlin. De Gruyter

Cassen, S, 1987, **Le Centre-Ouest de la France au IVème millénaire avant J.C** (= British Archaeological Reports International Series 342). Oxford. British Archaeological Reports

Cassen, S, 1993, Material culture and chronology of the middle Neolithic of western France. **Oxford Journal of Archaeology**, 12, 197–208

Cassen, S, Audren, C, Hinguant, S, Lannuzel, G, and Marchand, G, 1998, L'habitat Villeneuve-Saint-Germain du Haut-Mée (Saint-Etienne-en-Coglès, Ille-et-Vilaine). *Bulletin de la Société Préhistorique Française*, 95, 41–75

Cassen, S, and L'Helgouach, J, 1992, Du symbole de la crosse: chronologie répartition et interprétation. In C-T Le Roux (ed), *Paysans et Bâtisseurs. Actes du 17e Colloque Interrégional sur le Néolithique, Vannes (29–31 octobre 1990)* (= Revue Archéologique de l'Ouest, Supplément 5). 225–35

Cassen, S, and Scarre, C, 1997, *Les Enceintes Néolithiques de La Mastine et Pied-Lizet (Charente-Maritime). Fouilles archéologiques et études paléo-environnementales dans le Marais Poitevin (1984–1988)*. Chauvigny. Association de Publications Chauvinoises

Constantin, C, Mordant, D, and Simonin, D (eds), 1997, *La Culture de Cerny. Nouvelle économie, nouvelle société au Néolithique* (= Mémoires du Musée de Préhistoire de l'Ile de France 6). Nemours. Association pour la Promotion de la Recherche Archéologique en Ile de France

Coudart, A, and Demoule, J-P, 1982, Le site néolithique et chalcolithique de Menneville. *Vallée de l'Aisne. Cinq Années de Fouilles Protohistoriques* (= Revue Archéologique de Picardie, numéro spécial). 129–147

Despriée, J, 1986, *Un Village Néolithique: Fossé, Loir-et-Cher*. Blois. Centre Départemental de Documentation Pédagogique du Loir-et-Cher

Diot, M-F, Gomez, J, and Marinval, P, 1987, Le site fortifié du Fort-des-Anglais à Mouthiers-sur-Boême (Charente) et son environnement protohistorique. *Préhistoire de Poitou-Charentes. Problèmes actuels*. Paris. Editions du Comité des Travaux historiques et scientifiques. 331–46

Dubouloz, J, Mordant, D, and Prestreau, M, 1991, Les enceintes "néolithiques" du Bassin parisien. *Identité du Chasséen. Actes du Colloque International de Nemours 1989* (= Mémoires du Musée de Préhistoire d'Ile de France 4). Nemours. Association pour la Promotion de la Recherche Archéologique en Ile de France. 211–29

Evans-Pritchard, E E, 1940, *The Nuer: a description of the modes of livelihood and political institutions of a Nilotic people*. Oxford. Clarendon Press

Fouéré, P, 1998, Deux grands bâtiments du Néolithique final artenacien à Douchapt (Dordogne). In *Rencontres Méridionales de Préhistoire Récente, Arles 1996*. Antibes. ADPCA. 311–28

Giot, P-R, L'Helgouach, J, and Monnier, J-L, 1998, *Préhistoire de la Bretagne (2nd edition)*. Rennes. Ouest France

Gyulai, F, Corillion, R, and Gruet, M, 1996, Les macro-restes. In C Burnez, *Le Site des Loups à Echiré, Deux-Sèvres*. Bougon. Musée des Tumulus de Bougon. 153–4

Irribarria, R, 1998, Fouille d'une enceinte du Néolithique ancien à Villeromain (Loir-et-Cher). In X Gutherz and R Joussaume (eds), *Le Néolithique du Centre-Ouest de la France (Actes du XXIe Colloque Inter-régional sur le Néolithique, Poitiers, 14, 15 et 16 octobre 1994)*. Chauvigny. Association des Publications Chauvinoises. 61–66

Joussaume, R, 1981, *Le Néolithique de l'Aunis et du Poitou occidental dans son cadre atlantique*. Rennes. Travaux du Laboratoire d'Anthropologie, Préhistoire, Protohistoire et Quaternaire Armoricains

Joussaume, R, 1987, Les sépultures du site à triple enceinte de fossés interrompus de Champ-Durand à Nieul-sur-l'Autize. *Préhistoire de Poitou-Charentes. Problèmes actuels*. Paris. Comité des Travaux Historiques et Scientifiques. 271–288

Joussaume, R, and Pautreau, J-P, 1990, *La Préhistoire du Poitou*. Nantes. Editions Ouest-France

Kuper, R, Lohr, H, Lüning, J, Stehli, P, and Zimmerman, A, 1977, *Der bandkeramische Siedlungsplatz Langweiler 9, Gemeinde Aldenhoven, Kreis Düren*. Bonn. Rheinland Verlag

Lecerf, Y, 1986, Une nouvelle intervention archéologique au camp du Lizo en Carnac (Morbihan). *Revue Archéologique de l'Ouest*, 3, 47–58

Leroux, G, 1992, Découvertes de structures d'habitat néolithiques dans le bassin oriental de la Vilaine: l'apport de la prospection aérienne dans le sud-est de l'Ille-et-Vilaine. In C-T Le Roux (ed), *Paysans et Bâtisseurs. Actes du 17e Colloque Interrégional sur le Néolithique, Vannes (29–31 octobre 1990)* (= Revue Archéologique de l'Ouest, Supplément 5). 79–83

Letterlé, F, 1997, Le Cerny: sa place dans la néolithisation de l'Armorique et le développement des cultures armoricaines au Néolithique moyen I. In C Constantin, D Mordant and D Simonin (eds), *La Culture de Cerny. Nouvelle économie, nouvelle société au Néolithique* (= Mémoires du Musée de Préhistoire de l'Ile de France 6). Nemours. Association pour la Promotion de la Recherche Archéologique en Ile de France. 661–77

Letterlé, F, Le Gouestre, D, and Le Meur, N, 1990, Le site d'habitat ceinturé du Néolithique moyen armoricain de Sandun à Guérande (Loire-Atlantique). Essai d'analyse des structures. In D Cahen and M Otte (eds), *Rubané et Cardial*. Liège. ERAUL 39, 299–313

L'Helgouach, J, 1970, Le monument mégalithique du Goërem à Gâvres (Morbihan). *Gallia Préhistoire*, 13, 217–61

L'Helgouach, J, 1988, Le site néolithique final à fossés interrompus des Prises à Machecoul. In C Burgess, P Topping, C Mordant, and M Maddison (eds), *Enclosures and defences in the Neolithic of western Europe* (= British Archaeological Reports International Series 403). Oxford. British Archaeological Reports. 265–73

Le Roux, C-T, 1984, A propos des fouilles de Gavrinis (Morbihan): nouvelles données sur l'art mégalithique Armoricain. *Bulletin de la Société Préhistorique Française*, 81, 240–45

Le Roux, C-T, 1998, Quinze ans de recherches sur les mégalithes de Bretagne (19809–1995). Bilan des connaissances. In P Soulier (ed), *La France des Dolmens et des Sépultures Collectives (4500–2000 avant J.-C.)*. Paris. Errance. 58–66

Le Rouzic, Z, 1933, Premières fouilles au camp du Lizo (commune de Carnac, Morbihan). *Revue Archéologique*, 2, 189–219

Lüning, J, 1988, Zur Verbreitung und Datierung bandkeramischer Erdwerke. *Archäologisches Korrespondenzblatt*, 18, 155–58

Maguer, P, 1996, Les enceintes fortifiées de l'Age du Fer dans le Finistère. *Revue Archéologique de l'Ouest*, 13, 103–21

Marambat, L, 1995, *Paysages de la Façade Atlantique Girondine et de la Saintonge au Post-Glaciaire. L'empreinte de l'homme*. Paris. CNRS

Marambat, L, 1996, L'apport de la palynologie à la connaissance de l'environnement. In C Burnez, *Le Site des Loups à Echiré, Deux-Sèvres*. Bougon. Musée des Tumulus de Bougon. 173–6

Marsac, M, and Scarre, C, 1979, Recent discoveries of Neolithic ditched camps in West-Central France. *Aerial Archaeology*, 4, 37–57

Mercer, R J, 1981, Excavations at Carn Brea, Illogan, Cornwall, 1970–73. A Neolithic fortified complex of the third millennium bc. *Cornish Archaeology*, 20, 1–204

Mohen, J-P, and Bergougnan, D, 1984, Le camp néolithique de Chez-Reine, à Semussac (Charente-Maritime). I. Etude archéologique. *Gallia Préhistoire*, 27, 7–40

Mordant, C, and Mordant, D, 1988, Les enceintes néolithiques de la haute vallée de la Seine. In C Burgess, P Topping, C Mordant, and M Maddison (ed), *Enclosures and defences in the Neolithic of western Europe* (= British Archaeological Reports International Series 403). Oxford. British Archaeological Reports. 231–54

Ollivier, A, Leduc, M, and Diot, M-F, 1997, L'enceinte néolithique de Temps Perdu, commune de Migné-Auxances (Vienne). *Bulletin de la Société Préhistorique Française*, 94, 217–29

Petrasch, J, 1990, Mittelneolithische Kreisgrabenanlagen in Mitteleuropa. *Bericht der Römisch-Germanischen Kommission*, 71, 407–564

Poulain-Josien, T, 1965, Etude de la faune du gisement de Soubérac, Gensac-la-Pallue (Charente). *Bulletin de la Société Préhistorique Française*, 62, 316–27

Poulain-Josien, T, 1966, Etude de la faune du gisement néolithique des Matignons. *Gallia Préhistoire*, 9, 210–41

Poulain-Josien, T, 1984, La faune. In Le camp néolithique de Chez Reine à Semussac (Charente-Maritime), II: Le Milieu. *Gallia Préhistoire*, 27, 41–65

Rowley-Conwy, P, 1990, Annexe III. Un échantillon de grains carbonisés de Réjolles à Biron (Charente-Maritime). *Bulletin de la Société Préhistorique Française*, 87, 388–89

Scarre, C, 1982, Settlement patterns and landscape change: the late Neolithic and the Bronze Age of the Marais Poitevin area of western France. *Proceedings of the Prehistoric Society*, 48, 53–73

Scarre, C, 1992, The early Neolithic of France of western France and megalithic origins in Atlantic Europe. *Oxford Journal of Archaeology*, 11, 121–54

Scarre, C, 1998, Arenas of action? Enclosure entrances in Neolithic western France *c.* 3500–2500 BC. *Proceedings of the Prehistoric Society*, 64, 115–138

Sherratt, A, 1998, Points of exchange: the later Neolithic monuments of the Morbihan. In A Gibson and D Simpson (eds), *Prehistoric ritual and religion. Essays in honour of Aubrey Burl*. Stroud. Sutton Publishing. 119–38

Thomas, J, 1991, *Rethinking the Neolithic*. Cambridge. Cambridge University Press

Tinevez, J-Y, 1995, La Hersonnais à Pléchâtel (Ille-et-Vilaine): un vaste ensemble du Néolithique final. Résultats préliminaires. In C Billard (ed), *Evreux 1993. Actes du 20ème colloque interrégional sur le Néolithique* (= Revue Archéologique de l'Ouest, Supplément 7). 293–317

Whittle, A, 1996, *Europe in the Neolithic. The creation of new worlds*. Cambridge. Cambridge University Press

Whittle, A, 1997, Moving on and moving around: Neolithic settlement mobility. In P Topping (ed), *Neolithic landscapes* (= Neolithic Studies Group Seminar Papers 2). Oxford. Oxbow Books. 15–22

Neolithic enclosed settlements in Cornwall: the past, the present, and the future

R J Mercer

INTRODUCTION

The excavation of the site at Carn Brea, near Redruth, Cornwall, published in 1981 (Mercer 1981), represented a new departure in our understanding of the southern British Neolithic. It presented southern British archaeology, for the first time, with a phenomenon well known on the near European continent and in the north of Britain – an enclosure or defined area bearing ample evidence of structural complexity, midden accumulation, and traces of artefact production and usage in a style, and of a quantity, to suggest long-term use of the site for settlement. At Carn Brea, in this latter regard, some 550 vessels were represented in the recovered ceramic assemblage which emanated from about 10% of the excavable area of the site and 2107 implements were located among over 26,000 struck pieces of flint. Such figures, at least in terms of the ceramic assemblage, compare well with the yield per cubic metre excavated at sites like Eilean Domhnuill, Loch Olabhat, North Uist (Armit 1992) and the related site at Eilean an Tighe (Scott 1951) on the same island. In Orkney, and of broadly similar date, the Neolithic settlement at Knap of Howar (Ritchie 1983) produces a similar quantitative profile. In southern England comparison with, for example, Windmill Hill, Wiltshire (Smith 1965) and Hambledon Hill, Dorset (Mercer and Healy forthcoming) shows, immediately, that despite the vastly greater areas excavated on these sites, the "yield" of ceramic and even lithics (in a flint bearing area) are, by volumetric comparison, minute.

CARN BREA: AN ENCLOSED NEOLITHIC SETTLEMENT

Carn Brea introduced a new site type, the enclosed Neolithic settlement, to southern British archaeology – and offered a new and vital insight to social organization and development in the Neolithic. So great was the shock this administered that in a book entitled *Rethinking the Neolithic* (Thomas 1991) a study focusing on southern Britain, a decade after its publication, the site is not mentioned at all. The issue here, presumably, is the acceptance of Carn Brea as a settlement site and it is for that reason that I chose to introduce this retrospective note by emphasizing the quite extraordinary density of cultural material located on the site which perhaps has not been sufficiently generally appreciated.

It is also the case that much of this material was located on and in trampled surfaces, and within organic deposits (albeit ill-defined as no pollen, bone, or molluscan material survived the hostile nature of the site and even charcoal was generally converted to black "sludge"). With only one or two exceptions, where nearly complete vessels had apparently been crushed *in situ* by the collapse of formerly upright slabs, the vast majority of the ceramic assemblage was highly fragmentary with little evidence, if any, for carefully placed deposits of a "ceremonial" character. The abundance of well crushed-down ceramic in, where sufficient protection was offered, richly organic deposits on the site leaves the writer in no doubt that the site at Carn Brea was extensively used for settlement by a large social group, however intermittently. Extrapolation would suggest that the remains of in excess of 5000 vessels may have been deposited at Carn Brea and a quarter of a million fragments of struck flint and chert. The ceramics, there is now no doubt (despite some hints of doubt in the 1981 Report,) were all attracted to the hilltop from a manufacturing source in the Lizard Peninsula – some 25km to the south. Similarly large quantities of flint and chert must have been brought to the site from local beaches as well as from further afield in the form of polished axes as well as raw material. A total of *c.* 40 greenstone and other imported stone objects have been found on the hill, again only a tithe of the number that may remain there – which must suggest that the site saw the use and possibly the manufacture of polished stone axes (one axe polisher was also found).

It was, in fact, this extraordinary wealth of artefacts which led to the recognition of the site at Carn Brea in the first instance. The description of "Carnbray" by John Leland during his visit to Cornwall in 1541 as

> "on an hill a castelet or pile (of) Bassetts a mile west of Re(druth) town. There was sometime (a pa)rk now (defa)ced"

may well suggest the contemporary recognition of the massive "hillfort" defences that characterize today the southern slopes of the hill (Figure 3.1). So massive are these defences that the outer (southernmost) circuit proved beyond the resources of the 1970–73 campaign of excavations to examine. Indeed until the 1640s the hill was covered by oak forest, felled to pay the fines of the staunchly Royalist Francis Basset Baron de Dunstanville after the death of Charles I and these mighty fortifications must have been visible in this environment. Thence until the early 20th century the hill was under a turf grazed down by sheep and it is in this context of maximum visibility of the early remains that the first major archaeological investigation took place by Thurston Peter assisted by John Burnard (Peter 1896; Burnard 1896). Both men were skilled archaeologists by the standards of their time and spent several months on the site. The focus of their attention was, however, the extant southern ramparts already mentioned and the dozen or so hut-circles, of Iron Age date, set on the eastern saddle of the hill. At no stage in their account or indeed on plan, in the high quality survey of the site provided by Sampson Hill of Redruth, is there any hint that there was any understanding of the enclosure wall of the Neolithic eastern summit (1ha) *enceinte* nor any "joined up" understanding of the outer Neolithic defences as investigated on Site A3 of the 1981 report.

If these features were difficult to observe in 1896 under a sheep grazing regime this writer can aver that under the decayed state of upland grazings in Cornwall, and certainly at Carn Brea, where bracken and gorse have, in the interim, made major advances, it was

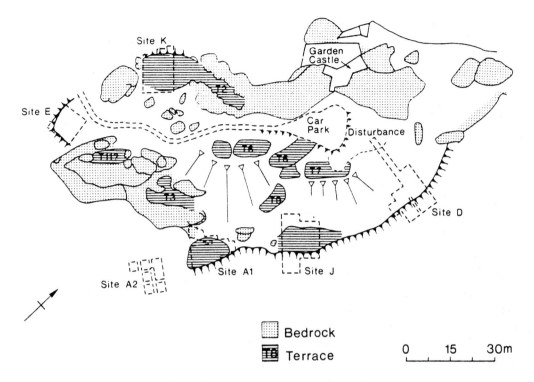

Figure 3.1: Plan of Carn Brea, Cornwall

quite impossible to locate, let alone appreciate the features that in the course of excavation emerged as the Neolithic defences of the site.

What indeed drew the writer to the site at Carn Brea was not the field remains, as visible, at all. It was the sheer quantity and quality of Neolithic artefacts that lay in tea-chests in the magazines of the County Museum, Truro, as it had been recovered by Peter and Burnard. What was absolutely clear from their accounts was that Neolithic material had been recovered all over the eastern end of the hill, wherever they had excavated. Within the hut-circles both diagnostically Neolithic material (leaf-shaped arrowheads, bowl pottery) and diagnostically Iron Age material in much lesser quantity (spindle whorls, wheel-made pottery) had been located. It was also abundantly clear that when, at the suggestion of Peter's little daughter, they dug "among the nooks and crannies of the Eastern summit" of the hill, the rate of recovery of Neolithic material, notably arrowheads, increased exponentially. *Prima facie* a case existed for settlement focused on the eastern summit. It was excavation carried out on "promising" terrace-like locations in the area that revealed the defensive circuit of the eastern summit. At first this was assumed to be Iron Age superimposed upon Neolithic levels but that view soon became unsustainable in the face of the evidence.

The moral of this story is that sites of this type are not likely to be easy to find. Even with the (quite accidental) intervention of Peter and Burnard, determined as much, one suspects, by the proximity of Carn Brea to the Redruth-Camborne conurbation, as by any research trajectory, it required relatively major archaeological input to disentangle the record and reveal the site for what it was.

OTHER ENCLOSED SETTLEMENTS

Since 1981, as with any new departure, there has been some concerted effort to locate parallel sites if only to confirm the interpretation of the Carn Brea evidence and to confirm its significance as a "type-site". This effort has been met with only partial success and has perhaps also brought a measure of obfuscation to which the writer himself, let it immediately be said (and with hindsight), has substantially contributed.

The search for parallel sites to Carn Brea has really only met with one unqualified success – the discovery of the site at Helman Tor near Lostwithiel in central Cornwall (Figure 3.2). The initial stimulus for investigation of this site came from the late Mrs Mary Irwin, a stalwart member of the Cornwall Archaeological Society, who knew the site well and was convinced that the site "had the same feel" as Carn Brea (and how right she was to adopt this approach!). Subsequent checking revealed that Neolithic material (struck flints and two stone axes) had been found on, and in the immediate vicinity of, the site.

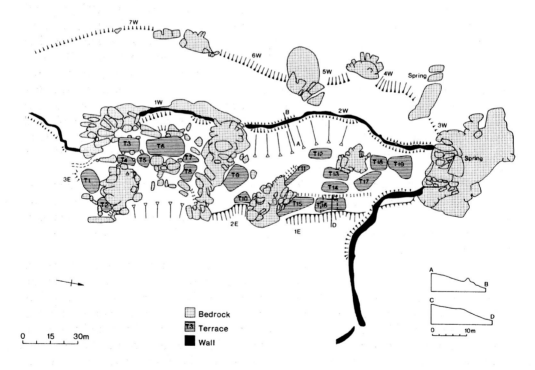

Figure 3.2: Plan of Helman Tor, Cornwall

Inspection of the site at the appropriate season, for bracken was again a major problem here, confirmed the presence on the hilltop of features (terraces and lengths of walling) that might offer parallels with Carn Brea. But the most compelling "evidence" lay in the "feel" to which Mrs Irwin had alluded. Set at almost exactly the same height as Carn Brea (220m OD), on a similarly orientated northwest-facing spur, Helman Tor overlooks a good flowing water source at no great distance (as does Carn Brea at *c.* 500m) and is set on a spur upon all sides of which ground exists that would or could have furnished both good grazing and arable resources. The water source in both cases is likely to have been unpolluted as it is very near its rising springs and, again in both instances, occupies, near the source, an area of rather indeterminate drainage which may have fostered the presence of other resources, notably wild fowl. In both instances ancient field lay-outs have been located (at Helman Tor by survey and at Carn Brea by excavation) in close proximity to the site on south and southwest facing slopes. Both sites are, of course, sited on granite, well drained, offering a prominent (and with their tors well signalled) position, easily defensible and perhaps conferring status within the broader landscape. Yet in both instances the site, while on granite, is within easy reach of other geologies offering a range of opportunities. Both sites are close to ancient east to west routes across Cornwall.

PREDICTIVE MODELLING AND ORIGINAL DISTRIBUTIONS

Above are listed ten diagnostic traits shared by Carn Brea and Helman Tor – a "fingerprint" that appears to offer meat and drink to a Geographical Information System. Predictive modelling through such a system, querying only topographical, land-use and geological information layers, should produce a list of likely locations in very short order. Then, of course, the hard work would begin, checking each location on the ground, at the appropriate season, in order to assess the likelihood of a Neolithic presence. Such searches must take into account the very great antiquity of such remains which has led to their obscuration at both Carn Brea and Helman Tor, by ruination and geomorphological factors such as soil creep. It may well be subtly shifting environmental and geological/geomorphological factors over distance will also change the structural response to the ten requirements expressed in the above diagnostic features.

Such an approach, however, will help to eliminate a number of sites suggested (by the writer among others) that palpably do not, even remotely fulfil even a minority of the suggested criteria. Sites such as Roughtor, on Bodmin Moor, set well within granite massifs at a height far in excess of 200m OD may be Neolithic, but they are not likely to be part of the Carn Brea/Helman Tor continuum.

It may, of course, be that Cornwall could only support two such centres (if that is what they were) and there are no more to look for. That this seems unlikely is suggested by the excellent fieldwork of Jacqui Nowakowski and Peter Herring at Carn Galver, near St Ives in West Penrith, Cornwall. Bracken (at its height on the only occasion that the writer has been able to visit the site) and the ubiquitous presence of granite "clitter" makes the site extremely difficult to appreciate but "the eye of faith" allowed him to accept the site as a "probable" and it certainly satisfies the majority (but not all) of the criteria set out above; it lacks the proximity to the ecotone between granite based and other soils and, as yet, lacks proximate field lay-outs, but is flanked by substantial peat deposits that could conceal these.

DISCUSSION

Why is it worth-while searching for such sites? As hinted at earlier in this paper such complex (defended) settlements, at a relatively early stage of the Neolithic in Britain may appear to cut across the path of current appreciations of the period – at least in southern Britain. This tension, however, makes it more important, not less, that we should investigate the potential of such sites.

The sites at Carn Brea and Helman Tor have profound disappointments to offer the archaeologist. As already indicated, the sites, for reasons associated with their geology and location, do not support fossil bone, molluscan, or pollen material, and therefore offer little in the way of palaeo-environmental or palaeo-economic information. Yet they do offer extraordinarily rich artefact assemblages within structures set within enclosures, themselves set within larger enclosive systems. Pottery manufacture and exchange systems hinted at from the wider south British context are shown within their local context. At Carn Brea, as has been indicated, the whole pottery assemblage, potentially 5000 vessels for the whole site, has been imported from manufactories set at a considerable distance to the south. At Helman Tor the proportion of such imported ceramic is much reduced although still very substantial (Mercer forthcoming). Locally manufactured ceramics, however, fill whatever vacuum was created and these display a distinctly eastward reflection, in terms of style, demonstrating links with known sites in Devon and Wessex. Yet the lithic tradition continues without, apparently, any significant variation. The grouped axes passing through these sites vary in accordance with proximity with their established sources.

Helman Tor (Mercer 1986; forthcoming) was a very small-scale excavation conducted, through the mediation of the late Bob Smith, as a site assessment, for English Heritage. The cost of the excavation (in 1986) was less than £4000. The amount of material and data gained was extraordinary. The area excavated was less than 75 square metres.

It will take a very great deal less simply to demonstrate the Neolithic assignation of such sites, if the density of evidence at Carn Brea and Helman Tor is to be anticipated. Sites exist in southwest Britain that have the potential to show us aspects of the economic structure and interrelational nature of human society in our early Neolithic. Let us take the relatively straightforward and inexpensive steps to establish their existence and ensure their protection for the future.

BIBLIOGRAPHY

Armit, I, 1992, The Hebridean Neolithic. In N Sharples and A Sheridan (eds), **Vessels for the ancestors**. Edinburgh. Edinburgh University Press. 307–21

Burnard, R, 1896, The exploration of Carn Brea. **Transactions of the Plymouth Institution and Devon and Cornwall Natural History Society**, 1–54

Mercer, R J, 1981, Excavations at Carn Brea, Illogan, Cornwall, 1970–73. A Neolithic fortified complex of the third millennium bc. *Cornish Archaeology*, 20, 1–204

Mercer, R J, 1986, *Excavation of a Neolithic enclosure at Helman Tor, Lanlivery, Cornwall, 1986: interim report* (= Department of Archaeology, University of Edinburgh, Project Paper 4). Edinburgh. University of Edinburgh

Mercer, R J, forthcoming, The excavation of a Neolithic enclosure complex at Helman Tor, Lostwithiel, Cornwall. *Cornish Archaeology*, 36 (1997)

Mercer, R J, and Healy, F, forthcoming, *The excavation of the Neolithic enclosure complex at Hambledon Hill, Dorset* (= English Heritage Archaeological Reports). London. English Heritage

Peter, T, 1896, The exploration of Carn Brea. *Journal of the Royal Institution of Cornwall*, 13, 92–102

Ritchie, A, 1983, Excavation of a Neolithic farmstead at Knap of Howar, Papa Westray, Orkney. *Proceedings of the Society of Antiquaries of Scotland*, 113, 40–121

Scott, Sir W L, 1951, Eilean an Tighe: a pottery workshop of the second millennium BC. *Proceedings of the Society of Antiquaries of Scotland*, 85 (1950–51), 1–37

Smith, I F, 1965, *Windmill Hill and Avebury. Excavations by Alexander Keiller 1925–39*. Oxford. Clarendon Press

Thomas, J, 1991, *Rethinking the Neolithic*. Cambridge. Cambridge University Press

Chapter 4

Early enclosures in southeast Cornwall

Keith Ray

INTRODUCTION

In many parts of Britain, the discovery and initial investigation of important prehistoric sites has understandably had a considerable impact on subsequent archaeological perceptions. This has sometimes too readily led to assumptions that such sites typify settlement or activity for certain periods and for whole regions. For the Neolithic of Cornwall and southwest England, the dramatic results from excavations at Carn Brea near Redruth, and limited exploration of other Neolithic hilltop sites such as Helman Tor south of Bodmin, may in this way have led to an expectation that tor enclosures were the characteristic form for early settlement sites in the region (Mercer 1986a). Generalization of this kind is, however, premature since despite the long and distinguished record of archaeological exploration, there are large areas of Cornwall that have been subject only to the most limited study.

One such area is southeast Cornwall, a distinctive sub-region of undulating hills and deeply incised valleys extending from the southern flank of Bodmin Moor southwards to the Atlantic coastline. The area is bounded to the east by the lower reaches of the River Tamar and to the west by the Fowey Estuary. The dramatic monuments on the edge of the moor such as The Hurlers stone circles and Trethevy Quoit are familiar from guides to British prehistory. Less well-known is the group of Neolithic sites that exists in the area of Balstone Down near Callington, or the barrows that survive in a series of clusters south and east of the lower valley of the River Fowey, not far from Lostwithiel (Figure 4.1).

The fieldwork reported here represents a limited exploration of the character of some of the known prehistoric enclosures in this area. Between 1994 and 1996, initial survey work and trial excavation was carried out at two sites, one on the most prominent hilltop south from the moor, and the other on a ridge overlooking the coast. The results of this fieldwork have raised more questions than they have answered, but do suggest that there are more early enclosures to be discovered in the region than might be supposed from the existing literature. This account provides some background to the investigations, describes their results, and weighs the implications both locally and more widely within southern Britain.

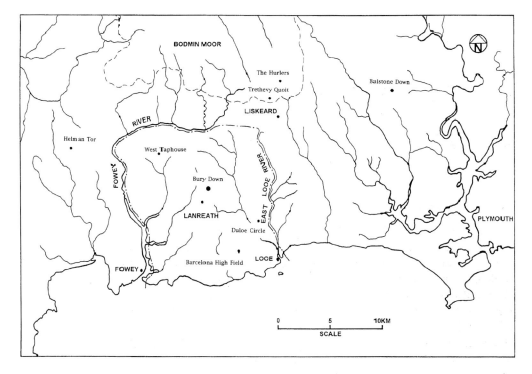

Figure 4.1: Southeast Cornwall showing the location of the principal sites mentioned in the text

THE NEOLITHIC OF SOUTHEAST CORNWALL

Trethevy Quoit is generally regarded as the earliest monument in the area. It was first recorded by Norden in 1610, and was described in detail by the younger Borlase (Borlase 1872, 45–51). Structurally similar to sites such as Chun Quoit in West Penwith (Barnatt 1982, 44–7), it is regarded as a classic portal dolmen, while nonetheless a rare example of this kind of monument in eastern Cornwall (Barnatt 1982, 131–4).

At Balstone Down south of Kit Hill near Callington a source area and quarry site has been claimed for greenstone (epidiorite) axes thought to constitute Group IV among petrologically characterized Neolithic stone implements (Stone and Wallis 1951, 113). Doubt has been cast upon the definition of these Cornish groups, and the existence of any definable Cornish axe production sites has also been questioned (Berridge 1994). However, what appear to be axe roughouts (albeit in material other than greenstone), and objects that are difficult to explain other than as hammerstones (in greenstone), have been found during fieldwalking on the slopes of Balstone Down (Walford 1994). These finds suggest that the manufacture of stone implements did take place in the area. They also reinforce a view that, while the coherence of Group IV and its quarrying in southeast Cornwall is doubtful, the existence of some kind of axe-manufacture in the Callington area is less so. Axes made of greenstone, or worked in other materials, have been recovered during fieldwalking in several other locations in southeast Cornwall, or as accidental finds. The latter includes a large axe lifted from a submerged reef at Barn Pool near Mount Edgcumbe, a location likely to have been above sea-level during Neolithic times (Ray 1994a).

The importance of the Balstone Down area to the south of Kit Hill in the Neolithic is underlined by the survival locally of the best example of a henge monument yet known in Cornwall, at Castlewich on the southwestern flank of the Down. This survives as a prominent earthwork with a pronounced external bank surrounding a raised central area (Mercer 1986a, fig 15). Moreover, a mound oriented east to west on the southern slopes of Kit Hill on Hingston Down (SX 38127078) has been claimed as a long barrow, although it might otherwise be explained as waste from mining operations. The existence of the placename "Sevenstones" just to the east, also on Hingston Down, could be taken to imply the former presence of a stone circle here.

The continuing significance of the Balstone Down area to prehistoric communities is further marked by the discovery of a Beaker burial cist at Harrowbarrow less than 1km to the east. Moreover, there are barrow cemeteries with visible mounds on Kit Hill to the north, again on Hingston Down to the northeast, and on Viverdon Down immediately to the south.

Apart from the sites on the southern flank of Bodmin Moor already noted, the only other concentration of sites of proven Neolithic date close to southeast Cornwall exists in the area just to the west of the Fowey and south of Bodmin. This group again includes the site of a megalithic burial chamber, at Lesquite, Lanivet (Miles and Trudgian 1976), and what appears to be another henge monument at Castilly (Thomas 1964; Mercer 1986a, fig 15). Close to both of these monuments is the tor enclosure on Helman Tor (Mercer 1986b and Chapter 3).

These groups of sites are all on, or close to, elevated land enclosed in recent centuries, or on ground that remains rough grazing today. Only very exceptional early sites, such as the stone circle at Duloe with its six massive quartzite stones, survive on lower ground, although even this site is close to the summit of a prominent ridge (Barnatt 1982, 192–5; Mercer 1986a, 71). Across the rest of southeast Cornwall, away from the moor, some earthwork sites of Bronze Age and later date do survive as above-ground earthworks, among them barrows and hilltop or hillslope fortifications.

In addition to the stone axes already mentioned, numerous scatters of worked flint have been located by fieldwalking and surface collection. Probable Neolithic flintwork has been noted among some of this material, but until the fieldwork reported below no investigations had been organized specifically to follow up such finds. In contrast, activity from later periods is represented by several reported findspots of bronzes, goldwork, and (from destroyed barrows) pottery of Bronze Age character.

THE BOCONNOC AREA PROJECT

One area where Bronze Age finds are concentrated is that immediately east of the lower reaches of the Fowey and west of the valleys of the East and West Looe rivers. Some of the earliest excavations in southwest Britain were carried out on barrows in this area, at Pelynt, between 1834 and 1845 (Borlase 1872, 188–96). Moreover, several finds of goldwork have been reported here, such as a chain from Little Larnick north of Pelynt

(Pearce 1983, 422), and an armring from Tremadart near Duloe (Pearce 1983, 405; Royal Institution of Cornwall Museum, catalogue number 1939/320).

The barrow groups mentioned at the beginning of this paper have not been published in detail, but the most prominent, on the crest of a ridge at West Taphouse, have been noted in several publications (*e.g.* Barnatt 1982, 204–5). The barrows are distributed across an area of high ridges that descend sharply to the Fowey to the north and west, but which slope more gradually southwards. To the east are further prominent ridges that nonetheless appear at present not to have contained such a high concentration of barrows.

Within the Boconnoc area there is a total of 46 barrows recorded (Ray forthcoming). The distribution of these barrows is focused upon Braddock Down and parish, and lies almost entirely within the lands of the Boconnoc Estate. For this reason the term "Boconnoc area" has been used to designate the focus for the study reported here. The landscape to the north towards Bodmin Moor and to the south towards the coast contains isolated barrows, but the only definite groups are (or were) located in the vicinity of Pelynt. There are seven main groups of barrows, containing between four and seven examples in each group. In common with most such barrow groups they consist of barrows of different sizes, although the largest are concentrated in the groups that are among the most northerly and easterly.

The dense distribution and nature of the barrows can be taken to indicate the presence of a significant population in the area over an extended period of time. Such a density might also imply that the communities represented by these cemeteries had occupied the area ancestrally, but if this was the case, the absence of traces of Neolithic monuments is curious. Of course, it may transpire that the barrows themselves originated in the Neolithic. To test whether this absence was more apparent than real as far as settlement was concerned, it was decided to look more closely at known monuments other than barrows.

BURY DOWN, LANREATH

Bury Down is the highest hilltop in southeast Cornwall, south of Bodmin Moor. At its west end are the prominent earthworks of a prehistoric enclosure with two roughly concentric circuits of banks and ditches. At first sight, it appears that the inner circuit is a well-preserved earthwork, while the outer circuit represents an eroded outer rampart. In part because of the existence of this outer circuit of ditch and bank, the site is widely regarded as a bivallate Iron Age hillslope fort (Preston-Jones 1996, 6).

On closer inspection it can be seen that the outer earthwork comprises an intermittent bank, with an equally vestigial ditch surrounding it. This latter extends around the hillside in a series of elongated scoops. The disappearance of the outer work along part of its southern circuit has led to the supposition that the monument was an unfinished Iron Age fortification with widely-spaced defensive circuits (Ordnance Survey field record 1971). It could be argued that ploughing has brought down the bank of this outer earthwork circuit and has partially infilled the ditch. However, the earliest published descriptions of the site suggest that in historically recent times, this outer earthwork was never comparable in scale with the inner bank and ditch (Lysons and Lysons 1814, 248; Polsue 1870, 33; Page 1906, 466). Moreover, aerial photographs of the site (*e.g.* CUCAP QD 19 taken in 1955 and

NMR SX 1859/7) demonstrate that it is more likely that the southern arc of the outer enclosure is present, but is obscured by a later hedgerow.

From the surface evidence alone, therefore, an alternative reading of the outer earthwork circuit at Bury Down is possible (Figure 4.2). The intermittent bank is represented by elongated dumps that correspond with the scoops noted above that can be seen as separate segments of ditch. On the northwestern arc of the circuit, there is a faint surface indication of yet another arc of these banks and dumps, but this time immediately inside the other. Were this monument to be situated on the Sussex Downs it would, long ago, have been identified as an interrupted ditch system or causewayed enclosure (Ray 1994c, 228).

In contrast, the form and features of the principal surviving (inner) earthwork enclosure at Bury Down is entirely consistent with a large Cornish round, or enclosed village, of the late Iron Age (extending through to sub-Roman times). This is represented by an oval-shaped defensive perimeter with a substantial near-vertically faced earthen rampart fronted by a simple ditch. The monument lies westward of the summit of the Down, and slopes from east to west. The single entrance is situated at the lowest point of the defences, and the terminus of both bank and ditch turn inwards from each direction to define the gateway. The front of the perimeter rampart is faced with a substantial stone wall visible at several points, and battered inwards. The interior of the fort is marked by the gentle

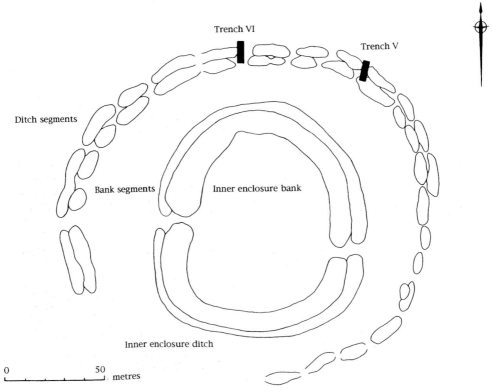

Figure 4.2: Bury Down, Cornwall. Plan based on the 1994 survey and the position of the 1995 trenches

slope of the rear of the earthen rampart. In all these particulars, and in its size (but not in its location), the site is closely comparable with the totally-excavated round at Trethurgy near St Austell some 20km to the west (Miles and Miles 1973).

The 1994 field season at Bury Down involved some test-pitting outside the outer enclosure eastwards from the site, and some exploratory mapping of the outer earthwork itself (Ray 1994c; 1994d). This reinforced the impression that the bank and ditch were segmented. In 1995, a ditch terminal on the northern side of the monument that had been located through surface mapping and geophysical survey (Figure 4.3) was test-excavated. A second trench was also excavated, located at the apparent mid-point of another segment. In one of these trenches the adjacent bank was also examined (Figure 4.4).

The expectation from excavations at other enclosures in the southwest where a Neolithic component has been traced (such as Raddon Hill, north of Exeter: Gent and Knight 1995) would be that the ditches would contain significant quantities of lithic and some ceramic material. It is perhaps worth emphasizing the small scale of the excavations and therefore of the sample examined at Bury Down, but nonetheless, the near-absence of such material was noteworthy. The rounded ditch terminal was shown to define the western side of a causeway, and was characterized by a complex series of silting episodes sealed by a substantial later deposit (Figure 4.3).

Figure 4.3 Bury Down, Cornwall. Plot of the 1998 geophysical survey with results from 1995 shown as an insert

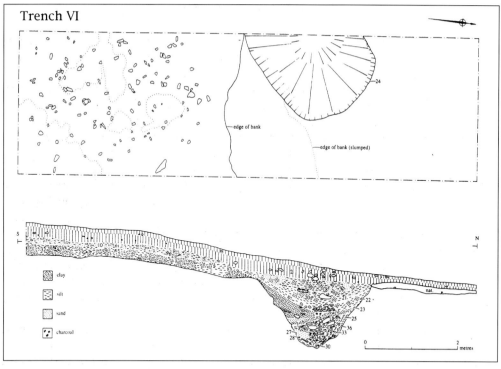

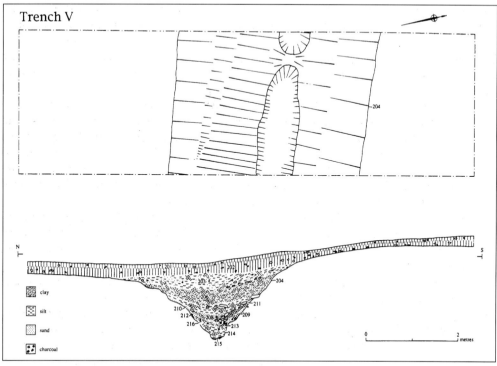

Figure 4.4: Bury Down, Cornwall. Plans and sections from the 1995 trenches

The primary silting (contexts 30 to 27 on the section drawing) in this terminal is interpreted as representing gradual erosion of the sides of the freshly cut ditch. These lowest deposits were then sealed by two layers representing a stabilization horizon, but without evidence of turf formation (contexts 36 and 33). Some deliberate infilling then occurred, from outside the ditch (contexts 25 and 23), followed by further stabilization (context 35). Erosion from or collapse of the bank into the ditch then took place (contexts 26 and 22), before further silting over an extended period (contexts 21, 20, 18, 16, 5).

A series of soil samples was taken from these contexts, and these were tested for pollen content (Charman 1996). Pollen was traced in adequate concentrations in six samples, although pollen grain condition was fair to good in only four of the samples. The sequence hints at several major changes in the local vegetation cover. The primary fill (analyzed sample 1, context 30) contained pollen that points to a light cover of hazel woodland interspersed with open areas of heathland and some grassland. The pastoral indicator *Potentilla erecta* present in the succeeding deposit (sample 2, context 27) suggests that while heathland was still present, grassland was by then more extensive, perhaps associated with the use of the monument. Pollen trapped within the deposits inferred as being part of the infilling from the direction of the bank (sample 3, context 26) formed during a period featuring extensive open grassland.

By the time that the deposit that sealed this was forming, the pollen (sample 4, context 22) provides evidence for a substantial regrowth of woodland with hazel and alder prominent, together with some heathland. The pollen sample from the next deposit (sample 5, context 20) was found to be dominated more than any other by hazel, but with heathland and grassland species also present. The final sample (sample 4, context 5) approximates context 6 on the section drawing. In addition to a mixed woodland flora (including hazel, alder, and oak), lime is also present, suggesting tree cover on the site itself, and while some open land existed nearby, no grass pollen was noted (Charman 1996).

Comparison was made with recently examined and dated pollen sequences on Bodmin Moor. These show that human land management was continuous on those uplands from the early Neolithic, with intensification especially evident during and immediately after the Bronze Age (Gearey and Charman 1996). It was concluded for Bury Down that while it is difficult to extrapolate from upland to lowland with confidence, the very fact that there are significant changes in the pollen spectra of the ditch fills suggests that the ditch dates from the earlier rather than the later prehistoric period (Charman 1996).

The bank was excavated to subsoil, and was shown to be of simple dump construction. No indications were present of a pre-bank soil, suggesting that any turf present had been stripped prior to its construction. Nor were there any traces of postholes or other timber elements.

The second trench produced further evidence for stabilization after intital silting in the ditch, then an episode of rapid infilling from outside the monument. A very fine silt deposit was taken to represent a long period during which the ditch was open, before further evidence for rapid erosion or collapse of the bank, and subsequent infilling over an extended period. The base of the initial cut for the ditch featured a deliberate interruption between segments, a feature that when observed in excavation explains the near-segmentation of ditches evident from geophysics.

Further geophysical survey was carried out in 1998 by staff of the Department of Geological Sciences of the University of Plymouth. This involved both magnetometry and resistivity, and showed that the arc of double bank and ditch traced for the northwestern part of the enclosure circuit continues southwards around the whole of the west-facing side of the monument. The distance between the recorded ditch centres is no more than 5m (Figure 4.3).

BARCELONA HIGH FIELD, PELYNT

In order to examine an enclosure that might be expected to yield more material, it was decided to look at a site where a dense surface scatter of worked flint had been collected during fieldwalking earlier in the 1990s. This site occupied another prominent ridge, this time closer to the sea and only 2km from the major Pelynt barrow cemetery. The site was first noted from the air by O G S Crawford in 1935. Aerial photographs (*e.g.* CAU F19/ 70–74 taken in 1989) suggested that the earthworks crowning the east to west ridge were circular or slightly oval in plan. This had led to contrasting speculations that the enclosure was another round, or even a henge.

A measured plane-table survey was made of the site. This showed that, rather than being sub-circular, its shape was in fact an extended oval, aligned along the ridge. A geophysical survey using a fluxgate gradiometer was then carried out over the earthworks using 20m by 20m grids. This revealed that the form of the enclosure is quite different from that diagnostic of rounds (Figure 4.5; the arc of ditch northwards is interpreted as a medieval deer-park enclosure bank and ditch, the former existence of which is attested by documentary evidence).

The enclosure is 180m east to west, and 100m wide. Its shape is oval, but not egg-shaped in the way that, for instance, the Raddon Hill enclosure in Devon appears to have been (Gent and Knight 1995). Rather, it is a rounded oval shape with almost symmetrical semicircular ends. Close to these ends are what appear to be four entrances, the most easterly and most southerly of which have very rounded terminals. The bank had eroded in a manner similar to that at Bury Down, and did not feature clearly in the geophysical survey. However, along the northern side, a length of bank is evident within two of the 20m survey grids. Through the centre it is possible to discern a narrow positive anomaly, possibly a palisade slot.

A trench was excavated across the southern arc of ditch 40m southwest of the most easterly entrance. The enclosure ditch was found to be sealed by over a metre of erosion deposits derived from the ridge-top above. This is the product of a very extended period of ploughing, indicated also from the geophysical results which appear to register the former existence of ridge and furrow cultivation trending northwest to southeast across the site. The profile of the ditch was much less steep than the ditch at Bury Down, with fewer silting episodes evident. Worked flint was recovered from each of a succession of contexts representing a simple series of fills within the ditch.

The extensive flint assemblage from the site is strongly characterized by small blade cores and narrow blades (Bellamy forthcoming). This is thought to be typical of many flint assemblages of early Neolithic date from southwest England (P Bellamy pers. comm.). It

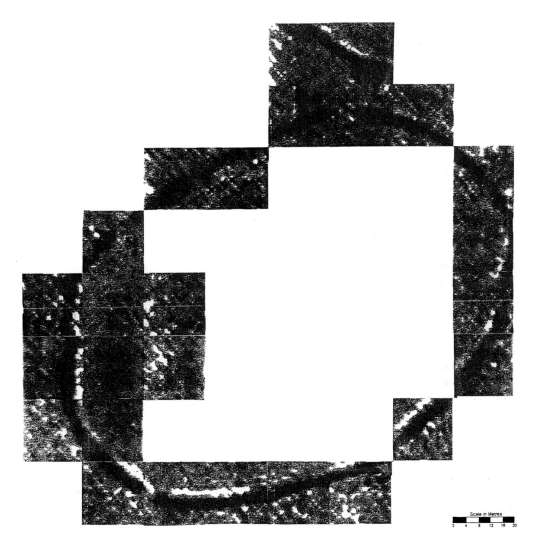

Figure 4.5: Barcelona High Field, Pelynt, Cornwall. Plot of results from the 1996 magnetometer survey

is possible that the flints were lying on the site when the enclosure was constructed. However, the small size and well-sealed context of the material from the excavation suggests, rather, that it is contemporary with it.

IMPLICATIONS FOR SOUTHEAST CORNWALL ENCLOSURES

The results of the investigations outlined above introduce a new element of complexity into the prehistory of this part of Cornwall. Hitherto, the monuments known to exist at

Bury Down and at Barcelona High Field could be fitted into a well-understood distribution of Iron Age sites. Bury Down was interpreted as one of a series of minor bivallate or multivallate hillslope forts, while the Barcelona High Field site was thought most likely to be one of the many hundreds of small homestead enclosures or rounds of the Iron Age and Romano-British periods (*cf.* Johnson and Rose 1982). The strong possibility emerges from the 1994–96 fieldwork that the Bury Down site contains, and the Barcelona High Field site represents, earlier prehistoric enclosures. These sites do not fit into the classifications so far developed for Iron Age defended sites, but they are also beyond what has so far been established as norms for Neolithic enclosures.

One further possibility, in view of the scarcity of material from the excavations, is that the sites can be attributed to a period either very early in the Iron Age, or in the middle or later Bronze Age. A ditch that might have formed part of a ridge-top enclosure at Liskeard was excavated in 1996 by Cornwall Archaeological Unit. This has tentatively been dated, albeit from undiagnostic pottery sherds, to the Bronze Age (Jones 1997). The ditch had a flat base with near-vertical sides quite unlike the Bury Down profile, and exhibited little complexity of infill.

The apparent multiplicity of entrances at Bury Down might be considered a curious feature for a Bronze Age site, and it would be difficult to establish any parallels for the two different forms of the enclosures. The narrow ditches at Bury Down, dug discontinuously with deliberate distinctions between segments of ditch marked by slight baulks between different lengths at the base of the ditch, and the creation of carefully cut butt-ended terminals by entrance causeways, together convey a strong impression of the practices associated with Neolithic monuments.

Such an impression is reinforced by the realization that in parts of the outer circuit at Bury Down two lines of such ditches were cut, separated from one another by as little as 2m. This would render them defensively useless, and also potentially explains the slight nature of the bank as found in the excavation of the ditch terminal. While other possibilities remain, it could be argued that what exists here is a variant form of the causewayed enclosure, the variability of which is now becoming more clearly evident. This cannot be more firmly established without further investigation and the recovery of reliable dating evidence, but would accord with the long sequence of vegetation change apparently indicated by the pollen analysis.

The form of the enclosure at Barcelona High Field is equally anomalous. The existence of four entrances, and their location close to either end of the enclosure, is in practical terms inexplicable for an Iron Age site. In a Neolithic context it could be suggested that the number of entrances and their location around the boundary circuit were determined by ceremonial considerations. This returns the discussion to the possibility that it is a henge. Against such an interpretation is the fact that the monument is quite different in character from such sites. In looking for parallels, it might be more instructive to make comparisons with the (albeit larger-scale) palisaded enclosures now known from Wiltshire and central Wales (Gibson 1998).

It remains to consider each of these enclosures in their landscape context. The Bury Down site occupies a hilltop that is visible (but not easily identifiable) from all parts of the landscape. Like May Hill in Gloucestershire, the crowning of the summit by a grove of trees would make it instantly recognizable from every direction. However, the enclosure commands the western end of the summit of the Down, and as a result faces westwards with an extensive prospect both north and south. This makes it visible from the valleys and ridges below it. The site stands at the extreme southern limit of the near-continuous distribution of barrows already noted.

Interestingly, while the Barcelona High Field site occupies the centre rather than the end of a prominent ridge, it too has extensive views both north and south. Again, it stands at the apparent southern limit of another dense distribution of barrows, represented by the Pelynt barrows already noted, but also by a group only 500m west of the ridge on which it stands. These barrows, at Greystone, Ashen Cross, are situated on the side of a valley. Although now almost obliterated by ploughing, some of them appear to have had mounds of large diameter and height.

FINDING THE UNEXPECTED: WATCHFIELD, OXFORDSHIRE

At Watchfield near Faringdon, in southwest Oxfordshire, on the western margin of the Vale of the White Horse, there exists a site well-known for the excavation of an early Anglo-Saxon cemetery (Scull 1990; 1992). During a rapid magnetometer survey in 1985 a marked linear anomaly was noted to the north of the area discovered and excavated in 1983. When revealed within the area of the 1988 excavations it produced small sherds of Iron Age pottery from the upper fills, and friable pieces of cattle bone and fragmentary potsherds from the lower fills. These last mentioned were subsequently dated by thermoluminescence to the mid-fourth millennium BC (Scull 1992, 144).

This linear feature (context 387 in Area 4: Scull 1992, 135, illustrations 10 and 18) was therefore interpreted as a straight ditch of early Neolithic date, the course of which could not be traced for any appreciable distance north of the excavated area (Scull 1992, 130 and illustration 6). However, reference should also be made to the published grey-tone plot of the enhanced data from the 1992 magnetometer survey (Skull 1992, 129 and illustration 5). This shows the ditch as a straight linear feature terminating some 30m northeast of Trench 4. A similarly marked and again very straight linear feature aligned southeast to northwest almost at right angles to the first ditch is then evident starting some 10m further northeastwards. This continues for around 90m before turning due north.

However, a very much slighter anomaly can also be traced on the plot. This extends northwards in a slight curve from the end of the first straight linear feature, eventually turning westwards in a curving arc 120m north of Trench 4. One tentative interpretation of the two distinct sets of linear features might be that the straight anomalies represent the later phases of the ditch examined in Trench 4, while the curving anomaly represents its Neolithic phase. If the course of this putatively earlier ditch is mapped onto the topography of the hilltop the further possibility emerges that this ditch formed the eastern perimeter of an oval enclosure perhaps 120m across (north to south) sited around the crest of a slight east-facing knoll here, commanding a wide view out over the Vale to the south.

What should be emphasized about the Watchfield case is not the specific nature of any enclosure here. Rather, what is evident is how easy it is to miss the possibility that such enclosures may exist as extremely subtle or vestigial features beneath later monuments and landscapes.

ANTICIPATING VARIABILITY: HEREFORDSHIRE

In Herefordshire, work is beginning on the task of locating a largely missing landscape of Neolithic monuments. While Arthur's Stone, Dorstone, near the Black Mountains is one of the best-known megalithic monuments in the west of England, the existence of similar sites in the north and east of the county that have vanished as obvious surface monuments within the last two centuries is less well appreciated. There are no certain Neolithic enclosures known in the county, but it can be anticipated that, when they begin to be discovered, they will not necessarily be limited in variety to the widely reported sites of the river valleys or hills of southern and eastern England. Indeed, given the topographical variety of the county and its mix of lowlands and upland areas a high degree of variability might be expected. For the moment, only hints of this diversity of form are available.

For example, an enclosure at Westington Camp, Grendon Bishop, near Leominster, is partly defined by a single scarp-edge bank around a promontory, with an extensive view westwards. Aerial photographs indicate a simple entrance facing northeast at the centre point of ditches across the neck of the promontory. The enclosure is described in the Schedule of Ancient Monuments as an Iron Age fortification. However, the only known finds from the site are a small collection of Neolithic flints and one or more stone axe fragments (Turner 1981, 28: site No.319; Herefordshire Sites and Monuments Record 1316). This may be coincidental, but does indicate the possibility of a Neolithic phase here, or indeed that the enclosure in its entirety is an early one.

Undated multiple-ditched enclosures also exist, known only at present from aerial photographs. One of these, at Garway in the southwest of the county, stands high above the River Monnow. It appears to comprise discontinuous lengths of ditch in two or more circuits. Another anomalous enclosure occupies a low ridge above the River Wye near Eaton Bishop. This site features what looks like a palisade within a succession of outer ditches. Moreover, the southern annexe to the hillfort at Croft Ambrey, northwest of Leominster, is undated despite sample excavation of the southwestern arc of its bank during the 1960–66 campaign of excavations (Stanford 1974). Its surveyed form exhibits a degree of segmentation of both bank and ditch (Stanford 1974, fig 1 and plate 1B). One of the few finds, albeit from a stratigraphically late level within the small trench excavated, was a flint flake (Stanford 1974, 131). The possibility exists here, therefore, that the outer ditch, which is very much slighter than that surrounding the main rampart, represents an earlier enclosure.

CONCLUDING DISCUSSION

It would be premature to make detailed comparisons between the Bury Down and Barcelona High Field enclosures on the one hand and other excavated or surveyed sites in southwest Britain on the other. The aim of introducing discussion of sites outside Cornwall is to propose that at last it is possible to recognize the wide-scale existence and diversity of Neolithic enclosures. The intention is also to contribute, as many of the papers in this volume do, to the process of breaking out from the confines of the inherited typologies that have led to the supposition that the full variability of Neolithic enclosures has been explored and understood.

Some consistent features of the kinds of site noted in this paper do emerge. Nonetheless, several such features stem from their field archaeology in the present rather than their form or development in prehistory. The first observation to emphasize about the recognition of these sites is that many of them are still visible in the landscape as earthworks. However, in almost every case these earthworks are very slight or vestigial, sometimes giving rise to the idea that the enclosures were unfinished. In the west of Britain, in areas newly brought under the plough, they may be traceable by crop-marks: but the results of oblique photography may be misleading.

Secondly, in many instances, they may have been confused (either as crop-mark sites or as earthworks) with enclosures of Iron Age date. In some cases, this may have resulted from the reuse of the same site at different times, but in many areas it is due to the uncritical attribution of all pre-Roman enclosures to the Iron Age. The presumption that all enclosures that survive as earthworks must be of late prehistoric date is largely an artefact of the development of archaeology in Britain (*cf.* Thomas 1991, 59, on readings of Neolithic pits from Iron Age practices). Such expectations have been sufficiently tenacious that the contradictory evidence of Neolithic finds from many enclosure sites (otherwise regarded on morphological grounds to have been of Iron Age date) has simply been discounted as being of no great significance.

ACKNOWLEDGEMENTS

I am especially thankful to David and Barbara Tamblyn, and to John Ede, for permission to excavate, and to John Aylett, Mark Knight, John Orme, Samantha Sage, David Stephens, and Nick Wright for their contributions to the fieldwork. Additionally, my thanks are due to Samantha Sage for her drawings of the sections and trench plans featured in Figure 4.4. I also gratefully acknowledge support and encouragement from staff of the Cornwall Archaeological Unit and especially from Nick Johnson and Pete Rose. Steve Hartgroves and Tony Bayfield kindly provided SMR data. Martin Fletcher and Henrietta Quinnell of the Cornwall Archaeological Society lent support and advice to the field project, and the Cornwall Archaeological Society made a small grant towards fieldwork costs. Rob Iles of English Heritage provided Scheduled Monument Consent monitoring. Andrew Chamberlain of the University of Sheffield conducted the geophysical surveys of 1994 and 1996. Dan Charman of the University of Plymouth carried out palynological sampling, and Grahame Taylor also of Plymouth University kindly provided copies of his recent (1998–99) and continuing geophysical surveys at Bury Down.

BIBLIOGRAPHY

Barnatt, J, 1982, *Prehistoric Cornwall. The ceremonial monuments*. Wellingborough. Turnastone Press

Bellamy, P, forthcoming, Lithics. In K Ray, The Boconnoc Project: investigations at prehistoric sites in south-east Cornwall, 1994–96. *Cornish Archaeology*

Berridge, P, 1994, Cornish axe factories: fact or fiction. In N Ashton and A David (eds), *Stories in stone* (= Lithics Studies Society Occasional Paper 4). London. Lithic Studies Society

Borlase, W C, 1872, *Naenia Cornubiae, the cromlechs and tumuli of Cornwall*. London. Longman. (Facsimile reprint by Llanerch Press, 1994)

Charman, D, 1996, *Bury Down: an assessment of pollen content of ditch fill*. Plymouth. University of Plymouth. [Limited circulation printed report]

Gearey B, and Charman, D, 1996, Rough Tor, Bodmin Moor: testing some archaeological hypotheses with landscape scale palynology. In D Charman, R Newnham, and D Croot (eds), *The Quaternary of Devon and east Cornwall: field guide*. London. Quaternary Studies Association. 101–119

Gent, T H, and Knight, M, 1995, *Excavation and survey of a multi-period enclosure site: Raddon Hill, Stockleigh Pomeroy. Interim report* (= Exeter Archaeology Report No. 95.68). Exeter. Exeter Archaeology. [Limited circulation printed report]

Gibson, A, 1998, Hindwell and the Neolithic palisaded sites of Britain and Ireland. In A Gibson and D Simpson (eds), *Prehistoric ritual and religion. Essays in honour of Aubrey Burl*. Stroud. Sutton Publishing. 68–79

Johnson, N, and Rose, P, 1982, Defended settlement in Cornwall, an illustrated discussion. In D Miles (ed), *The Romano-British Countryside* (= British Archaeological Reports British Series 103). Oxford. British Archaeological Reports. 151–208

Jones, A, 1997, *Liskeard Junior and Infant School, Cornwall: an archaeological investigation at Liskeard, Cornwall, December 1996*. Truro. Cornwall County Council. [Limited circulation printed report]

Lysons, D, and Lysons, S, 1814, *Magna Britannia, III: Cornwall*.

Mercer, R J, 1986a, The Neolithic in Cornwall. *Cornish Archaeology*, 25, 35–80

Mercer, R J, 1986b, *Excavation of a Neolithic enclosure at Helman Tor, Lanlivery, Cornwall, 1986, interim report* (= Department of Archaeology, University of Edinburgh, Project Paper 4). Edinburgh. University of Edinburgh

Miles, H, and Miles, T, 1973, Excavations at Trethurgy, St Austell: interim report. *Cornish Archaeology*, 12, 25–30

Miles H, and Trudgian T, 1976, An excavation at Lesquite Quoit, Lanivet. *Cornish Archaeology*, 15, 7–10

Page, W (ed), 1906, *Victoria County History of Cornwall, Volume 1*. London

Pearce, S, 1983, *The Bronze Age metalwork of south western Britain* (= British Archaeological Report British Series 120). Oxford. British Archaeological Reports

Polsue, J, (ed), 1870, *Lake's parochial history of Cornwall*.

Preston-Jones, A, 1996, *Management work at Bury Down Fort, Lanreath, Cornwall*. Truro. Cornwall County Council. [Limited circulation printed report]

Ray, K, 1994a, A Neolithic stone axehead from Barn Pool, Mount Edgecumbe. *Cornish Archaeology*, 33, 225–6

Ray, K, 1994b, The barrow group at Viverdon Down, St Mellion: some observations. *Cornish Archaeology*, 33, 229

Ray, K, 1994c, *An interim report on investigations at Bury Down Fort, Lanreath, Cornwall, July 1994*. Truro and Plymouth. Cornwall Archaeological Society and Geographical Sciences, University of Plymouth. [Limited circulation printed report]

Ray, K, 1994d, Bury Down, Lanreath: investigations in 1994. *Cornish Archaeology*, 33, 227–8

Ray K, forthcoming, The Boconnoc Project: investigations at prehistoric sites in south-east Cornwall, 1994–96. *Cornish Archaeology*

Scull, C J, 1990, Excavation and survey at Watchfield, Oxfordshire, 1983–89: an interim report. *Oxoniensia*, 55, 42–54

Scull, C J, 1992, Excavation and survey at Watchfield, Oxfordshire, 1983–92. *Archaeological Journal*, 149, 124–281

Stanford, S C, 1974, ***Croft Ambrey***. Hereford. Privately published

Stone, J F S, and Wallis, F S, 1951, Third Report of the Sub-Committee of the South-Western Group of Museums and Art Galleries on the Petrological Identification of Stone Axes. ***Proceedings of the Prehistoric Society***, 57, 103–57

Thomas, A C, 1964, The Society's 1962 excavations: the henge of Castilly, Lanivet. ***Cornish Archaeology***, 3, 3–14

Thomas, J, 1991, ***Rethinking the Neolithic***. Cambridge. Cambridge University Press

Turner, J, 1981, ***Herefordshire Register of Countryside Treasures***. Leominster. Hereford and Worcester County Council

Walford, G F, 1994, Prehistoric stone implements found near Callington, Cornwall, and their significance. ***Cornish Archaeology***, 33, 5–21

Chapter 5

Recent work on Neolithic enclosures in Devon

F M Griffith

INTRODUCTION

The last substantial discussion of the Neolithic enclosures of Devon was presented by Roger Mercer in 1981, in his consideration of parallels for the hilltop enclosure at Carn Brea in Cornwall (Mercer 1981). For some time previously, and indeed, until recently, there were four possible Neolithic enclosures in Devon: Hembury, High Peak, Haldon, and Hazard Hill. Of these, only the first two had confirmed enclosing features. The object of this paper is to summarize some recent developments in the study of Neolithic enclosure sites in Devon. All sites mentioned in the text are shown on Figure 5.1.

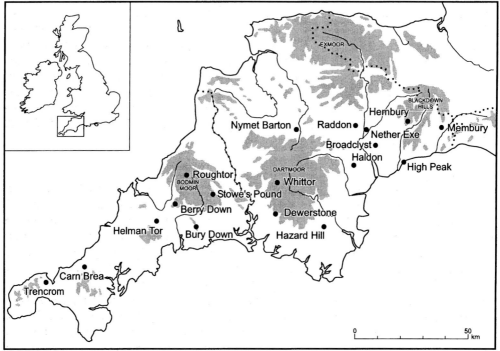

Figure 5.1: Devon and Cornwall: sites mentioned in the text, and by Mercer 1981

ESTABLISHED AND PROBABLE ENCLOSURES

Hembury

Hembury, in east Devon, is one of the classic sites of the southern British Neolithic. It was excavated in the 1930s by Dorothy Liddell (1930; 1931; 1932; 1935). She recorded a causewayed ditch cutting off the southern tip of a spur of the Blackdown Hills, forming a defensible enclosed promontory. The Neolithic enclosure was smaller than the subsequent hillfort occupying the same spur-end location. Inside the entrance to the causewayed enclosure a sub-rectangular house was excavated. The close similarities of the finds from Hembury with those from the contemporary excavations at Windmill Hill provided an important stimulus to pre-war consideration of the southern British Neolithic. In 1960, Lady (Aileen) Fox, who had participated in the Hembury excavations, submitted charcoal samples from the excavations for radiocarbon dating (Fox 1963). Calibrated, these yielded dates of 4350–3500 BC (5100±150 BP, BM-130); 4350–3650 BC (5190±150 BP, BM-136), and 4450–3700 BC (5280±150 BP, BM-138). In the 1980s, excavation by Malcolm Todd (1984) produced more material of Neolithic date, and confirmed Liddell's identification of a length of ditch as Neolithic within the hillfort but beyond (north of) the causewayed enclosure, perhaps suggesting a complex of enclosures. Full publication of Todd's work is awaited. More recent re-examination of the Neolithic ceramics by Henrietta Quinnell is discussed below.

High Peak

On a cliff on the east Devon coast, virtually due south of Hembury, lies High Peak. This now only survives as a fragment of an enclosure, but is seen as a site that probably once had a complete defensive circuit, now largely lost through erosion of its clifftop. Parts of a ditch of Neolithic date were excavated by Sheila Pollard (1966), though most of the putative line of the ditch had been obscured by the later post-Roman ditch on the site. Pollard's small excavation produced a surprising volume of finds: ceramics comparable with those from other sites discussed here, lithics, and five ground stone axes, including one of jadeite. Samples of charcoal, from a pit, gave a date of 4000–3100 BC (4810±150 BP, BM-214) (Pollard 1967).

Hazard Hill

Hazard Hill is a hilltop in southern Devon investigated by Christopher Houlder to elucidate a concentration of fieldwalking finds. Pits, postholes, ten hearths and six "cooking holes" were recorded, as were "linear depressions" (Houlder 1963). Houlder suspected the presence of an enclosing ditch to the settlement, but the published air photographic evidence was doubtful and this was not clarified by excavation. He felt "it is safer to regard the main settlement areas as lying within the 460 ft [140m] contour" (Houlder 1963, 21). Aerial reconnaissance by the writer in 1989 produced the faint crop-mark of a possible ditch on the north side of the hilltop (Figure 5.2), but more recently a limited geophysical exercise undertaken as an undergraduate project did not identify a ditch. Since there is limited help from the topography in determining a plausible extent for any putative enclosure circuit on the ground, this point must remain unproven at present, although the existence of an enclosure still seems likely. The assemblage of material (whose volume, from limited excavations, is again striking) recovered by Houlder fits well with that from

Figure 5.2: Hazard Hill in the drought of 1989. (Photograph DAP/PG 14 (27 July 1989) F M Griffith, Devon County Council. Copyright reserved)

demonstrably enclosed sites in Devon, and the close resemblance of the material to the Hembury assemblage was remarked upon by the excavator. Charcoal from a pit and from a spread provided dates of 4050–3350 BC (4920±150 BP, BM-149) and 3800–2900 BC (4700±150 BP, BM-150) respectively.

Haldon

Haldon lies on a dominant hilltop immediately south of Exeter. In the 1930s, an extensive collection of material from the site was made by Dr E H Willock, who subsequently carried out the excavations that recovered the celebrated plan of a rectilinear house (Willock 1936; 1937; most recently discussed by Darvill 1996). However, to non-prehistorians the site at Haldon is better known as the site of Haldon Belvedere, a memorial tower built in the late 18th century AD. By the 1990s this had fallen into poor condition, and on the death of its owner was left to a preservation trust, which, with the aid of very substantial grant aid from English Heritage, Devon County Council and other bodies, proceeded to carry out extensive restoration. In the course of this work, an unfortunate sudden change of the architect's plans meant that a cut (A on Figure 5.3) was made with the intention of installing a septic tank very close to the summit of the hill, and this went straight into a pit containing Neolithic material. Subsequent observation of other stripped areas recorded

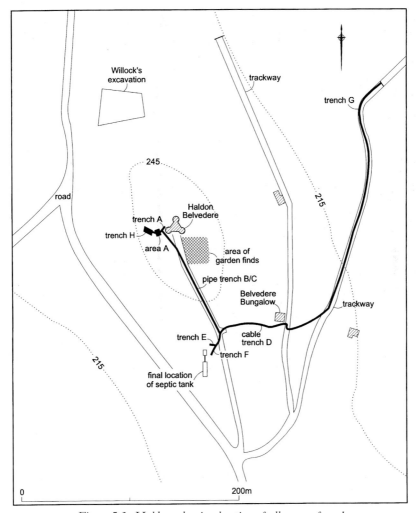

Figure 5.3: Haldon, showing location of all areas of work

further Neolithic features, chiefly small, probably truncated, pits (especially in Trench H), although unfortunately their fills, though artefact-rich, were heavily disturbed by intense activity from roots. These had preferentially colonized the archaeological features cut into the hard cherty subsoil, which underlay a very thin topsoil. Full publication of this work is in progress (Gent and Quinnell forthcoming a) but the principal value of this discovery, and the watching brief on sundry other pipe runs etc. that followed it, lies in the further information it provides for us on the extent of the Neolithic site at Haldon.

The Belvedere, or Lawrence Castle, at Haldon is sited on the summit of one of two hilltops which form the highest point of the northwest to southeast Haldon Ridge. Willock's original excavations, which were quite extensive, were sited some 150m northwest of the Belvedere, below the top of the hill (Figure 5.3). His excavation site was chosen because it was the focus of his finds made during fieldwalking of an area recently cleared of trees and cultivated. The house itself was the only "feature" recognized by Willock within the rather irregular area of his excavation (he appears not to have excavated fully the whole area of his trench), but he recovered a very substantial volume of both high quality flintwork and ceramics, as well as fragments of stone axes (Willock 1936; 1937). John Allan, Curator of Antiquities at Exeter Museum, has remarked on the fresh quality of both lithics and ceramics from Willock's work, and observes that it is difficult to square these with the very slight and weathered appearance of site and features under excavation as seen in Willock's published photographs (1936). It is possible, therefore, that other undisturbed features were excavated but not fully recorded.

However, the summit itself, in the area around the tower, has long produced copious finds comparable with those from Willock's excavations. Some were recorded in the 1930s, from the drive, while in the 1980s the former owner of the Belvedere, Mr Dale, reported and showed to the writer and others a fine collection of material from his vegetable garden (shown on Figure 5.3), downslope to the southeast of the building. This included both ceramic and lithic material, generally comparable with Willock's finds, which they have now joined in Exeter Museum. The site of the initial 1994 trench lay about 10m to the west of the tower, a little off the top of the hill. The 1994 finds closely resemble those from the 1930s, comprising a good collection of Hembury-type wares and good quality lithics.

Further examination of the hilltop at Haldon is impeded by the existence of dense rhododendron and laurel cover (vegetation whose clearance has not yet been agreed by the site managers) and thus the obvious step of commissioning geophysical survey has not yet been possible. However, the pieces of evidence summarized above, and shortly to be fully published, do when taken in total appear to suggest use of the hilltop in the Neolithic period extending over an area of at least 200m by perhaps 80m, and incorporating the top of the hill. No enclosing features have yet been positively identified, although irregularities which might be the vestiges of a low bank, only partly accessible, to the north of the Belvedere, bounding the present garden area, may be prehistoric in origin. Observation of the pipe trench down the drive running south away from the hilltop (Figure 5.3) did not identify any enclosure features, although in this area these might have been completely removed by subsequent work associated with the construction of the Belvedere and drive. However, the overall pattern of discovery suggests that this site should be considered alongside other hilltop sites of demonstrable enclosure.

POSSIBLE ENCLOSURE SITES

Mercer's 1981 discussion referred to two other Devon hilltop enclosed sites which had been suggested (*e.g.* Silvester 1979) not to fit well into the general pattern of southwestern hillforts. These were Dewerstone and Whittor, both lying on the western side of Dartmoor. Both of these sites are characterized by a low double wall of granite rubble, that at Whittor completely enclosing the tor and that at Dewerstone cutting off a promontory. No invasive work has been undertaken on either site since that time, but a recent survey of Dewerstone by Al Oswald and Iain Sainsbury of RCHME (Oswald 1994) has once again concluded that the nature of the boundary of this site is "abnormal" and suggestive of a Neolithic date. The writer would concur in suggesting that at least Dewerstone should be included within the group considered here.

Fieldwalking has been responsible for the identification of another possible enclosed hilltop site, at Crib House, Membury, in East Devon. Here, on the eastern edge of the Blackdown Hills, Mrs Nan Pearce has for many years carried out detailed and systematic fieldwalking, which has, among other things, resulted in the recognition of a substantial series of mesolithic occupation sites (Berridge 1985). At Membury, on very thin soils, ploughing revealed the presence not only of Neolithic lithics but also ceramic material. As a result of this, Peter Berridge carried out a small-scale excavation in 1986, and more recently this has been pursued by Martin Tingle. Very truncated ditch or pit remains and good ceramic assemblages have been retrieved, although no radiocarbon dates have yet been obtained. The site remains resistant to geophysical survey and so the extent of the putative enclosed area is not yet known (Tingle 1998).

IDENTIFICATIONS THROUGH AERIAL PHOTOGRAPHY

In more recent years, the Devon Aerial Reconnaissance Project has also contributed to the picture of the Neolithic period in lowland Devon, as it has for other periods of the county's prehistory (*e.g.* Griffith 1994). Some sites, notably the two large enclosures discussed below, suggested themselves as possibly Neolithic from an early stage, while the existence of others has only made itself evident in excavation.

Bow

An example of this (though certainly not a major Neolithic enclosure) was a small (45–50m) sub-square single-entrance enclosure at Nymet Barton, Bow. Aerial reconnaissance since 1984 has identified a concentration of prehistoric sites, both ceremonial and apparently non-ceremonial, including a henge, numerous ring-ditches, and many small enclosures, in the Bow area of central Devon north of Dartmoor (Griffith 1985). A limited programme of fieldwork and environmental sampling was devised by a small group, including the writer, to examine the apparent concentration of these sites on the red sandstone soils, and to test whether this was the product solely of their differential visibility in crop-mark form or represented a "real" pattern. As part of this exercise, a small trench was cut in the square enclosure in the hopes of enhancing information from a pollen core from the adjacent bog. Here it suffices to say that what had been seen as "obviously" a small Romano-British enclosure proved to seal a fine group of Neolithic ceramics and lithics in perfect fresh condition which were almost certainly not part of an everyday rubbish deposit (Caseldine *et al.* 2000). The ceramics, discussed below, are of the same fabrics as the other sites discussed here. The date of the enclosure itself remains unclear: no post-Neolithic material was recovered, but no dating material was recovered from the enclosure itself. The excavation thus shed very little light on the land utilization represented by the pollen core – which was of roughly Roman date – but further emphasizes the picture of the Bow area as a focus of Neolithic and Bronze Age ceremonial activity (as well as promoting caution in the interpretation of small square enclosures).

Raddon

A more substantial Neolithic discovery was that at Raddon. This lies on a ridge among the rolling hills to the west of the Exe Valley. In 1986, a multiple ditched hilltop enclosure, initially interpreted as a hillfort, was discovered on top of the ridge through aerial reconnaissance (Figure 5.4; for geophysical survey plot see Griffith 1994, fig. 1). In subsequent years this was seen in both crop-mark form and as slight surviving earthworks, visible especially in winter. Works associated with the construction of an access road to a reservoir necessitated the excavation by Exeter Archaeology, in 1994, of a strip along the axis of the enclosure (Gent and Quinnell forthcoming b). Like other "hillforts" before it, Raddon proved surprising on excavation, and the strip provided a sample across the defensive circuit as well as some internal features.

The hilltop at Raddon shows evidence of several phases of enclosure. A Neolithic interrupted ditched enclosure, with, possibly, part of an outer circuit, was identified, and this was succeeded by an early Iron Age hillfort sequence with several dates bracketed by 830–400 BC (2545±70 BP, AA-29725) and 780–400 BC (2475±55 BP, AA-29722); at least one phase had a timber-revetted rampart. The Neolithic enclosure, within the area excavated, showed ditch widths between 2.7m and 3.9m, with an average surviving depth of 0.8m (the hilltop has been truncated by cultivation). The excavated ditch produced lithic and ceramic finds, including three leaf-shaped arrowheads and a classic Hembury trumpet-lug. The ditch gave a radiocarbon date of 3370–3030 BC (4525±50 BP, AA-

Figure 5.4: Raddon, Mid Devon. (Photograph DAP/RN5 (7 June 1990) F M Griffith, Devon County Council. Copyright reserved)

29723), and similar dates came from redeposited Neolithic material, 3370–3030 BC (4520±50 BP, AA-29721) and 3650–3100 BC (4615±60 BP, AA-29729). Several internal features were excavated, including the top of a deep shaft or well, other pits, and a post-setting.

The overall plan and form of the enclosure at Raddon has many parallels with other similar sites, in part no doubt due to its situation along a ridge-top site. Of particular interest are a series of small cellular enclosures recorded by the magnetometer survey radiating out from the Neolithic enclosure. These are tentatively interpreted as small cultivation plots, which, if contemporary, would add a very interesting further dimension to the interpretation of the activities at this particular enclosure.

Other possible Neolithic enclosures
Apart from small square enclosures with an unsuspected Neolithic dimension, such as Nymet Barton, the aerial reconnaissance programme has identified two further large enclosures which may well warrant consideration as early sites. Unlike all the major enclosures so far considered, and their Cornish counterparts, these are low-lying sites in valley locations, comparable with others recorded in southern England. Both have only been pieced together over a period of time, as elements of their plans emerged in crop-mark form in different years under different crops. Broadclyst (Figure 5.5), in east Devon near Exeter, has an overall diameter of about 300m, and is bisected by a small stream. The

Figure 5.5: Broadclyst, East Devon. (Photograph DAP/AAM11 (20 July 1996) F M Griffith, Devon County Council. Copyright reserved)

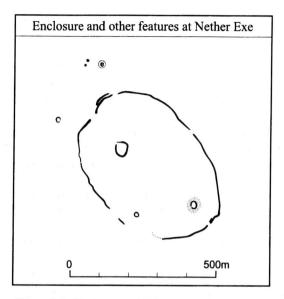

Enclosure and other features at Nether Exe

0   500m

Figure 5.6: Enclosure at Nether Exe. Composite plot from air photographs 1984–97

enclosure has at least two phases, the inner one having a narrow internal ditch which may represent a palisade trench within the main ditch. The larger enclosure intersects with a ring-ditch at one point, though the chronological relationship is not clear.

In the Exe Valley, in an area which has produced a substantial concentration of both early and later Neolithic lithic scatters, the circuit of a very large enclosure has gradually been pieced together at Nether Exe (Figure 5.6). Some of the breaks in the ditches appear to be genuine, although other gaps on the plot represent areas where crop-marks are not visible (_e.g._ roads). Barrows, ring-ditches, and a small enclosure of early first millennium BC date lie within and outside it, and other enclosures of demonstrated Romano-British date lie in the immediate vicinity. The Nether Exe cursus/oblong ditch complex (Griffith 1989, 24–5) lies to the south. Whether any of these relationships is significant cannot at present be demonstrated, since the lower Exe Valley is generally rich in archaeological sites of all periods, but the scale of this enclosure is something not encountered elsewhere in lowland southwest England. These two lowland sites are currently the subject of further work.

FINDS FROM NEOLITHIC ENCLOSURES IN DEVON

The fairly substantial developments in the study of both known and newly discovered Neolithic enclosures in Devon already discussed have prompted work on the new finds and a review of those from earlier excavations, notably Hembury and Haldon, by Henrietta Quinnell. Her work, and a programme of macroscopic examination of the petrology of the ceramics by Roger Taylor, have produced interesting developments. No new forms have been identified, but consideration of the fabrics has been much refined.

David Peacock, re-examined southwestern Neolithic pottery in the 1960s at a time when much of the 1930s material was not accessible. Nonetheless, he identified two main types of fabric for material from Hembury and related sites – the gabbroic wares, whose origin was seen as somewhere in the Lizard in west Cornwall, and local coarse gritted fabrics (Peacock 1969). Since then, we have of course seen further debate about the actual origin of the gabbroic fabrics (_e.g._ Smith in Mercer 1981, 161; Sofranoff in Mercer 1981, 179–81). The term will be used here without prejudice. This material has been identified at all the excavated Devon sites discussed above.

The gabbroic wares tend to form the finer part of each assemblage. Peacock's suggested percentage of this fabric at Hembury, 10%, still stands, but at Haldon and at Hazard Hill the quantities are between 5 and 10% rather than 35 and 30%. Peacock was working on excavation data which had grouped all igneous rock inclusions together and so grouped gabbroic fabrics with those now identified as granitic. Raddon's small assemblage has about 6% gabbroic wares. These figures provide a fairly consistent pattern for Devon sites, rather than showing a fall-off across the county. Exceptions are in the possible structured deposit at Nymet Barton, with 15 out of 39 sherds, mainly carinated bowls in a gabbroic fabric (Quinnell in Caseldine *et al.* 2000), and at Seaton, 17 out of 18 sherds, again mainly carinated forms (Smith 1981, 57–60). These variations may indicate complex processes of selection and deposition.

The other fabrics now recognized by Quinnell exploited more local materials. One group is granitic, indicating the use of clays from rivers flowing off Dartmoor or the careful selection of pockets of granitic clays weathered from the Permian breccias. The other group has obvious visible temper of crushed vein quartz or of greensand chert and, while it forms around 80% of total Devon Neolithic assemblages, demonstrates considerable variations. At Haldon most of this group has greensand chert temper, but at Raddon crushed vein quartz has been added to local ferruginous carboniferous clays providing a visually distinctive white tempered ware. This latter fabric appears to form more than half the local wares at Hembury (*contra* Liddell 1931, 92), with the remainder having greensand chert temper. It is possible that the use of white quartz temper may be for visual effect, and relate to the frequent discoveries of quartz pebbles in Neolithic and Bronze Age ceremonial deposits, and its occasional use for architectural decoration in barrows. However, heavily gritted wares are used in many periods, and the explanation may be more utilitarian.

All these three fabrics have been recognized at all the excavated enclosure sites discussed above, and the fillip given to southwestern ceramic studies by the recent work in Devon and Cornwall has been a welcome product of the work outlined here. It is interesting to note that all three types of pottery were described by Isobel Smith in her report on the finds from High Peak (in Pollard 1966), but that subsequent discussion has until recently tended to merge the two groups of local coarse wares there identified.

CONCLUSIONS

The above only briefly summarizes recent developments in our understanding of enclosed sites in Devon, and most of the excavations discussed should be published within the next two years to provide full information. Limited excavations and other work have provided a fair volume of new material for thought, and even the small trench at the poorly-understood site at Nymet Barton has contributed to the review of ceramic assemblages, as have collections from other excavations and watching briefs. Most of these excavations were not on a scale that would warrant overall conclusions about the function of the enclosures, but it is striking that, insofar as they are datable, all the sites discussed here appear to fall into the earlier Neolithic. Much more work is required before we can tell whether our failure to recognize later Neolithic sites is because they are not here, or because we have not found them, or because our 'earlier' Neolithic may continue rather later than we at present suppose.

It is a stimulating time for the Neolithic in the southwest, and thoughts are burgeoning of aspects beyond the individual sites. For example, it is noted that the sites of Raddon, Hembury, and Haldon are all intervisible. In this context, I have also been thinking of the paper presented by Roy Loveday to the Autumn 1997 meeting of this Group. His title was "Mother Dunch's Buttocks", and his subject turned out to be a consideration of recurrent patterning of the hilltop location of some Neolithic sites in central England. Without reiterating his discussion, I would point out that two of the major sites discussed here, Raddon and Haldon, occupy not only hilltop locations but, in each case, one of a pair of hilltops. In neither of these two cases has it yet been possible to ascertain definitively the presence or absence of material on the other of the twin peaks, but his work will remain in the mind as we continue to enjoy the exploration of these sites in Devon.

ACKNOWLEDGEMENTS

This paper summarizes the work of many organizations and individuals. Work at Haldon was commissioned by the Devon Historic Buildings Trust and carried out by C and N Hollingrake, Oxford Archaeotechnics, and Exeter Archaeology. Excavations at Raddon, funded by South West Water, were carried out by Exeter Archaeology, supervised by Mark Knight, with geophysical survey by Oxford Archaeotechnics. The Bow project was a collaboration between the writer, Chris Caseldine and Bryony Coles of Exeter University, funded by the University Research Fund and the British Academy, and carried out with the help of Exeter Archaeology and Devon Archaeological Society. The Devon Aerial Reconnaissance Project has been carried out by the writer, with, since 1992, Bill Horner, for Devon County Council, and has been funded successively by English Heritage, RCHME, and Devon County Council. I am grateful to Dominic Sheldon for news of his work at Hazard Hill, and to Martin Tingle for discussions about Membury and the lithics from Raddon.

The paper reports work by the above and, in particular, by Henrietta Quinnell, to whom I am grateful for frequent discussion on these topics, for information from current post-excavation work, and for comments on this text. I have enjoyed discussions with Lady Fox about the Hembury excavations. I am also grateful to Chris Henderson and Peter Weddell and the staff of Exeter Archaeology for discussion and collaboration. The figures were prepared by Tony Ives of Exeter Archaeology.

BIBLIOGRAPHY

Berridge, P J, 1985, Mesolithic sites in the Yarty Valley. ***Proceedings of the Devon Archaeological Society***, 43, 1–22

Caseldine, C J, Coles, B J, Griffith, F M, and Hatton, J, 2000, Conservation or change? Human influence on the mid Devon landscape. In T P O'Connor and R A Nicholson (eds), *People as an Agent of Environmental Change* (= Symposia of the Association for Environmental Archaeology 16). 60–70

Darvill, T, 1996, Neolithic buildings in England, Wales and the Isle of Man. In T Darvill and J Thomas (eds), *Neolithic houses in northwest Europe and beyond* (= Neolithic Studies Group Seminar Papers 1). Oxford. Oxbow Books. 77–112

Gent, T, and Quinnell, H, forthcoming a, Salvage recording on the Neolithic Site at Haldon Belvedere. *Proceedings of the Devon Archaeological Society*

Gent, T, and Quinnell, H, forthcoming b, Excavation of a Causewayed Enclosure and Hillfort on Raddon Hill, Stockleigh Pomeroy. *Proceedings of the Devon Archaeological Society*

Griffith, F M, 1985, Some Newly-discovered Ritual Monuments in mid Devon. *Proceedings of the Prehistoric Society*, 51, 310–15

Griffith, F M, 1989, Aerial reconnaissance in mainland Britain in 1989. *Antiquity*, 64, 14–33

Griffith, F M, 1994, Changing perceptions of Dartmoor's prehistoric context. *Proceedings of the Devon Archaeological Society*, 52, 85–100

Fox, A, 1963, Neolithic charcoal from Hembury. *Antiquity*, 37, 228–9

Houlder, C H, 1963, A Neolithic settlement on Hazard Hill, Totnes. *Proceedings of the Devon Archaeological Society*, 21, 2–30

Liddell, D M, 1930, Report on the excavations at Hembury Fort, Devon, 1930. *Proceedings of the Devon Archaeological Society*, 1.2, 39–63

Liddell, D M, 1931, Report on the excavations at Hembury Fort, Devon: Second Season 1931. *Proceedings of the Devon Archaeological Society*, 1.3, 90–120

Liddell, D M, 1932, Report on the excavations at Hembury Fort, Devon, Third Season 1932. *Proceedings of the Devon Archaeological Society*, 1.4, 162–190

Liddell, D M, 1935, Report on the excavations at Hembury Fort, Devon, 4th and 5th Seasons 1934 and 1935. *Proceedings of the Devon Archaeological Society*, 2.3, 135–75

Mercer, R J, 1981, Excavations at Carn Brea, Illogan, Cornwall, 1970–73. A Neolithic fortified complex of the third millennium bc. *Cornish Archaeology*, 20, 1–204

Oswald, A, 1994, *The Dewerstone, Devon*. RCHME. Swindon. [Limited circulation printed field survey report]

Peacock, D P S, 1969, Neolithic pottery production in Cornwall. *Antiquity*, 49, 145–9

Pollard, S H M, 1966, Neolithic and Dark Age Settlements on High Peak, Sidmouth, Devon. *Proceedings of the Devon Archaeological Society*, 23, 35–59

Pollard, S H M, 1967, Radiocarbon dating, Neolithic and Dark Age settlements on High Peak, Sidmouth, Devon. *Proceedings of the Devon Archaeological Society*, 25, 41–2

Silvester, R J, 1979, The relationship of first millennium settlement to the upland areas of the South West. *Proceedings of the Devon Archaeological Society*, 37, 176–90

Smith, I F, 1981, The earlier prehistoric pottery. In R J Silvester, Excavations at Honeyditches Roman Villa, Seaton, in 1978. *Proceedings of the Devon Archaeological Society*, 39, 37–87

Tingle, M, 1998, *Membury Excavation 1998. Interim Report*. [Limited circulation printed report; Devon SMR]

Todd, M, 1984, Excavations at Hembury, Devon, 1980–3: a summary report. *Antiquaries Journal*, 64, 251–68

Willock, E H, 1936, A Neolithic site on Haldon. *Proceedings of the Devon Archaeological Society*, 2.4, 244–63

Willock, E H, 1937, A further note on the Neolithic site on Haldon. *Proceedings of the Devon Archaeological Society*, 3.1, 33–43

Clegyr Boia: a potential Neolithic enclosure and associated monuments on the St David's peninsula, southwest Wales

Blaise Vyner

INTRODUCTION

This paper, inevitably speculative, presents the interim conclusions of a review of the nature, chronology, and context of activity at Clegyr Boia, Pembrokeshire, southwest Wales. In particular, comment is made concerning the landscape setting of this and other Neolithic monuments on the St David's peninsula and the evidence this presents for their contemporary association (Figure 6.1).

The small stone-walled enclosure at Clegyr Boia is usually ascribed to the extensive group of later prehistoric enclosures of southwest Wales (Crossley 1963), but the existence of Neolithic buildings within and beneath the enclosure rampart is evidence for much earlier use of the location. The site has been the subject of three field investigations, the first a campaign of excavation undertaken in 1902 (Baring Gould *et al.* 1903), the second a programme of excavation carried out during the Second World War in advance of projected quarrying which never materialized (Williams 1952), and, most recently, a programme of field analysis reported on here.

Some years ago the writer, visiting Clegyr Boia in the course of analysis of some of the numerous Pembrokeshire pre-Roman Iron Age enclosures, was struck by its small scale in relation to other enclosures in northwest Pembrokeshire and the potential of a Neolithic date for the defences as well as the structures. It was resolved to undertake more detailed analysis of location, area enclosed, scale and techniques of construction, association with other sites, and continuing archaeological potential. Field survey was undertaken in 1989, and a brief comparative analysis of local enclosures, usually presumed to be pre-Roman Iron Age in origin, was undertaken in September 1991. Intermittent fieldwork has been undertaken since, but events have conspired to delay the completion of the project. Its continuing relevance finds support in the evidence of the excavation of the Neolithic enclosure at Carn Brea, Cornwall (Mercer 1981, 194), and by further doubts cast on the Iron Age credentials of the defences at Clegyr Boia (Barker 1992, 69).

NEOLITHIC SETTLEMENT AT CLEGYR BOIA

The enclosure at Clegyr Boia occupies a low rocky outcrop, roughly rectangular in plan.

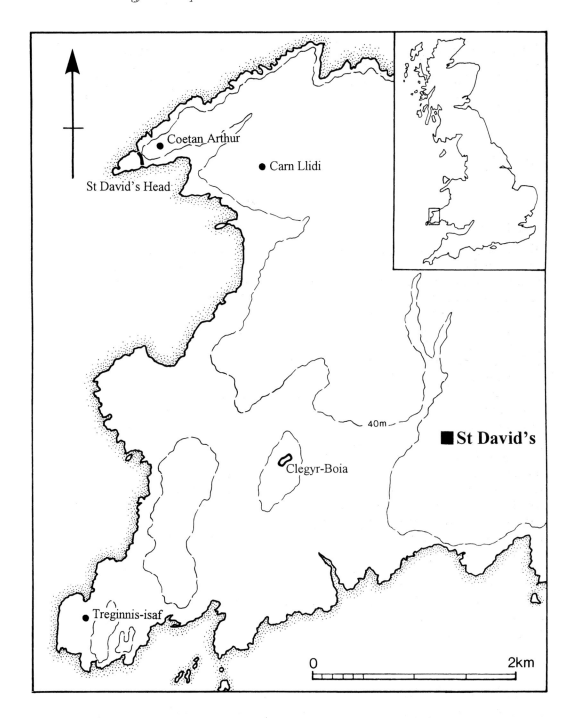

Figure 6.1: Map of St David's peninsula showing Clegyr Boia and potentially associated sites

Figure 6.2: Clegyr Boia from the north

The outcrop is one of a number on the western and northern sides of the peninsula, but appears to have offered a larger area of level surface than others (Figure 6.2), although its eastern end, now damaged by quarrying, seems not to have been usable. The summit is most easily approached from the west side, with a short but steep climb needed from any other approach. The enclosure interior is uneven and covered in tussocky grass which disguises the surface evidence of any underlying features, although the persistent legend of the 8th century AD Irish pirate, Boia (Baring Gould 1903, 3–4), suggests that the site was the location of post-Roman settlement which might have disturbed any pre-existing surface evidence. The outcrop has an apparently natural bowl-like profile, with an irregular edge further marked by occasional low rock stacks. A low rampart, of which more details are provided below, follows the outer edge of the outcrop, extending from one stack to another, but not riding over any (Figure 6.3).

Clegyr Boia is best known for the evidence it has produced for Neolithic occupation. The structural evidence, and its association with a fire pit and midden deposits containing pottery, charcoal, and faunal fragments, suggests that this was principally domestic in nature (Figure 6.4).[1] Baring Gould's excavations uncovered the remains of a rectangular structure, his feature J, which was re-excavated by Williams and renamed Hut 1 (Williams 1952, 24–27). This was set in a hollow in the bedrock measuring 6.7m by 3.7m. The chief structural component comprised two parallel rows of postholes, not opposed, with a linear bank of stone set between the edge of the hollow and the nearest long side of the structure. Williams' Hut 2, which was sealed beneath the stone rampart, had a similar arrangement of postholes masked by a larger circular area of dark deposits; a gully led from the hut interior (Williams 1952, 27–29). Both structures are likely to have been subrectangular in plan, Hut 1 approximately 6.7m by 2.1m, and Hut 2 approximately 4.6m by 3m. They may be placed tentatively in Darvill's Type A grouping of early Neolithic buildings (Darvill 1996, 85, 108), characterized by rectangular modular timber frames.

Figure 6.3: Aerial view of Clegyr Boia from the south-east; the enclosure occupies the western part of the rock outcrop, the southern end of which has quarry scars. (AP88–98–30 Photograph by Terry James, reproduced courtesy of Cambria Archaeology. Copyright reserved)

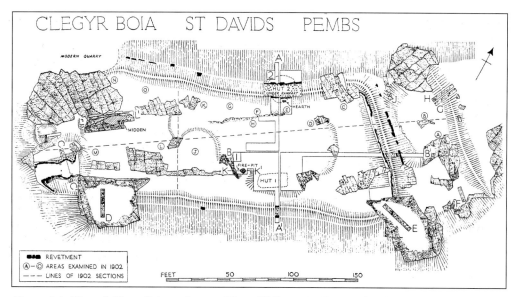

Figure 6.4: Plan of Clegyr Boia settlement. (From Williams 1952, reproduced courtesy of the Cambrian Archaeological Association)

The enclosure rampart, more properly a wall, is made up from small stone rubble and soil placed within a revetting of stone blocks, many of which have now become dislodged. Its width as excavated varies from 2.7m on the east side to 4.6m at the north end, while the average surviving height is 0.6m (Williams 1952, 30–31). In places, especially where the revetting blocks are absent, material has slipped downslope. The original height of the rampart is difficult to establish, but the width suggests that the maximum height is unlikely to have been more than 2m if it was to remain stable, while the absence of stone rubble within the enclosure also supports the suggestion that it never achieved any great height. It has been suggested that the construction material was quarried from the hollow at the east end (Williams 1952, 34), but it does not seem likely that the scale of the rampart would have required resort to quarrying and moving material from one specific point, and stone was more probably gathered from around the outcrop and from its interior surface, accentuating its bowl-like profile. An outlying ridge at the eastern end of the outcrop, beyond the putative quarry, has the appearance of a further stretch of rampart, although excavation suggests that this is not the case (Williams 1952, 34).

The rampart was constructed directly on top of deposits containing Neolithic pottery and charcoal, a fact which has been taken to suggest that the area had been stripped of topsoil to provide material for the rampart core when it was constructed during the pre-Roman Iron Age (Williams 1952, 43). However, it seems unlikely that the area to be occupied by the rampart would have been stripped in this way since this would have negated the height advantage offered by stripping of the interior and at the same time would increase the required height of the rampart. Additionally, if the area to be occupied by the rampart had been stripped the derived material would have had to be stockpiled until rampart construction had proceeded sufficiently to allow the stripped material to be added.

The structure of the entrance is not visible, although its location, suggested by the relative ease of approach from the southwest, was confirmed by excavation (Williams 1952, 31–34). The entrance comprised a pair of orthostatic walls, 6.1m long, leading to opposed elliptical embrasures which had a massive post-setting at each end. Each of the embrasures was 2.4m long and had a maximum depth of 0.6m, while the postholes averaged 0.9m by 0.76m and 0.46m deep. Considerable quantities of charcoal showed that the timber elements of the construction had been destroyed by fire. In 1973 charcoal samples preserved from the excavation were used for radiocarbon dating. Although one of the samples was thought to be associated with Neolithic domestic debris, both samples produced dates late in the first millennium BC: 760–380 BC (2370 ± 29 BP, BM-1109) and 350 BC – AD 400 (1950 ± 116 BP, BM-1110). The date for charcoal thought to have been associated with the entrance destruction (BM-1110) was cautiously accepted, but the sample relating to putatively Neolithic material was rejected (Burleigh and Hewson 1979, 349). However, there are no grounds for preferring one over the other and, given the lapse of time between excavation and analysis, it is suggested that both must be rejected.

CLEGYR BOIA AND PEMBROKESHIRE ENCLOSURES

Pembrokeshire, indeed, southwest Wales as a whole, is notable for the large number of surviving enclosed sites, still best appreciated by reference to the Ordnance Survey's *Map of Southern Britain in the Iron Age* (1967). Only a very few of these sites have been the subject of detailed survey, and still fewer have been excavated in recent times (for a review see Williams 1988). Excavation does now at least allow a broader chronology for some of these sites to be suggested, with the antecedents of some lying in the later Bronze Age and others continuing in use into the Roman period, with most seeming to have been constructed and used from the 5th century BC. A few, it may be suggested, have morphologies which suggest an altogether different chronological horizon.

The enclosures have usually been considered in terms of their defensive potential, referring to a combination of topographical attributes, size, and number of enclosing banks and ditches, and area enclosed (*e.g.* Williams 1988, 31). This has allowed the identification of some sites as readily-defended "hillforts" and others, with less potential for defence, as "ringforts". However, the approach continues to be unsatisfactory in providing a basis for the understanding of these sites, not least because a number of enclosures which satisfy the hillfort criteria in terms of area enclosed and size of rampart are placed in manifestly indefensible locations. The prehistoric enclosures of southwest Wales do potentially fall into two groups, but not on this basis.

Although the distribution of earth-ramparted enclosures extends into the north of the county it appears to be related to the availability of good quality land. Indeed, the visitor fairly readily observes that the site distribution corresponds closely with that of the modern bovine population. These were settlements which potentially had a strong agricultural economy and where status was expressed through the size and elaboration of enclosing boundaries. Today the stone-constructed enclosures are located in areas where sheep are the basis of the agricultural economy. It is tempting to see the distinctions between the stone- and earth-ramparted enclosures reflecting cultural differences which may be attributed to a dichotomy of agriculture in prehistory which mirrors that seen in Pembrokeshire today.

The first group of enclosures comprises substantially embanked univallate and multivallate enclosures in hillslope, hilltop, promontory, and headland locations. The distinguishing characteristic of most of these sites is an emphasis on monumentality. Massive banks, usually made up from earth and shale excavated from associated ditches, are combined with a lack of overt defensive capacity, and in a situation with good agricultural potential. Excavation shows that some of these sites developed from palisaded or more lightly ditched settlements (Vyner 1986). The principal distribution of these sites, which make up the majority, is in central and southern Pembrokeshire.

The second group of enclosures is characterized by stone ramparts which, now fallen, for the most part appear originally to have been mostly of dump construction. These are distributed across the northwest and northern parts of Pembrokeshire, areas where outcropping rock facilitated the gathering of construction material and provided focal points for settlement. The different construction materials, combined with the markedly different topographical background, makes comparison with the earth-ramparted enclosures difficult. The little excavation that has been undertaken on the stone-built sites suggests that these were, if anything, even poorer in archaeologically-visible material culture than the earth-ramparted enclosures appear to be. Like the earth-ramparted enclosures, enclosures with rubble ramparts also vary considerably in size and complexity of construction, but a few of these can be described as more overtly defensive in nature. The multi-ramparted enclosure on the summit of Moel Trigarn certainly qualifies as a hillfort, while the natural defences of the nearby small rock outcrop at Carn Alw have been augmented by a stone rampart and outlying *chevaux de frise* (Mytum and Webster 1989). Apart from their stone construction and the utilization of rock outcrops and scarps, other substantial stone-constructed enclosures, such as Gaer Fawr or Carn Ingli (Hogg 1973), have rather less claim to a defensive function and may be more directly comparable with earth ramparted enclosures such as those at Crundale or Keeston. Clegyr Boia lies within, but close to the southern edge of, the topographical zone containing the stone-constructed enclosures, yet it differs from other stone-constructed enclosures in its small scale, combined with the care in which the rampart has been constructed, and also in the way in which soil has also been utilized in its construction.

While Clegyr Boia finds a poor comparison with the later prehistoric enclosures of Pembrokeshire, there are a number of similarities between this enclosure and the enclosure complex at Carn Brea, Cornwall (Mercer 1981). True, the rampart at Carn Brea is constructed on very much more massive scale than at Clegyr Boia, with the use of much more substantial stone blocks, and encompasses a greater area, but this may have much to do with topographical opportunity. Other components of the Carn Brea site provide a closer comparison, with the Central Summit and the Eastern Summit enclosures each being of comparable extent to Clegyr Boia. The Central Summit has not been excavated, but the Eastern Summit proved to contain a rectangular structure similar in construction, but slightly larger than, Hut 2 at Clegyr Boia (Mercer 1981). The similarity of the pottery assemblages from the two sites has also been commented upon (Lynch 1976, 65).

If it is accepted that Clegyr Boia stands apart from the main groups of Pembrokeshire enclosures, and potentially of Neolithic date, it seems reasonable to ask if any other similar enclosures may be identified. Two sites which in their later phases show evidence of pre-Roman Iron Age use also display features which are certainly of earlier date, although how much earlier has yet to be established. By chance, or perhaps not, one of these is the coastal promontory fortification at Clawdd y Milwyr, on St David's Head, close to the Coetan Arthur chambered cairn and just 1km to the north of Clegyr Boia, from which the promontory can be seen. A second, Castell Coch, Trevine, is set on another coastal promontory 15km to the northeast of St David's Head.

The rocky promontory location of Clawdd y Milwyr is notable among Pembrokeshire coastal enclosures for its substantial stone rubble rampart and the survival of a number of sub-circular stone building foundations within its interior. Excavations in the late 19th century retrieved an assemblage of glass and stone artefacts which demonstrate activity, probably occupation, during the pre-Roman Iron Age (Baring Gould *et al.* 1900). In the absence of modern excavation evidence its chief interest lies in its visible defensive sequence. From the outer, eastern, approach the defences comprise two low banks of orthostatic boulders facing a core of soil derived from a shallow ditch in front, beyond these is a very much more substantial bank of clean stone rubble (Figure 6.5). An entrance passage of orthostatic walling extends from the outer of the two low ramparts to terminate in the innermost massive rubble bank which dominates the site today. The defences are clearly of two periods, the entrance passage and the two outer ramparts are the earliest visible features, while the fact that the entrance passage extends to the line of the innermost, massive, rampart suggests that there was originally a third low rampart along its course.

Figure 6.5: Clawdd y Milwyr, St David's Head, showing the orthostatic entranceway leading through two low ramparts to the massive inner rubble bank.

The single massive stone rampart is similar to those at Moel Trigarn or Gaer Fawr, potentially defensive but perhaps simply a monumental construction. The earlier orthostatic stone and earth banks, however, are best paralleled by the bank surmounting the rocky outcrop at Clegyr Boia, or, indeed, one of the ramparts cutting off the similar promontory at Castell Coch. Here, again, two phases of rampart construction are in evidence, this time a massive ditch and upcast bank lies outside a much less substantial stone and earth bank with facing shallow ditch. The substantial bank and ditch is similar in scale to those found at the earth-ramparted enclosures, but not so the less substantial and presumably earlier one. The smaller stone and earth ramparts, however, are not a feature of the pre-Roman Iron Age enclosures of the area, and while these enclosures do quite frequently possess multiple ramparts, these tend to be much more nearly equal in size. It is suggested, therefore, that the smaller banks at these sites are earlier than the pre-Roman Iron Age, that they may belong to the Neolithic is suggested on the basis of spatial association and intervisibility. Interestingly, for the purposes of this argument, Castell Coch lies only 1km to the northwest of Carreg Samson, Mathry (Barker 1992, 34), a chambered cairn set in a very similar location to that at Lower Treginnis, at the head of a short cwm, although the two sites are not currently intervisible.

CHAMBERED CAIRNS

Some 3km north-northwest from Clegyr Boia, and only 250m east of Clawdd y Milwyr is a chambered cairn, Coetan Arthur, described as a substantial capstone resting on bedrock at the western end and raised by a single megalith at the east end (Barker 1992, 36). There is more, though, that can be added to this somewhat bald description, although the site, and a nearby pit, was explored in 1898 with little result (Baring Gould *et al.* 1899, 130). The remains of a low kerbed facade at the east end, not previously remarked upon, and the pit discovered and excavated by Baring Gould, suggest that the structure was formerly more complex. Thus, although it is unlikely that any cairn originally enclosed the capstone – here, as elsewhere, a substantial mound would have been required and who could have robbed it so completely as to leave no trace? – the monument may not have had the open structure which now presents such an impressive skyline profile.

The setting of the cairn is worthy of comment, since it has been carefully located in a bowl-like depression on the spine of a ridge (Figure 6.6). This declivity is clearly visible from Clegyr Boia to the south, or by any approach from the southwest, while the cairn itself appears clearly on the skyline at a distance of around 0.5km. From the Clawdd y Milwyr enclosure, only 250m distant to the west, the view of the cairn as it is now survives is obscured by the west end of the outcrop which effectively marks its location, but to move four paces from the cairn brings the enclosure into sight. Since the traces of kerb and Baring Gould's discovery of a pit indicate that the monument was once more extensive, a strong claim for original intervisibility can be made.

About 3.75km north of Clegyr Boia, and around 1km east of Clawdd y Milwyr and Coetan Arthur, on the low but sharply defined rocky spine of Carn Llidi, is a pair of rectangular megalithic chambers placed less than 2m apart. By contrast with Coetan Arthur, these are diminutive monuments, the chambers of each being around 1.5m square (Barker

Figure 6.6: Coetan Arthur chambered cairn in its setting

1992, 36). Given their size it is not surprising that the chambers themselves are not readily visible from any distance (Tilley 1994, 90). The location of the Carn Llidi monuments, however, has been carefully chosen so as to be readily recognizable from Clegyr Boia to the south, or from Coetan Arthur chambered cairn and the Clawdd y Milwyr enclosure to the west. The chambers are set immediately below the most prominently marked outcrop at the western end of Carn Llidi, so that even if the cairns themselves could not be seen, their location was clearly marked from any of these three locations.

Less well known is the damaged chambered cairn at Lower Treginnis (Freeman 1976; Barker 1992, 49), situated to the south of St David's Head. Again, its location is worth remark. The monument is sited in the lee of a low rock outcrop, in a position which does not, as claimed, overlook Ramsey Island and the intervening strait. The placement appears to have taken no advantage of the opportunities of establishing a relationship with either the rocky outcrop, the sea, or the island features. The monument lies at the head of a very shallow cwm, or valley, which debouches northwards. This is best seen from the north, the direction in which Coetan Arthur, Carn Llidi, and Clawdd y Milwyr lie; all these locations are intervisible with the head of the cwm where the Lower Treginnis chambered cairn is situated. Lower Treginnis is the only one of the chambered cairns which cannot be now seen from Clegyr Boia, although an additional metre of rampart, which surely once existed, might well have brought the site into view, vegetation allowing.

CLEGYR BOIA: A SETTLEMENT IN A NEOLITHIC LANDSCAPE

The earliest phase of activity at Clegyr Boia appears to have comprised an open settlement which was established on the largest and most prominent of the rock outcrops on St David's Head. Activity continued over an unknown period of the Neolithic. It is argued that the settlement was enclosed within a stone-walled rampart, the wooden gateway to which, set in an orthostatic entrance, was destroyed by fire. There is no evidence for repair or continued activity thereafter. It is possible, perhaps even likely, given that there is no evidence for the rebuilding of the structures, that the site was used over a fairly short period of time. Use of the site may have been episodic or seasonal, but there is no evidence for this. If the case for enclosed settlement is accepted Clegyr Boia has increased importance as a Neolithic settlement which is closely comparable with Carn Brea in terms of structure and material culture.

Further interest attaches to Clegyr Boia because it is one of a group of sites on the St David's peninsula which may be broadly contemporary, and for which there is some evidence for association by intervisibility within the Neolithic landscape (Figure 6.7). The settings and location of Neolithic monuments in southwest Wales has been the subject of recent discussion (Tilley 1994, 87–110), who draws attention to the fact that the coastal monuments have been placed so as to have an inland visual field, and, frequently, an association with rock outcrops which serve to identify location and to obscure the monuments themselves (Tilley 1994, 93–94). A few further points may be made, with particular reference to the sites under discussion here. Monument location appears to be concerned with the inland area to such an extent that it is difficult to argue an interest in sea and littoral resources, although the location of the Lower Treginnis and Carreg Samson chambered cairns at the head of well-defined cwms leading to the coastal cliffs should be noted. Positions on or adjacent to landmark rock outcrops are favoured, but it should be noted that only the minority of the many rock outcrops in the area have been utilized in this way. The monuments themselves were not conspicuous in the landscape, but their size and scale militates against this possibility. The small group of monuments on St David's Head appear to have been placed so that their positions were intervisible (Table 6.1), although not all potential locations were utilized.

It has been suggested that the chambered cairns of the area served principally as ritually and symbolically important meeting and reference points (Tilley 1994, 109), and there is

Figure 6.7: View looking north from Clegyr Boia towards Carn Llidi and St David's Head

Table 6.1: The intervisibility of monuments on the St David's peninsula

	Clegyr Boia	Coetan Arthur	Carn Llidi	St David's Head	Treginnis
Clegyr Boia		X	X	X	
Coetan Arthur	X		X	X	X
Carn Llidi	X	X		X	X
St David's Head	X	X	X		X
Treginnis		X	X	X	

some evidence to suggest that these sites were structurally more complex than they at first appear. Mention has been made of the possible eastern cairn facade at Coetan Arthur, St David's Head, a detail to which may be added the observation that at Carreg Samson the capstone and two supports on the western side are a conglomerate rock containing substantial chunks of milky quartz, by contrast, the three supports on the east side are igneous rock which contrasts in its simplicity.

If the chambered cairns were important meeting points, the sites to which they related should be expected to occupy the same landscape arena. It is suggested here that Clegyr Boia and Clawdd y Milwyr may have been the enclosed settlements from which the living participants journeyed to the chambered cairn.

ACKNOWLEDGEMENTS

Access to Clegyr Boia was kindly allowed by the land-owner, Mr J Senior-Stern. Fieldwork at Clegyr Boia and the vicinity has been undertaken with grant support from the Cambrian Archaeological Association, the Prehistoric Society, and the Royal Archaeological Institute. For assistance with survey work during 1989 thanks are due to Robin Daniels and Pip Robinson, I am grateful for help during 1991 to Terry James, then of Dyfed Archaeological Trust and to Chris Delaney and Gavin Evans at the then Dyfed Museum Service. For exploration of, and comment on, the monuments of St David's peninsula I am grateful to Gillian Cobb and Anthony Gilmour. Eleanor Breen at Cambria Archaeology has kindly made available Terry James's air photographs of Clegyr Boia.

NOTE

1   Some comment on the nature and potential of the archaeological resource represented at Clegyr Boia might be relevant here. The excavations of both Baring Gould and Williams demonstrate the survival of considerable amounts of charcoal from occupation and other levels; despite the extent of previous excavation the potential for the recovery of charcoal and other carbonized material from contexts associated with structural evidence is considerable. In

contrast to many Welsh prehistoric sites, some animal bone survives in stratified contexts, while limpet shells were also noted in the midden deposit.

Pottery excavated in 1943 is described as being either "corky" due to the loss of grass tempering, or calcite-gritted. Examination of the material shows that the "corky" material is so because of the leaching out of angular calcite grits; the pottery described as calcite-gritted is for the most part tempered with quartz.

Finds from the 1899 excavations were deposited in Tenby Museum, but of these, only the damaged stone axe now survives. Finds from the 1943 excavations are maintained in the National Museum of Wales, Cardiff.

Extensive areas of low-lying marshland are to be found in the immediate vicinity of Clegyr Boia. At first glance these offer the encouraging possibility of obtaining palaeo-environmental evidence which might extend back to the Neolithic. However, sampling undertaken in 1991 with the assistance of Mike Warren of the University of Lampeter shows that these contain only silts of fairly recent origin.

BIBLIOGRAPHY

Baring Gould, S, Burnard, R, and Enys, J D, 1900, Exploration of the stone camp on St David's Head. *Archaeologia Cambrensis*, 55 (Series 5.17), 105–31

Baring Gould, S, 1903, The exploration of Clegyr Voya. *Archaeologia Cambrensis*, 58 (Series 6.3), 1–11

Barker, C T, 1992, *The chambered tombs of south-west Wales* (= Oxbow Monograph 14). Oxford. Oxbow Books

Burleigh, R, and Hewson, A, 1979, British Museum natural radiocarbon measurements XI. *Radiocarbon*, 21, 339–52

Crossley, D W, 1963, List of hill-forts and other earthworks in Pembrokeshire. *Bulletin of the Board of Celtic Studies*, 20 (1962–64), 171–205

Darvill, T, 1996, Neolithic buildings in England, Wales and the Isle of Man. In T Darvill and J Thomas (eds), *Neolithic houses in northwest Europe and beyond* (= Neolithic Studies Group Seminar Papers 1). Oxford. Oxbow Books. 77–111

Freeman, M D, 1976, Lower Treginnis, St David's. *Archaeology in Wales*, 16, 27

Hogg, A H A, 1973, Gaer Fawr and Carn Ingli: two major Pembrokeshire hill-forts. *Archaeologia Cambrensis*, 122, 69–84

Lynch, F M, 1976, Towards a chronology of megalithic tombs in Wales. In G C Boon and J M Lewis (eds), *Welsh Antiquity. Essays mainly on prehistoric topics presented to H N Savory*. Cardiff. National Museum of Wales. 63–79

Mercer, R J, 1981, Excavations at Carn Brea, Illogan, Cornwall, 1970–73. A Neolithic fortified complex of the third millennium bc. *Cornish Archaeology*, 20, 1–204

Mytum, H C, and Webster, C J, 1989, A survey of the Iron Age enclosure and chevaux-de-frise at Carn Alw, Dyfed. *Proceedings of the Prehistoric Society*, 55, 263–67

Ordnance Survey, 1967, *Map of Southern Britain in the Iron Age*. Southampton. Ordnance Survey

Tilley, C, 1994, *A phenomenology of landscape: places, paths and monuments*. Oxford. Berg

Vyner, B E, 1986, Woodbarn, Wiston, a Pembrokeshire rath. *Archaeologia Cambrensis*, 135, 121–33

Williams, A, 1952, Clegyr Boia, St David's (Pemb.): excavation in 1943. *Archaeologia Cambrensis*, 102, 20–47

Williams, G, 1988, Recent work on rural settlement in later prehistoric and early historic Dyfed. *Antiquaries Journal*, 118, 3–54

Bridging the Severn Estuary: two possible earlier Neolithic enclosures in the Vale of Glamorgan

Steve Burrow, Toby Driver, and David Thomas

INTRODUCTION

The search for earlier Neolithic enclosures in south Wales has for many years been a barren quest, with the Severn Estuary proving a formidable barrier to the apparent westward extension of well-populated English distribution maps (*cf.* Piggott 1954, fig 1.I; Palmer 1976, fig 1; Darvill 1987, fig 26).

In many parts of south Wales the failure to identify such enclosures might plausibly be explained away on topographical grounds. In the uplands that dominate the region it is possible that the Neolithic population may have adopted a social system which did not require the building of enclosures like those of southern England. Alternatively, perhaps the population was too small or too transient to warrant them, or possibly the thin soils and solid bedrock of the uplands made the digging of ditches too arduous when hilltops and landscape features may have served as natural cues for gatherings (see Tilley 1994 and *cf.* Fleming 1999).

In the Vale of Glamorgan such reasons appear less convincing. The Vale is an area of rich low-lying land flanked to the north by uplands and bordered on the remaining three sides by the Bristol Channel to the south and west, and the Severn Estuary to the east (Carter 1980). The low rolling hills of the Vale of Glamorgan bear closer comparison with western England than with much of Wales, with the limestone geology of the Vale extending into Gloucestershire and Somerset. It is unlikely therefore that environmental factors alone will have caused the Neolithic population of these two areas to adopt different social systems (Webley 1969).

For the last 2000 years the agricultural wealth of the Vale of Glamorgan has made it a valuable possession, encouraging cultural links with southern England both overland (Webley 1976) and via the natural routeways of the Severn Estuary and Bristol Channel (Sherratt 1996). It would seem surprising if such cultural links did not also exist in the Neolithic period, and the presence of Cotswold-Severn tombs at Tinkinswood and St Lythans support this view (see Webley 1969; Houlder 1976; Darvill 1982). Support can also be found in the large number of polished flint axe fragments that have been found within the Vale, since the nearest reliable sources for the large pieces of flint required for these axes are in southern England (Darvill 1989).

The missing piece in this picture of regional conformity has been the earlier Neolithic enclosures of causewayed or related form. However, in the past decade two possible examples have come to light from aerial photography, the first at Norton (SS 87467578) and the second at Corntown (SS 926765). The evidence for these two potentially Neolithic sites is presented below.

DISCOVERY OF THE SITES

As with many other low-lying agricultural areas, the bulk of upstanding prehistoric archaeology within the Vale of Glamorgan has long since been removed, with aerial photography providing the best indication of the quantity that was once present. While the impact of archaeological aerial photography since the 1950s is well appreciated for better studied landscapes, like the central Borderlands (Musson 1994, 19), significant discoveries are still being made in other parts of Wales. A number of crop-marks of plough-levelled prehistoric and Roman enclosures are known from lowland Glamorgan (Musson 1994, 27). The Corntown enclosure was itself discovered by Chris Musson during RCAHMW flying in July 1995. However, the occurrence of heavy clay subsoils and flying restrictions over urban centres and military and civilian airports in parts of Glamorgan can restrict exploratory aerial photography. It is only recently that studies of vertical air photographs have begun to contribute to our archaeological knowledge of this area. In 1995, eight previously unknown defended enclosures and related sites were identified at Aberthaw, Glamorgan, from vertical aerial photographs (Driver 1995), in a zone of restricted air space. The further discovery of the Norton enclosure in 1996 from vertical air photographs shows that it is this source, coupled with continuing archaeological reconnaissance, which offers some of the greatest potentials for future discoveries in lowland Glamorgan.

The two newly discovered enclosures are situated on the southern side of the Ogmore Valley (Figure 7.1), which is itself now largely occupied by the town of Bridgend. As well as providing sheltered ground, the valley also offers a natural routeway into the Vale of Glamorgan, and north into the Welsh uplands. Its importance in the earlier Neolithic is illustrated by the range of archaeological sites and finds contained within it. At the mouth of the Ogmore River is the site of Ogmore-by-Sea which has produced large earlier Neolithic lithic and ceramic assemblages from buried land surfaces exposed by coastal erosion and is the subject of continuing excavation (Webley 1969; Hamilton and Aldhouse-Green 1998). On the north side of the valley, as it opens to the coast, is the site of Mount Pleasant which, upon excavation in 1952, revealed an earlier Neolithic house partially preserved beneath a Bronze Age barrow (Savory 1952). Also on the north side of the valley is the megalithic tomb of Tythegston (Daniel 1950, 210; Houlder 1976, 36–37).

Large quantities of earlier Neolithic material have also been recovered from the valley itself. The shifting sands of Merthyr Mawr Warren have produced a range of leaf-shaped arrowheads and stone axes (*e.g.* Evans 1911). Further stone axes have also been recovered from higher up the Ogmore Valley. Mention should also be made here of the two finds of Neolithic mace-heads (Grimes 1929; Savory 1980, 228) and a Seamer-style axe (Green 1981) from the vicinity of the current study area. These indicate a continued importance for the Ogmore Valley into the latter part of the Neolithic period.

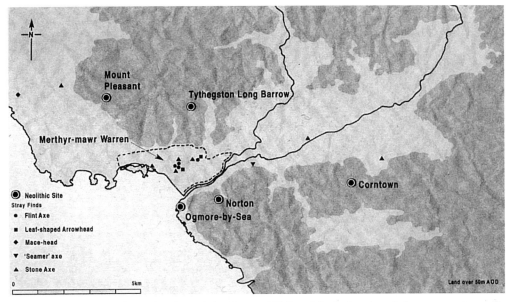

Figure 7.1: The Neolithic archaeology of the Ogmore Valley with the location of the two putative earlier Neolithic enclosures. (Source for artefact information: National Museums and Galleries of Wales accession records)

NORTON (NPRN 90000; SS 87467578)

The enclosure at Norton was initially recognized on Ordnance Survey vertical air photographs (taken 30th May 1984) by Toby Driver, and confirmed during Royal Commission aerial photography in July 1996 by Chris Musson (see Driver 1997a; 1997b; Topping and Varndell forthcoming).

The enclosure consists of two subcircular ditch circuits with an internal diameter of *c*. 191m by 176m (Figures 7.2 and 7.3). The ditches are narrow (*c*. 2m-4m wide) and close set (3.8m–7.2m apart). Interruptions are clearly visible in the ditches, with these often being displaced from those in the adjacent circuit. Two possible entrances are apparent. An antenna ditch extends from the eastern entrance, apparently enclosing a large pit, whilst breaks in the circuit on the western side of the enclosure may represent a second entrance, although the clarity of the crop-mark evidence here is poor. Within, and adjacent to, the enclosure are a number of large pits, although these are not necessarily contemporary with the enclosure itself.

Although situated only a few hundred metres from the Ogmore River, the enclosure at Norton seems to have been placed with other siting factors in mind. It is set back from the valley-edge in a position which hides it from visitors following the adjacent river course. It does, however, occupy a commanding position overlooking a steep-sided offshoot of the main valley which provides it with access to the adjacent low ground. From this semi-concealed position the enclosure offers extensive views to the north and east as far as the Welsh uplands.

Figure 7.2: Norton enclosure, aerial view from the northeast showing the out-turned entrance. (Photograph 965110–50 (25 July 1996), Crown Copyright RCAHMW)

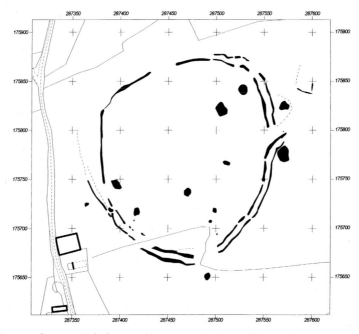

Figure 7.3: Norton enclosure, aerial photographic transcription from oblique and vertical sources. Grid at 50m intervals. (Crown Copyright RCAHMW. Based upon Ordnance Survey map with permission. All rights reserved)

Morphologically the site bears comparison with causewayed enclosures in Cambridgeshire (Great Wilbraham), Staffordshire (Mavesyn Ridware and Alrewas) and Gloucestershire (Eastleach) although the elaborate entrance at Norton is less easily paralleled.

A preliminary programme of gradiometry survey was conducted over a small portion of the site in 1997, and this was sufficient to establish the potential of the technique for refining the aerial photographic evidence. When the main field was ploughed in the spring of 1998 it was also fieldwalked by Steve Burrow and Mark Lodwick (NMGW), although bad weather prevented a systematic survey. At this time a transverse arrowhead (NMGW: 99.63H) and a small number of flint flakes were found. However, material was generally sparse and failed to reinforce the earlier Neolithic date attributed to the site. Although the form of the Norton site presents the most convincing evidence for an earlier Neolithic enclosure in the Vale of Glamorgan, in the absence of excavation its dating remains unproved.

CORNTOWN (NPRN 300311; SS 926765)

The site at Corntown was first recognized in 1976 when a lithic scatter was identified by Gareth Dowdell. Subsequent walking over a number of years by Steve Sell and Gerald Gregory has shown the site to cover an area approximately 200m in diameter, although it was only in 1995 that aerial reconnaissance by Chris Musson for RCAHMW identified a crop-mark enclosure at the same location (Burrow *et al.* forthcoming).

At Corntown, the enclosure is not of a typical earlier Neolithic form, and its attribution to the Neolithic period is based largely on the supporting grounds indicated by the character of the lithic scatter described below.

The enclosure, as revealed by aerial photography, is obscured in places by washes of alluvium and cracks in the underlying limestone. For this reason, the air photo transcription prepared in AutoCAD and ArcView GIS by David Thomas, is most reliable as a record of the southern half of the site (Figure 7.4 and 7.5). There appear to be three sets of ditches, an inner enclosure with two outer concentric circuits. The inner enclosure, 127m by 150m, is egg-shaped and defined by a narrow ditch, possibly a palisade trench. There is a space of about 33m before the middle concentric enclosure about 199m by 218m, which has a possible entrance gap to the southwest. The outer concentric circuit, measuring about 283m northwest to southeast, is set a further 32m away. Many pits occur across the site, as at Norton, but may of course date from any period. It is situated on the northern slope of a low east to west ridge. To the south of the enclosure the landscape consists of gently undulating hills, whilst to the north the land drops away, offering commanding views across the lowlands of the Ogmore Valley. It seems highly likely that the enclosure was constructed with this in mind.

It is difficult to find parallels for the Corntown site, except perhaps in some of the more complex Neolithic enclosures being discovered by aerial reconnaissance in central and eastern Europe. Without better evidence of the exact morphology of the site, from remote sensing or excavation, it would be unwise to make firm comparisons.

The lithic assemblage from the site consists of 2,866 pieces weighing a total of 3.24kg. In these gross terms the collection is therefore the largest yet found within the Vale of

Figure 7.4: Corntown enclosure, aerial view from the northeast (Photograph 955150–66 (4 July 1995), Crown Copyright RCAHMW)

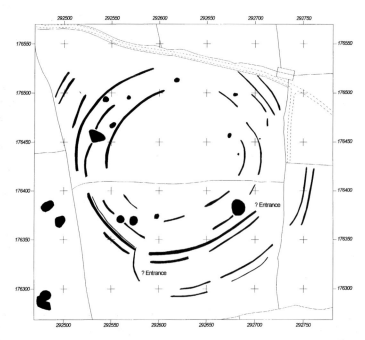

Figure 7.5: Corntown enclosure, aerial photographic transcription from oblique sources. Grid at 50m intervals. (Crown Copyright RCAHMW. Based upon Ordnance Survey map with permission. All rights reserved)

Glamorgan, and one of the most substantial to have been found in south Wales. With the exception of one piece of chert, the entire assemblage is of flint. It has not been possible to undertake detailed plotting of finds from the site, and the assemblage must therefore be considered as a single unit (Table 7.1).

Table 7.1 - Summary of the lithic artefacts recovered during fieldwalking at Corntown.

	Total	% of assemblage
Debitage		
Unretouched flake	2671	93.19
Chunk	12	0.42
Core fragment	6	0.21
Core	3	0.10
Total debitage	*2692*	*93.92*
Retouched pieces		
Knife	23	0.81
Leaf-shaped arrowhead	30	1.06
Microburin	1	0.03
Microlith	2	0.06
Notched flake	4	0.14
Oblique arrowhead	1	0.03
Piercer	1	0.03
Polished axehead fragment	8	0.28
Retouched flake	41	1.43
Retouched point	2	0.07
Scraper	34	1.19
Worked piece	11	0.38
Utilized flake	16	0.57
Total retouched pieces	*174*	*6.08*
ASSEMBLAGE TOTAL	**2866**	**100**

Only three diagnostic Mesolithic pieces has been recovered from the site (one microlith, one microlith fragment, and a microburin). It might also be noted that only five blades of Mesolithic proportions have been identified within the assemblages 400+ intact pieces of debitage. However, recent work by Barton on the late Mesolithic site of Goldcliff (43km to the east) has shown that hunter-gatherers in the area at this time also employed a flake-based technology (Barton 2000). On balance one can, however, note that Mesolithic material appears to form only a minor contaminant within the collection. Similarly the presence of only one oblique arrowhead and no diagnostically later pieces within the assemblage suggests that little if any of the collection is of later Neolithic or Bronze Age date.

All the remaining chronologically specific material – such as leaf-shaped arrowheads (30 examples), and flakes from polished artefacts (8 examples, probably from axes) – can be dated to the earlier Neolithic. It therefore seems reasonable to assume that the vast majority of material found at Corntown belongs to this period.

It is probable that the inhabitants of the site derived their flint from marine deposits along the Glamorgan coast, and in this context the large lithic scatter only 6.5km away on the coast at Ogmore-by-Sea is particularly interesting (Hamilton and Aldhouse-Green 1997). With few exceptions, such coastal sources are unlikely to have contained large high quality pieces, a point reinforced by the small size of the 405 intact flakes (all <40mm long) and the low mean weight of the cores/chunks from Corntown (5.27gr). The presence of primary and secondary flakes within the lithic scatter as well as 88 small chips (length <10mm) strongly indicates that some of this raw material was carried to the site and worked *in situ*.

The size of the assemblage is unusual within the Vale of Glamorgan and suggests that Corntown was either occupied for a considerable span of time, or was subject to repeated short-lived visits. Whichever is the case, the range of retouched pieces in the assemblage indicates that the location was used for a variety of activities.

The most striking component of the assemblage are the 30 leaf-shaped arrowheads. Whilst this quantity is perhaps a little higher than one might expect from an occupation site, particularly one which has only been subject to cursory examination, it is not high enough to suggest that violent events overcame its inhabitants.

To summarize, Corntown has produced an important earlier Neolithic assemblage from an area delineated by a sub-circular enclosure. To date no later finds have been recovered which might lead one to suggest that this crop-mark enclosure belongs to a more recent period. However, without the lithic artefacts the morphology of the site alone would make this a reasonable conclusion.

CONCLUSION

Without excavation it is impossible to be certain that these two enclosures within the Ogmore Valley are of Neolithic date. In the case of the Norton enclosure the case for a Neolithic date rests on morphological comparisons with the causewayed camps of southern and central England. In this instance only a handful of flint has been recovered from the surface and only one piece can be dated to the later Neolithic. At Corntown the situation is reversed, a large lithic assemblage has been found confirming the presence of an earlier Neolithic site at this location. It is not, however, possible to make an indisputable link between the surface scatter and the atypical enclosure that lies beneath.

In the absence of proof it would be foolhardy to explore too far the cultural significance of either of these sites within a strictly Neolithic context. At present their chief value is as pointers for further work and as a reminder that modern notions of cultural identity should not deter us from seeking out further links between southern Wales and western England. It is possible that both sites will prove to be of later date. However, their potential is sufficient to remind us that somewhere within the Vale of Glamorgan is likely to lie the remains of an earlier Neolithic enclosure which will push back the limits of decades of distribution maps beyond the boundary of the Severn Estuary.

ACKNOWLEDGEMENTS

The aerial photographic interpretation and mapping of both enclosures was undertaken by Toby Driver and David Thomas. They would like to extend their gratitude to Chris Musson, for his useful observations on the enclosures, to Dr Alex Gibson for his comments on the Norton enclosure, to David Wilson for his original comments on the Corntown enclosure, and to the staff and secretary of RCAHMW for their help and support.

Preliminary fieldwork at Norton and analysis of the Corntown lithics was undertaken by Steve Burrow with the support of staff in the Department of Archaeology and Numismatics, National Museums and Galleries of Wales (notably Richard Brewer, Mark Lodwick, and Elizabeth Walker). The collection of the lithic assemblage was undertaken by Steve Sell (Glamorgan – Gwent Archaeological Trust) and Gerald Gregory, and is retained by the landowner.

The authors would like to offer their thanks to Professor Tim Darvill for his invitation to contribute this article.

BIBLIOGRAPHY

Barton, N, 2000, The late Mesolithic assemblages. In M Bell, A Caseldine, and H Neumann (eds), *Prehistoric intertidal archaeology in the Welsh Severn Estuary* (= Council for British Archaeology Research Report 120). York. Council for British Archaeology. 39–47

Burrow, S, Driver, T, and Thomas, D, forthcoming, Corntown Neolithic lithic scatter (SS926765). *Archaeology in Wales*

Carter, H, (ed), 1980, *National atlas of Wales*. Cardiff. University of Wales Press

Daniel, G E, 1950, *The prehistoric chamber tombs of England and Wales*. Cambridge. Cambridge University Press

Darvill, T C, 1982, *The megalithic chambered tombs of the Cotswold-Severn region*. Highworth. Vorda Publications

Darvill, T C, 1987, *Prehistoric Britain*. London. Routledge

Darvill, T C, 1989, The circulation of Neolithic stone and flint axes: a case study from Wales and the mid-west of England. *Proceedings of the Prehistoric Society*, 55, 27–43

Driver, T, 1995, New crop mark sites at Aberthaw, South Glamorgan. *Archaeology in Wales*, 35, 3–9

Driver, T, 1997a, Norton: the first interrupted ditch enclosure in Wales? *AARGnews*, 15, 17–19

Driver, T, 1997b, Norton, Ogmore-by-Sea. *Archaeology in Wales*, 37, 66–67

Evans, W F, 1911, Prehistoric remains in the Ogmore sandhills. *Archaeologia Cambrensis*, 66 (Series 6.11), 441–43

Fleming, A, 1999, Phenomenology and the megaliths of Wales: a dreaming too far? *Oxford Journal of Archaeology*, 18.2, 119–26

Green, H S, 1981, A polished flint axe from Ogmore, Glamorgan. *Bulletin of the Board of Celtic Studies*, 29 (1980–82), 340–41

Grimes, W F, 1929, A fragmentary stone axe from Sker, Glamorgan. *Archaeologia Cambrensis*, 84, 147–49

Hamilton, M, and Aldhouse-Green, S, 1998, Ogmore-by-Sea (SS 861 756 to SS 861 751). *Archaeology in Wales*, 38, 113–15

Houlder, C H, 1976, Burial and ritual structures – Neolithic period. In *An inventory of the ancient monuments in Glamorgan. Volume 1: Pre-Norman. Part 1, the Stone and Bronze Ages*. Cardiff. HMSO. 23–42

Musson, C, 1994, *Wales from the air, patterns of past and present*. Cardiff. HMSO

Palmer, R, 1976, Interrupted ditch enclosures in Britain: the use of aerial photography for comparative studies. *Proceedings of the Prehistoric Society*, 42, 161–86

Piggott, S, 1954, *The Neolithic cultures of the British Isles*. Cambridge. Cambridge University Press

Savory, H N, 1952, The excavation of a Neolithic dwelling and Bronze Age cairn at Mount Pleasant Farm, Nottage (Glamorgan). *Transactions of the Cardiff Naturalists Society*, 81, 75–89

Savory, H N, 1980, The Neolithic in Wales. In J A Taylor (ed), *Culture and environment in prehistoric Wales: selected essays* (British Archaeological Reports British Series 76). Oxford. British Archaeological Reports. 207–31

Sherratt, A, 1996, Why Wessex? The Avon route and river transport in later British prehistory. *Oxford Journal of Archaeology*, 15.2, 211–34

Tilley, C, 1994, *A phenomenology of landscape: places, paths and monuments*. Oxford. Berg

Topping, P, and Varndell, G (eds), forthcoming, *The genesis of monuments: Neolithic causewayed enclosures*.

Webley, D, 1969, Aspects of Neolithic and Bronze Age agriculture in south Wales. *Bulletin of the Board of Celtic Studies*, 23 (1968–70), 285–90

Webley, D, 1976, How the west was won: prehistoric land-use in the southern Marches. In G C Boon and J M Lewis (eds), *Welsh Antiquity. Essays mainly on prehistoric topics presented to H N Savory*. Cardiff. National Museum of Wales. 19–35

Chapter 8

Survey at Hindwell Enclosure, Walton, Powys, Wales

Alex Gibson, Helmut Becker, Eoin Grogan, Nigel Jones, and Barry Masterson

INTRODUCTION

No volume on the theme of Neolithic enclosures would be complete without a brief account of current work being undertaken at the Hindwell Enclosure (Powys SMR PRN19376) which, more than any other yet discovered in Britain, truly warrants the epithet "monumental". However, despite having a perimeter of 2.35km and enclosing an area of 34ha, this site is invisible from the ground. It survives only as a crop-mark and even then shows from the air but rarely. The enclosure lies in the Radnor Valley on the Powys – Herefordshire border (Figure 8.1). The site today presents the visitor with a pleasant aspect over rural lowland mid-Wales surrounded by the upland moorland of the Radnor Forest. The area is given to a mixture of arable and pasture agriculture and the only features of archaeological note enclosed by the site are the plough-truncated remains of two round barrows (PRN309 and PRN314). This is not strictly true. A lane curves from east to west and in doing so has been recognized as fossilizing part of the northern perimeter of the site. This was totally unexpected and was understood only after the other parts of the perimeter had been discovered. Presumably, the palisade trench, measuring some 5–7m across, had been evident as a slight sunken earthwork in this area and had been utilized by the medieval inhabitants of the region for a hollow-way.

DISCOVERY AND ASSOCIATIONS

Accounts of the scale and discovery of the enclosure have already been published (Gibson 1995; 1996; 1998; 1999) and no repetition of these facts is necessary here. Suffice it to say that the internal details of the site are largely unknown. Crop-marks within the enclosure comprise the ditches and camber of a Roman road emanating from the Hindwell Fort, which lies over the eastern perimeter of the Neolithic site, and part of a large Roman marching camp (Figure 8.2). This monument covers some 18ha, was therefore capable of having held 12–13000 soldiers and probably dates to the early Flavian campaigns in Wales and the Marches. Some aerial photographs of the northern of the two barrows within the enclosure reveal a triple ring-ditch surrounding what would appear to be the central burial. The barrow sequence is complicated further by traces of a pit-circle also visible below the mound.

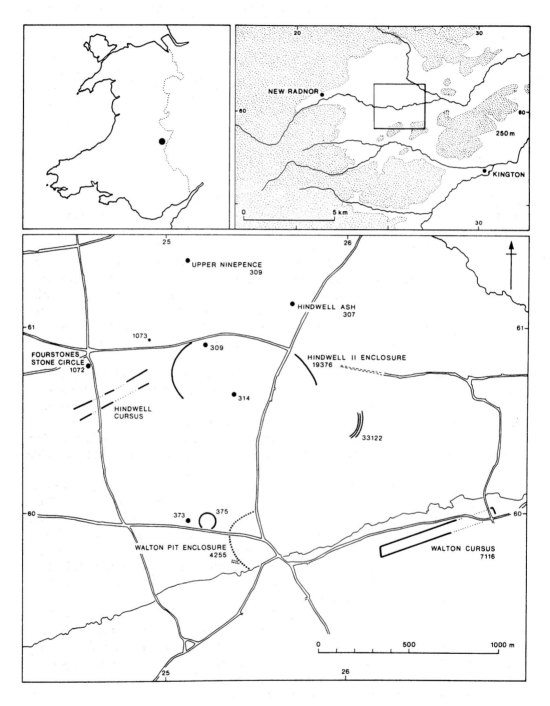

Figure 8.1: Location of the Radnor Valley and Hindwell Enclosure

Over half the interior of the enclosure is covered by land-use generally unsuited to the production of crop-marks. These land-uses include farmyards, buildings, roads and pasture. Speedy clover regeneration in the grass fields from which hay crops have been taken have produced some crop-marks, but never in those fields which are permanently grazed. Accordingly, a programme of geophysical survey was devised to investigate further the perimeter of the site and to research the pasture areas of the interior. The arable fields in which crop-marks had already been recorded (albeit of different dates to the enclosure) were regarded as of lower priority.

GEOPHYSICAL SURVEYS

Geophysical survey had been undertaken at the enclosure previously. Limited work on the western portion of the perimeter prior to the 1994 excavation had been undertaken by Stratascan Ltd, financed by Staffordshire University (Gibson 1997), while work on the northeastern perimeter was carried out by Claire Thomas and John Milson of University College London (UCL) prior to the 1996 excavation. The Stratascan survey located the post-pits and post-ramps, associated features which comprise the ditch of the enclosure, in both the ground penetrating radar and resistivity surveys but no trace was recorded with the magnetometry (fluxgate gradiometer). The UCL resistivity survey again located the enclosure's perimeter. Experiments with a magnetometer proved unsuccessful. It appeared that the soils of the Walton Basin were not conducive to the production of magnetic anomalies.

Accordingly, Helmut Becker from the Bayerisches Landesamt für Denkmalpflege in Munich was invited to Wales to try caesium-vapour magnetometry. This technique has two very obvious advantages. First, it is very fast (covering about 3ha per day) and, second, it is 1000 times more sensitive than conventional magnetometry. This degree of sensitivity allows the detection of minute changes in the magnetic signatures of the soils caused by microbacterial action. Some 20ha of the interior of the enclosure was surveyed at 0.25m intervals.

Prior to this work, the entire site was surveyed by Nigel Jones of the Clwyd-Powys Archaeological Trust and a grid was laid out to facilitate the geophysics (Figure 8.2). Fixed base points were surveyed in to the national grid to ±6mm accuracy. Field boundaries and other features were added to the survey to allow it to be compared with the Ordnance Survey data. This survey confirms the lack of relief within the enclosure although the crop-mark Roman road can be traced as a relief feature running through the western half of the enclosure from the centre to the northwest. Staff from the City Archaeology Service, Zwolle, Netherlands, assisted with both surveys.

The area of the Roman fort was surveyed by Eoin Grogan and Barry Masterson from the Republic of Ireland's Discovery Programme. This area was surveyed because the fort appeared to lie partly within the enclosure and therefore would be included within the geophysical survey. Furthermore, aerial photographs had detected an arc of what appeared to be a triple-ditched enclosure to the east (Figure 8.1, PRN33122). When the curvature of these ditches was projected, it suggested that they would intersect with the main enclosure somewhere in the vicinity of the fort. If this were to be the case, then it would be

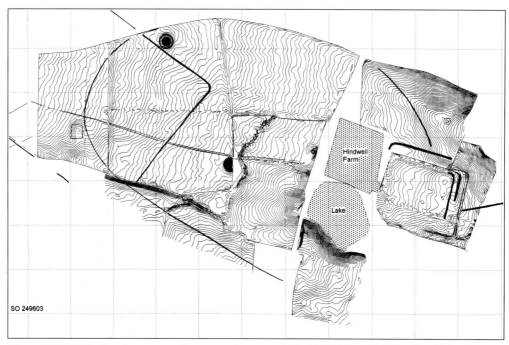

Figure 8.2: Hindwell enclosure: ground survey and crop-marks in 1998. The grid is based on 100m by 100m squares; contour intervals are 0.1m. The Hindwell marching camp overlies the western arc of the Neolithic site while the fort overlies the eastern

interesting to note whether a stratigraphic relationship could be detected in the geophysical survey.

While the ground and geophysical survey results from this area provide important information on the internal arrangements and phasing of the Roman fort and its previously unlocated *vicus*, and in so doing make a valuable contribution to the history of the Flavian campaigns into Wales, this aspect of the survey is hardly relevant in the present context. What is more important is the fact that the palisade trench of the Hindwell enclosure can be detected as a negative anomaly running below the eastern portion of fort (Figure 8.3). Two ditches almost certainly belonging to the triple-ditched enclosure can also be seen running through the *vicus* and clearly must intersect with the main enclosure ditch. Unfortunately, the point of intersection is obscured by the high level of background noise produced by the burning of the fort on its abandonment. The ramparts of the fort, however, appear to overlie the ditches of this triple-ditched (here double-ditched) enclosure since the signatures of the ditches are weaker in this area. There seems to be little doubt that the enclosure is prehistoric in date. Clearly this point of intersection would be a key area for targeting in any further excavation programmes.

Also important from the prehistorian's viewpoint are the results of the physical survey of the fort, for here it can be seen that the Neolithic palisade trench survives as a slight depression (Figure 8.3 upper). When the geophysics are superimposed on the digital

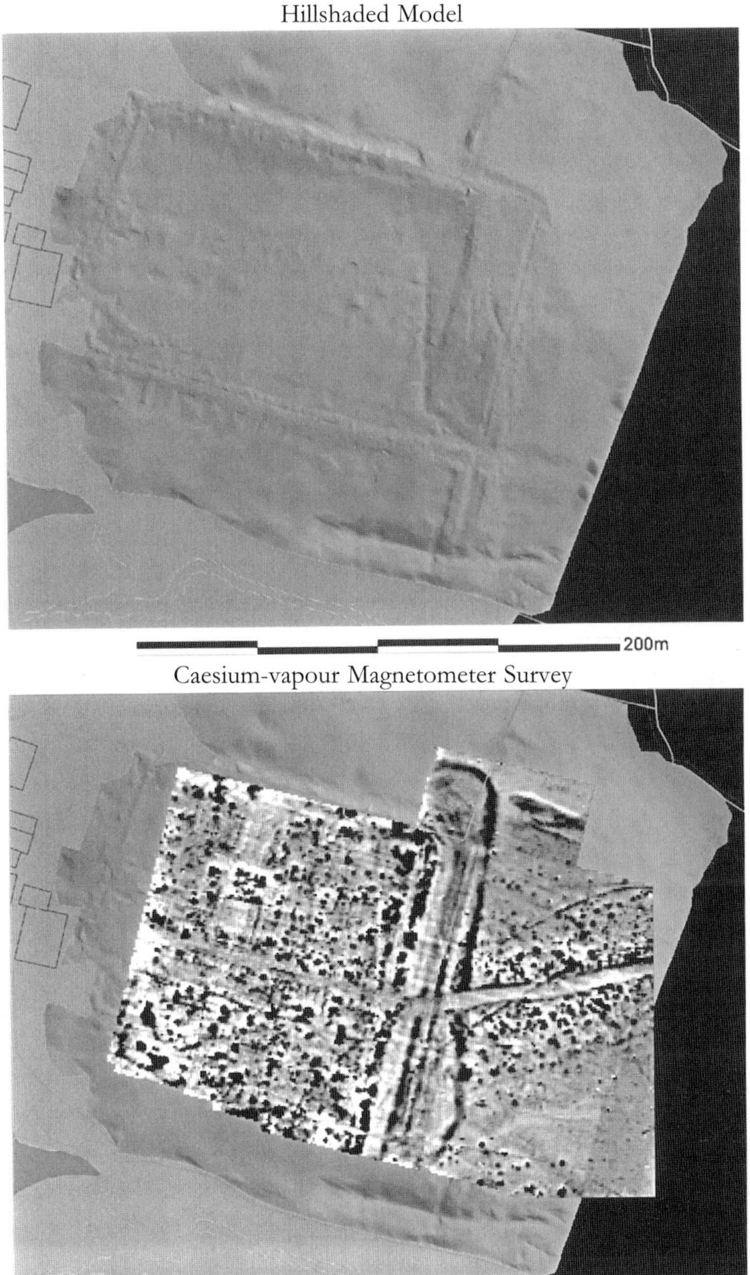

Hillshaded Model

Caesium-vapour Magnetometer Survey

Figure 8.3: Caesium-vapour magnetometer survey of the Roman fort superimposed on the hill-shaded digital terrain model. two ditches curving from the east and crossing the vicus *may belong to the triple-ditched enclosure to the east. The line of the Neolithic palisade trench can be seen as a curving negative anomaly just within the ramparts of the Roman fort*

terrain model, then the coincidence of the depression with the geophysical anomaly is remarkable. This earthwork feature was not noted prior to the survey because its significance was lost in the undulations of the earthworks of the ramparts in this area.

This survival must be due to the restricted arable agriculture that has taken place over the fort. It also suggests by inference that the enclosure may have been detectable at the time of the Roman advance, if not later, and that its area may have retained some symbolic significance. Similar claims have been made to explain the presence of Iron Age smithing at the early Bronze Age barrow at Four Crosses (Warrilow *et al.* 1986) and at the timber circle at Sarn-y-bryn-caled (Gibson 1994). That this earthwork survival of the enclosure continued much later than the Roman period is further suggested by the presence of the road forming the northern perimeter of the enclosure, presumably where the depression had been formalized by a hollow-way. Mr C Goodwin of Hindwell has noted that there is a considerable hard-core build-up beneath this road. This was observed while laying a water-pipe and suggests the in-filling of the hollow-way prior to the metalling of the present lane.

INTERPRETATION

The geophysical survey of the enclosure perimeter revealed some interesting phenomena. First, the entrance was located in the western arc of the ditch (Figure 8.4). Like Mount Pleasant, Dorset, the entrance was formed by two massive postholes each some 6m across defining a narrow entrance 2m wide. The significance of these narrow entrances on palisaded sites has already been discussed (Gibson 1998). Furthermore, the perimeter

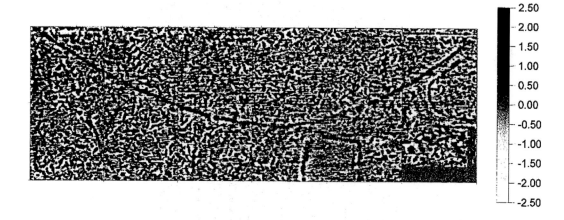

Figure 8.4: Caesium-vapour magnetometer results from the western arc of the Neolithic enclosure (north is to the left). The narrow entrance, marked by large post-pits, can be seen about 100m from the left (northern) edge of the survey. The total length of the survey area is 240m

appears to be double in sections in the northeast and southeast. This phenomenon is difficult to explain. The anomalies detected may indeed represent secondary post-pits, or they may have another function. The strength of the anomalies suggests some sort of pyro-technic activity. The excavations revealed that the posts had been water-proofed by charring the outer rings below the ground but that this burning had taken place prior to the insertion of the posts in their post-pits. These pits, revealed on the geophysical survey, may therefore represent the fire-pits in which the posts were charred. They may also suggest that the palisade had been, at least partly, destroyed by fire and that the collapsed and burning posts have left a micro-magnetic signature on the subsoil. In support of this theory it was noted that the Mount Pleasant perimeter had been destroyed in a number of ways; dismantling in some areas, burning in others (Wainwright 1979, 240). This may also have been the case at Hindwell. These regions must also be regarded as targets for further work.

Internally, the results were less spectacular but by no means less interesting. The enclosure seems to have been largely empty unless the structures that it contained were so flimsy as to have left few detectable traces in the gravel subsoil. There are, however, only a very few flint finds from the ploughed fields within the enclosure in contrast with the high flint densities on the ridge to the north. With the exception of a portion from a polished flint axe, all the flint finds (9 flakes plus two Mesolithic blades) are small and may well have been imported to the site on mud adhering to tractor tyres. This, with the negative results from the geophysics, may suggest that the interior of the enclosure had not been densely populated. Some random test transects over the interior may shed further light on this question. Some large pits were, however, detected, particularly in the northeast. Their association with the enclosure cannot be proven, they may equally

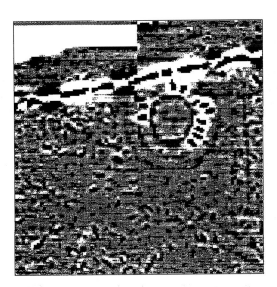

Figure 8.5: Caesium-vapour magnetometer results from the Hindwell barrow (PRN309). Unprocessed data. North is to the top of the lot. The total length of the survey area is 80m

represent activity associated with the Roman fort, and some test excavations in these areas would also prove beneficial to our understanding of how the enclosure functioned.

Below the northern of the two barrows, however, the geophysics results were more spectacular (Figure 8.5). As mentioned above, the aerial photographic evidence from this barrow suggests that a triple ring-ditch and a pit-circle underlie the mound. This has been supported by the geophysical survey but the strength of the pit-circle anomalies is remarkable. There is a difference in the interpretation of these features between the archaeologist and the geophysicist in the project. While both agree that the strength of these signals is probably the result of *in situ* burning, the archaeologist prefers to see them as belonging to a pre-mound phase while the geophysicist prefers to see them as secondary. The archaeological interpretation being offered is that they represent a pre-mound pit-circle, possibly the primary monument, the contents of which were burnt *in situ*. The rectangular nature of the anomalies many suggest that they are post-pits with ramps radiating outwards and belonging to a timber circle which had burnt down. The unevenness in the degree of burning may be the result of the predominantly southwesterly wind directions. The geophysicist's interpretation is that they represent secondary graves, dug into the mound and radiating from the centre, with *in situ* cremations. Further work needs to be undertaken to resolve this difference. If they are indeed secondary graves then a Roman or later date cannot be ruled out.

DISCUSSION

The Hindwell complex grows more interesting as more work is undertaken. Current knowledge suggests an enclosure of monumental proportions involving considerable human effort in its construction, and enclosing a largely empty space. While flimsy structures may have been present, certainly the usual settlement detritus seems missing from the ploughsoil. The entrance was restricted and massive. A **possible** timber circle existed within the site and there is the potential for episodes of pit-deposition. The history of the actual perimeter also seems to have been more complicated with external pits suggesting the possibility of a double palisade in places.

The relationship of this enclosure with other Neolithic monuments in the basin remains to be resolved. Excavation at the Meldon Bridge type enclosure less than 1km to the south at Walton (Figure 8.1, PRN4255) proved the pits to have held posts but recovered no dating evidence (Dempsey 1998). The 100m diameter ring-ditch within the marching camp complex at Walton, less than 1km to the south-southwest (Figure 8.1, PRN375) remains undated. Artefactual evidence alone suggested a date somewhere in the Neolithic for the Walton Green cursus approximately 1km to the southeast (Figure 8.1, PRN7116). The triple-ditched enclosure at Hindwell, with which the main enclosure intersects, also remains undated. These relationships clearly remain fundamental research priorities as does the extrapolation of an environmental history for the area. The sparse environmental data so far recovered from the acid and neutral soils comprise solely carbonized plant remains.

There is no doubt that the area was important in the Neolithic. However, the evidence does suggest a division between settlement and ritual areas. This is clearly a difficult distinction to make, and it may be safer to talk more in terms of "mundane" and "monumental". The mundane (settlement/domestic sphere) seems to have concentrated on the ridge above and to the north of the enclosure. It is represented by abundant flint scatters dating from the Mesolithic to the Bronze Age. Excavation of a preserved ground surface protected by a mound within this area of dense scatter produced a complex of pits and stakeholes including the ground-plans of two ostensibly domestic structures. These structures were contemporary (in radiocarbon terms) with the Hindwell enclosure and were associated with Grooved Ware. The first phase of this complex, represented by pits only, was associated with Peterborough Ware and is, therefore, likely to be contemporary with the Meldon Bridge type enclosure at Walton. The contents of the pits, as evidenced by absorbed residue analysis of the ceramics and microwear analysis of the flints, were clearly derived from domestic contexts (Gibson 1999).

In contrast, on the basin floor, flint scatters of any period are generally absent. Fieldwalking has produced a few isolated flint finds but no scatters. As mentioned above, these isolated flakes could easily have been transported from richer artefact scatters on mud adhering to the tyres of tractors and other forms of agricultural machinery. Yet it is on the basin floor that the monumental archaeology clusters: ring-ditches, barrows, stone circle, standing stones, a possible hengiform, the Walton Green cursus, the possible Fourstones cursus, the Walton and Hindwell enclosures, the Hindwell triple-ditched enclosure, and so on.

There appears to be a distinct division of space and the use of space within the landscape in the Walton Basin. Perhaps the lower, monumental areas were marginal. The better-drained soils of the ridge may have been more conducive to settlement and agriculture. The lower regions, prone to some seasonal water-logging, may have presented more of a risk to arable and yet have been perfectly suitable for pastoral purposes and, of course, the construction of communal monuments. The valley floor and the complexes it contains, may therefore have linked the communities inhabiting the fertile valley sides and which overlooked the communal terrain which served them agriculturally as well as ritually. This central place would unite the various Neolithic communities in shared land, shared effort, and shared economy. The monuments would present points of reference for the communities which they served. The rituals performed there would ensure the preservation of the *status quo* and the continued fecundity of the ecosystems on whose bounty their survival depended.

ACKNOWLEDGEMENTS

This paper was completed in April 1999. The following are thanked for their funding and/or support for the project. In alphabetical order: Bayerisches Landesamt für Denkmalpflege, Cadw: Welsh Historic Monuments, The Discovery Programme, English Heritage, The European Commission, and Sectie Archeologie van Gemeente Zwolle. Free access to the site was granted by the landowners Colin and Ann Goodwin who have provided tremendous support throughout the project.

BIBLIOGRAPHY

Dempsey, J, 1998, *The Walton pit circle, Radnorshire, trial excavation 1998/99* (= CPAT Report 298). Welshpool. Clwyd-Powys Archaeological Trust. [Limited circulation printed report]

Gibson, A M, 1994, Excavations at the Sarn-y-bryn-caled cursus complex, Welshpool, Powys, and the timber circles of Great Britain and Ireland. *Proceedings of the Prehistoric Society*, 60, 143–223

Gibson, A M, 1995, Walton. *Current Archaeology*, 12.11 (Number 143), 444–5

Gibson, A M, 1996, A Neolithic enclosure at Hindwell, Radnorshire, Powys. *Oxford Journal of Archaeology*, 15.3, 341–8

Gibson, A M, 1997, Survey in the Walton Basin (Radnor Valley), Powys. *Transactions of the Radnorshire Society*, 67, 20–62

Gibson, A M, 1998, Hindwell and the Neolithic palisaded enclosures of Britain and Ireland. In A Gibson and D Simpson (eds), *Prehistoric ritual and religion. Essays in honour of Aubrey Burl*. Stroud. Sutton Publishing. 68–79

Gibson, A M, 1999, *The Walton Basin Project: excavation and survey in a prehistoric landscape 1993–7* (= Council for British Archaeology Research Report 118). York. Council for British Archaeology

Wainwright, G J, 1979, *Mount Pleasant, Dorset: excavations 1970–1971* (= Reports of the Research Committee of the Society of Antiquaries of London 37). London. Society of Antiquaries

Warrilow, W, Owen, G, and Britnell, W J, 1986, Eight ring-ditches at Four Crosses, Llandysilio, Powys, 1981–85. *Proceedings of the Prehistoric Society*, 52, 53–88

Chapter 9

A time and place for enclosure: Gardom's Edge, Derbyshire

John Barnatt, Bill Bevan, and Mark Edmonds

INTRODUCTION

This paper is concerned with aspects of recent fieldwork at Gardom's Edge in the Derbyshire Peak District. In particular, it focuses on the results of recent survey and excavation along the line of a large, stone built, enclosure boundary. Attributed to the Iron Age for some time, it is now thought that the monument is actually rather older, belonging to the Neolithic. In what follows, we shall outline the reasoning that has led to this reassessment, drawing on the results of work to date. At the same time, we want to follow the purpose of the meeting that led to this volume, by using the vantage of Gardom's Edge to review some more general problems. To this end, we offer a series of interim comments concerning the broader classification of earlier Neolithic enclosures and the nature of regional traditions.

PLACE

Gardom's Edge is part of the gritstone scarp which forms the eastern side of the Derwent Valley. Behind the edge is a broad shelf which contains many archaeological features. Like other components of the Eastern Moors of the Peak District, the Gardom's Edge shelf is remarkable for the density of upstanding field evidence for settlement and other forms of activity during later prehistory (Barnatt 1986; 1987; 1999). Though the area has seen quarrying, coal mining, and use as a grouse moor, here at least, the plough has not bitten that deeply. The archaeological potential of Gardom's Edge has long been recognized. Preliminary surveys pointed to the presence of prehistoric fieldsystems, cairns, and other structures (Barnatt 1986; Beswick and Merrills 1983; Hart 1985). These observations have recently been augmented by a detailed 1:1000 survey of the dip slope behind the scarp (centred SK 273730) by the Royal Commission on the Historical Monuments of England and the Peak Park Joint Planning Board (Ainsworth and Barnatt 1998; RCHME 1987; RCHME and PPJPB 1993).

About 2000 archaeological features have been identified across Gardom's Edge as a whole. In addition to the enclosure, there are four examples of rock art – cup and ring marks and more complicated designs. Later prehistoric cairnfields and fieldsystems can also be seen across much of the better, if stony, land, associated with a rich variety of features. Potential house sites, clearance cairns, and linear banks are common. A linear rubble boundary and a pit alignment cross the central area of the shelf. Other monuments include standing stones, burial cairns, and a ring-cairn.

The patterned relationship of ritual monuments to fieldsystems throughout the Eastern Moors suggests that the farmed landscape was established as early as the earlier Bronze Age (Barnatt 1987; 1999). Artefacts and radiocarbon dates indicate that the settlements and fields on the Eastern Moors were used for upwards of a thousand years. Although reasonably fertile, the light sandy soils of the area were relatively stony, and boulders frequently needed to be cleared into heaps before cultivation or the improvement of pasture. In certain areas, excessively stony patches and lines of boulders were barriers to cultivation, thus individual bounded fields may have contained several cultivation plots. Other parts of the area have heavier clay soils which, with a few exceptions, appear to have been avoided for cultivation. Here though, the relative lack of naturally distributed boulders has the effect of making boundaries and other features less visible unless they survive as earthen banks. Subtle evidence for circular houses lies scattered amongst the fields, taking the form of slight platforms and stone banks. Pollen evidence and differences in field lay-out suggest that farming may have continued in more favourable areas into the Iron Age (Barnatt 1996; 1999; Bevan 1999; 2000; Long 1994; Long *et al.* 1998).

Work on the enclosure forms part of a larger project which aims to produce a long-term biography of Gardom's Edge, ultimately from prehistory to the present (Barnatt *et al.* 1995; 1996; 1997; 1998; 2000). The Project has involved excavation, remote sensing, survey, and the analysis of environmental and soils data. Conceived as an exercise in landscape archaeology, we are trying to trace the changing ways in which this land was inhabited, and the manner in which communities at different times were articulated within broader social geographies (Barrett 1994; Bender 1993). The Gardom's Edge Project is a joint undertaking by the Department of Archaeology and Prehistory at the University of Sheffield and the Archaeology Service of the Peak District National Park Authority.

FIELD SURVEY

What of the enclosure itself? The site lies on the highest part of the Gardom's Edge shelf, centred at SK 27207290 and between 266m and 278m OD. It is defined by a rubble bank between 5m and 10m wide, up to 1.5m high, and around 600m long. The bank comprises weathered, surface collected gritstone boulders, the majority between 0.2m and 0.5m in diameter. At various points, larger slabs of gritstone have also been used, some being positioned on the outer face to form a basic, if intermittent, façade. Detailed survey (Ainsworth and Barnatt 1998; RCHME and PPJPB 1993) has demonstrated the existence of at least five entrances through the bank, though it is likely that more may have been obscured by various forms of disturbance. Some entrances show signs of deliberate blocking.

The bank delimits one side of a large area at the crest of the edge, the other being the precipitous natural scarp that looks out across the Derwent Valley (Figure 9.1). Much of the *c.* 6ha interior of the enclosure is heavily boulder strewn, and there are many large gritstone earthfasts outcropping through the heather, peat, and coarse grasses. Most of the

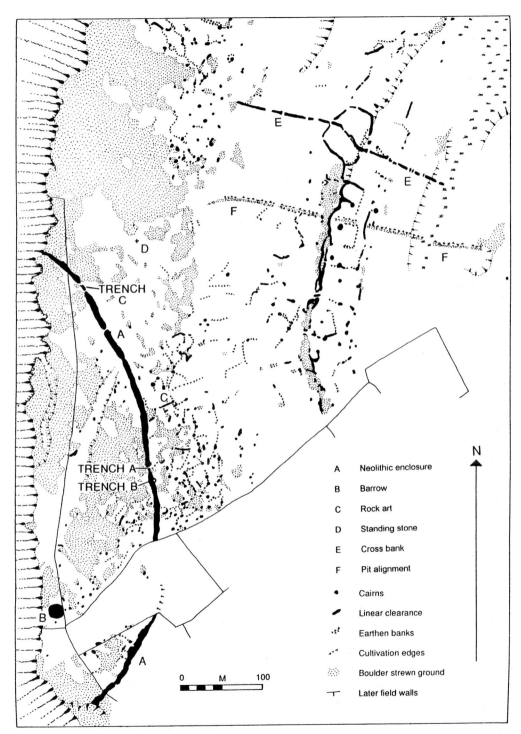

Figure 9.1: Plan of part of Gardom's Edge, showing the enclosure and location of trenches referred to in text

site lies on unimproved moorland, but at its southern end, the bank runs into an area of more recently enclosed fields. Here the pasture has been improved and the monument has been largely destroyed.

Detailed survey and excavations have shed light on the character, setting, and structural history of the enclosure. The bank as it appears today displays significant variations in character along its line. Some of the variation is due to later episodes of robbing and disturbance. The bank has been cut by post-medieval trackways, and stone has been taken towards either end in close proximity to more recent walls. One part of the central area has suffered minor remodelling during the construction of a sheep fold and lea wall. Elsewhere there are small delves and quarry features suggesting the sporadic use of the monument as a source of stone for various purposes. Many are consistent with individual episodes of turning over the upper portions or outer face of the bank to obtain larger gritstone boulders and slabs.

While robbing has certainly made a contribution to the current form of the monument, it accounts for only part of its character. A walk along its line confirms that the bank has probably always been varied. In places, it takes the form of a simple pile of rounded boulders rising no more than 0.5m above the ground surface. In others, it rises to *c.* 1.5m and there are equally marked variations in breadth reflecting different volumes of stone used in construction. The bank also rises and falls where it encounters large gritstone earthfasts. These are numerous in the immediate area of the bank, but in several places, it seems that the builders of the monument actually designed its alignment to incorporate these prominent natural features. Lower but equally massive earthfast slabs have been identified in the vicinity of a number of entrances. The terminals of the bank where it meets the precipitous scarp are also relevant here. To the south, the line of rounded boulders terminates at a massive naturally-placed gritstone block. A similar arrangement can be seen at the northern end, though here the boulder is rather smaller. However, the line of the bank at this point can be extended visually across the valley to the northwest, where it falls close to the Eagle Stone, a prominent gritstone tor on Eaglestone Flat (D Lee pers. comm.).

There are other significant variations in the build. Stretches comprising a simple rubble pile can be contrasted with others where a rudimentary and discontinuous outer façade has been established by placing larger gritstone slabs more or less on end. These changes in character are frequently associated with slight changes in direction at entrances, as if particular stretches were built as separate elements, perhaps even constructed or embellished as distinct steps or episodes in the broader process.

EXCAVATIONS

Three excavation trenches have added detail to these surface impressions. In the first, the bank took the form of a simple gritstone rubble heap; a fairly diminutive pile of rounded and weathered boulders which were presumably collected from the surrounding area (Figure 9.2: Trench A). At least some of the stone may have come from close at hand. However, relatively stone-free areas in the vicinity of the bank are also the product of geomorphological variations and of much later episodes of clearance and cannot be directly

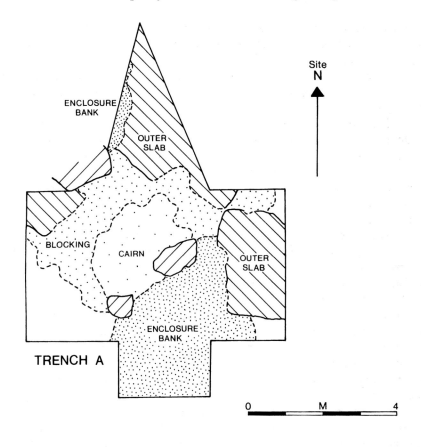

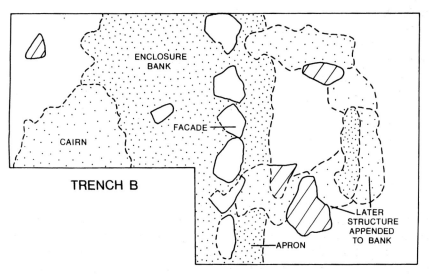

Figure 9.2: Simplified plans of enclosure elements excavated in Trenches A and B

related to the building of the enclosure. Variations in the character of the gritstone in the bank also suggest that some material was brought from further afield, principally from the low spine of "Redmires Flags" grit that runs approximately north to south across the moor (Barnatt *et al.* 1995; 1998).

Our first trench also investigated one of the entrances. This was defined on one side by a large earthfast boulder, on the other side by a large outcropping block of gritstone, and to the outside by two large flat earthfast slabs. There are no discernible signs of a clear structure or of distinct phasing to the build of the bank, nor any marked differences between inner and outer edges. The only sense of change in this area is that the entrance had been deliberately blocked by a low bank of rubble, probably some time before the clearance of the surrounding land had begun. Later on, the entrance received further blocking by the addition of a clearance cairn.

This pattern can be contrasted with another stretch of the bank excavated quite close at hand (Figures 9.2 and 9.3: Trench B). Here a façade of larger boulders was placed close to the outer edge. A narrow apron of small stones was placed in front, creating a sloping outer edge to the bank and giving support to the façade itself. Large boulders were placed on the ground behind the façade and smaller rounded and angular stones were then piled on top. The construction was designed so as to form a flat-top to the bank lying just below the level of the top of the façade. The deliberate creation of a façade and the levelling of the bank-top suggests that here, care had been taken to create a particular, even dramatic, visual impression (Barnatt *et al.* 1996).

Our third trench was considerably larger (Figure 9.4). In this case, we exposed 23m of the bank, specifically to look at variations in the character of the build towards the northern

Figure 9.3: Enclosure façade in Trench B after removal of outer apron of gritstone boulders

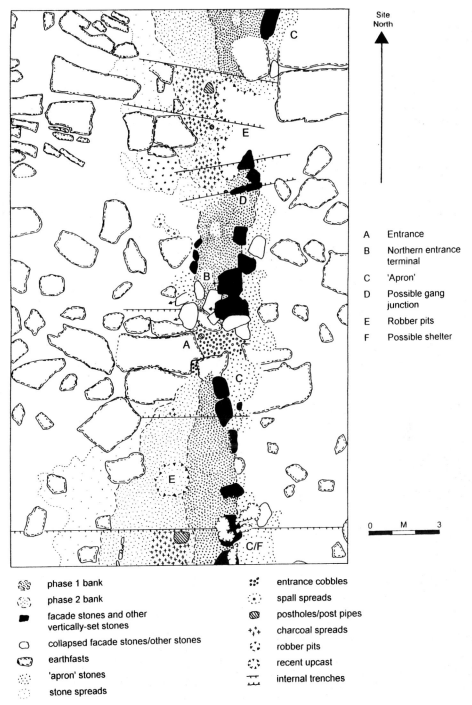

Site North

A   Entrance
B   Northern entrance terminal
C   'Apron'
D   Possible gang junction
E   Robber pits
F   Possible shelter

0   M   3

phase 1 bank
phase 2 bank
facade stones and other vertically-set stones
collapsed facade stones/other stones
earthfasts
'apron' stones
stone spreads

entrance cobbles
spall spreads
postholes/post pipes
charcoal spreads
robber pits
recent upcast
internal trenches

Figure 9.4: Simplified plan of enclosure elements excavated in Trench C

end of the enclosure. In this area, the bank was far more massive; rising to approximately 1.5m on the substantial boulders that flank an impressive entrance. As with the first entrance, this was located to incorporate large flat earthfasts, though here the gaps between the earthfasts were infilled with cobbles. There is also evidence that elements of the bank may have been constructed and perhaps embellished in distinct sections, as if it was built in a series of shorter lengths which together made the line. Distinct breaks or butted relationships run across the bank, and there are marked variations in the width of the bank that cannot be explained as a product of later robbing (Barnatt *et al.* 1998).

Trench C also revealed evidence of phasing. A line of substantial timber posts ran along the line of the bank, either preceding it or contemporary with its first stone phase. The latter took the form of a bank of substantial gritstone boulders with an outer façade of vertically placed stones of varied height. The largest of these stones were used in the immediate area of the entrance. Behind this bank, and perhaps after an interval of some time, a second phase of stone was added to the inner side of the bank, doubling its width. This was preceded by the removal of the posts. The second phase comprised many burnt stones which were placed above a thick deposit of charcoal. Many of these stones show the reddened and degraded characteristics that are often a consequence of heat alteration.

There are two interpretations for the charcoal deposit and the burnt stones above. It may be that a substantial fire was raised behind the bank, and the stones of the second phase thrown onto the fire while it was still alight. Alternatively, the charcoal and burnt stone may have been brought in after burning elsewhere. This suggestion is supported by the "placed" character of the charcoal deposit, and by the fact that none of the underlying soils or the larger stones of the first phase, which are in direct contact with the charcoal, show any signs of heat alteration. This might be expected if the fires had burnt *in situ*. However, the much larger boulders of the first phase may have responded to heat in a very different way to the smaller stones of the second phase. A decision will have to wait until we have experimented with the effects of heat on similar boulders and our soil columns have been analyzed. One thing is clear. The charcoal did not derive from the burning and collapse of some form of palisade. Good survival shows that it was produced from burning brushwood and branches.

What of the setting of the site? Looking west, the view is impressive. The ground falls away at your feet and down towards the River Derwent. It is possible to gaze across the valley towards the more distant reaches of the moors and the limestone plateau. From below, the cliff marks the location of the enclosure. For those passing through the valley, the cliff would have been prominent and perhaps a point of reference; a dominant feature on the skyline. The bank itself would have been out of sight from this direction. Significantly, the enclosure lies between the two main watercourses that break the Eastern Moors scarp, forming visually distinctive cuts in this dominant landscape feature. It is thus well placed to be approached from a number of directions. To the north and south, the ground falls away gently towards these valleys. From the east, the approach is gentler still. Here the shelf behind the cliff runs back into dips where the underlying rock is soft shale, and to another low gritstone ridge, before rising again to the face of the higher upper scarp of Birchen Edge. In strict topographic terms, the elevation of Birchen Edge allows a good view of the lower shelf, and of the enclosure. However, the ability to see into the interior from this vantage is heavily dependant on the nature and density of tree cover, something that may well have been an issue at many prehistoric enclosures, Neolithic or otherwise (Thomas 1982).

Although more detailed survey is currently underway, it is already apparent that differences in the form of the monument are responsive to the immediate local topography. The bank is at its highest in those places where the land immediately outside is more or less level. It is at its lowest in those areas where the ground falls away, albeit as a gentle slope. Just how significant these differences are, and how far they have been influenced by robbing, is difficult to determine. However, it is tempting to conclude that differences in the scale of the monument were tied to the impression that would be formed by approaching on foot from outside. Where the slope helped create a sense of elevation, the bank could afford to be relatively diminutive yet still be visually striking; where the approach was more level, the boundary had to be rather more substantial. We should not assume that it was only the **appearance** of the monument as it was being approached that was an important factor during construction. But impressions gained so far suggest that this theme was certainly caught up in the process.

TIME

The particular ways in which this monument has been forgotten and "discovered" over time is something that we shall be exploring within the broader remit of the Project. For the shepherds who built the fold and lea wall, or the delvers searching for suitable stone, the antiquity of the enclosure may not have been an issue, if indeed, it was even recognized as such. For now though, dating is one of our principal concerns. As yet, we have no absolute dates with which to answer the question, though samples are being prepared for submission. That said, several lines of evidence make a strong circumstantial case for a Neolithic date.

In the recent past, the site, like many others in central, western, and northern Britain, has been assigned to a variety of periods. Though it may have been known locally for far longer, its entry into the literature came in the 1940s. An intense fire removed much of the cover on the moor and made it possible for the eye to trace the pattern of the bank (Ward 1942; 1943). Referred to as "Meg Walls" (a field a little to the south of the enclosure was given this name in the 19th century), and linked by hearsay to cattle and milking, it was interpreted at this time as a "British defence wall". The term is by no means unusual. In the first half of the 20th century, it was used in many areas to attribute elevated enclosures to a period of assumed tension in the centuries around the Roman occupation. These attributions were often based on the superficial appearance and topographic setting of sites. This seems to have been the case at Gardom's Edge.

Survey in the following 20 years by Leslie Butcher added more detail to descriptions of the site and the complex cairnfields that lie across the moor (Beswick and Merrills 1983). But it was with the publication of the North Derbyshire Archaeological Survey that a more specific attribution emerged (Hart 1981). For Clive Hart, comparisons with other enclosures in the region suggested an Iron Age date:

> "The Gardoms site is similar in both size and location to Ball Cross and Fin Cop and all three may have been used primarily as stock enclosures. Each is sited so as to command and to

have exit on to a wide plateau with perched water tables or high spring lines providing good summer grazing" (Hart 1981, 75).

Further weight to this argument was added by the suggestion that the enclosure was demonstrably later than the surrounding Bronze Age cairnfield (Hart 1985, 72).

These attributions can be questioned on a number of grounds. In a number of places, the enclosure is actually overlain by features that are part of the Gardom's Edge central fieldsystem (Ainsworth and Barnatt 1998, 17). Cairns lie on its sides and block entrances, and in parts, the cairnfield runs across the interior. In these cases, the stratigraphic relationship is clear and there are no instances where it is reversed. A relative chronology can also be inferred by looking at broader relationships. Though few have a direct physical association with the bank, many cairns lie nearby. Given the volume of stone involved in the bank's construction, it is difficult to conceive of the monument being built after these cairns without there being some evidence that they served as sources of gritstone boulders. In fact, there is no evidence for the robbing of these features in the vicinity and this again suggests an earlier date. These and other cairnfields were established during the Bronze Age (some perhaps at a relatively early stage) and may have persisted into the first millennium BC (Barnatt 1986; 1987; 1999; Barnatt and Smith 1991; Everson 1989). The enclosure must therefore be at least that old and perhaps considerably older. Here it is interesting that the cairnfields extend into relatively stone-free parts of the southern area of the enclosure interior. Though precise stratigraphy is lacking, this suggests that the enclosure was no longer recognized or respected by the time these features were created. In places, it may have become no more than a suitable location to dump clearance stone.

The probability that the monument is Neolithic in date can also be inferred from the details of its landscape setting and morphology. In contrast to many late Bronze Age and early Iron Age hilltop enclosures, the constructed elements of the site are actually rather hidden. It only gains prominence when close at hand and lacks the physical presence and high visibility from a distance that is shared by many later Bronze Age and Iron Age sites. Though some Neolithic enclosures are prominent, and can have specific viewsheds (Edmonds 1999), there are many that are not (Palmer 1976). This might mean little in itself, but the morphology of the site also raises questions. The diminutive and variable character of the bank along its line has few late parallels and is most closely echoed in the form of many Neolithic enclosures. These parallels extend to the frequency of entrances and the sense of segmented construction revealed by survey and excavation (Palmer 1976; Mercer 1990). To this could be added the tendency to augment specific stretches of the monument through the addition of greater volumes of material or the creation of façades (Evans 1988a). Parallels for stone enclosures of this date include Carn Brea (Mercer 1981) Helman Tor (Mercer 1986) and perhaps Stowes Pound (Fletcher 1989; Tilley 1996) and Carrock Fell (Edmonds 1999). In at least two cases, these sites also display a tendency for banks to be carefully positioned so that they highlight and/or incorporate prominent natural outcrops.

Excavation lends further support. Work on and close to the enclosure has so far resulted in the recovery of a small number of Neolithic stone and flint artefacts, including two flakes from stone axes, arrowheads, blades and relatively narrow flint flakes, some of which come from secure contexts. These cluster around the enclosure bank, falling dramatically in frequency with increasing distance from the line. No later material has been found within or beneath the bank during any of our excavations; a stark contrast to the material recovered from Bronze and Iron Age features elsewhere on the moor. Though artefact densities are also low, an on-going programme of test-pitting in the interior has produced no conflicting evidence. There are no significant densities of later material and the only diagnostic artefacts recovered thus far are either later Mesolithic or Neolithic.

CATEGORIES

Definitive statements must await the completion of our work. However, we feel that even at this interim stage, the argument for a Neolithic date for the enclosure is a compelling one. It is only difficult to accept if we assume that Neolithic enclosures occupy a more restricted geographic distribution and conform to the tight morphological conventions established by work on "classic" sites. This was certainly a common assumption a few decades ago. But for some time now, it has been recognized that the formal and geographic boundaries of the category are actually rather blurred.

Perhaps this should not surprise us. Neolithic enclosures have been classified as a distinct archaeological category since the early part of the 20th century (Crawford 1937; Crawford and Keiller 1928; Curwen 1930; Kendrick and Hawkes 1932). Focused to a large extent on Wessex and Sussex, field research drew attention to the character of the ditches on these sites, seeing in their form a definitive trait. The broken, segmented character of their boundaries was the inspiration for many of the terms that have been used since then for description and definition: causewayed camp; interrupted ditch enclosure; causewayed enclosure. Situated for the most part on downland crests and promontories where they survived as earthworks, these sites set a pattern for recognition and classification. Since that time, the category has seen a number of revisions (Evans 1988b). Aerial reconnaissance has shown that many enclosures lie below the chalk hills that dominated early syntheses: on lower ground, on river terraces, and on the slopes of broad lowland valleys (Palmer 1976; Wilson 1975). New sites have also appeared beyond the margins of older distributions; along the Thames Valley, in the Midlands and on the edges of the East Anglian fens.

Work in these new areas has brought with it a greater flexibility in definition, and an acknowledgement that alongside setting, there are important differences of scale and form (Mercer 1990; Whittle 1977; 1988). Some sites enclose several hectares and have substantial ditches. Others are quite diminutive, with narrow, shallow ditches and circuits that enclose less than half a hectare. There are even examples, like Gardom's Edge itself, where one part of the boundary is formed by what we would recognize as a natural feature, a scarp edge, cliff, or river (Avery 1982). Many take the form of a single line of pits or ditches, often with an internal bank. Others have two, three or even four concentric circuits. Sequences also vary. Enclosures can be either short-lived or persistent, and often show changes in character over time; the addition of circuits (Bamford 1985; Whittle and Pollard 1998), or the development of more continuous boundaries and even palisades (Evans 1988a; Mercer 1981; 1988).

To these differences of form can be added a variety of functions. As Chris Evans has pointed out, the history of enclosure interpretation shows a variety in the use made of analogy (Evans 1988b). But it has often proceeded on the assumption that formal parallels could be equated with similarities of both history and purpose. Where attributes were shared, sites were presumed to have been used and understood in similar ways. As evidence has accumulated, we have had to acknowledge that this does not hold (Whittle 1988). Though there may be common themes, there are also uncommon histories. Episodic or "event-like" occupation has been suggested for a number of sites (Bamford 1985; Evans 1988c; Pryor 1998), together with their use as "rallying points for a dispersed population" (Smith 1966; 1971). Other accounts have emphasized a view of enclosures as bounded places and times, and as liminal arenas for varied rites of passage (Edmonds 1993; Evans *et al.* 1988; Thomas 1999). And in cases where the evidence allows, we find places in which persistent settlement developed before ceasing in the face of attack and destruction (Dixon 1988; Mercer 1990). In the fragmented landscapes of the time, there was no singular character to the ways these places developed. Though many saw the interweaving of "the rational and the irrational" (Pryor 1988), these could be combined in different ways.

One response to this variety has been to search for regional traditions (Palmer 1976; Whittle 1977). Using scale and the frequency and spacing of ditch circuits, lines have been drawn between areas like the Thames Valley and Wessex; and between the Midlands and the east of England. To these groups can now be added the growing number of hilltop enclosures in southwest England. This, in its turn, has encouraged a further broadening of definitions, and the recognition of sites with different characteristics in more distant areas. There are now acknowledged examples in Cumbria, Wales, Yorkshire, Northumberland, and Scotland; new names are continually being added to the list. Though some have been new discoveries, many have sat in the literature for some time as unexcavated hillforts, or as Iron Age enclosures with residual Neolithic material.

An interest in the regionalization of the Neolithic is by no means new, though it has tended to focus on the latter half of the period (Piggott 1954; Bradley 1984; Thorpe and Richards 1984; Thomas 1998). Recently though, this interest has grown in step with a questioning of the integrity of the period as a standardized "package" or "blueprint" (Thomas 1999; Whittle 1995) and a view of the landscapes of the earlier Neolithic as dispersed in both practical and social terms (Bradley 1998a; 1998b). In southern Britain, though not perhaps elsewhere (*cf.* Cooney 1997), this has been linked to the pattern of routine experience (Pollard 1999), and to traditions of what Alasdair Whittle has called "tethered mobility" (Whittle 1997). Viewed from the vantage of Gardom's Edge, these developments have been important. But it is unclear whether our interest in regions has been taken to its logical conclusion. Suggested geographies are again rather blurred and there are more localized patterns. Similarities in the form of sites within an area suggest more focused traditions; places like Etton, Uffington, Barholm, and Northborough around the edge of the East Anglian fens, or Bury Hill, Court Hill, and Halnaker Hill on the South Downs (Russell 1997). A sense of an interplay between broader traditions and local histories can also be traced in the tendency towards the pairing of sites in the Thames Valley.

What are our patterns telling us? In the absence of suites of radiocarbon dates from a wide range of sites, there is much that remains uncertain. However, one response would be that this blurring reflects a fluidity and complexity to regional traditions, and a variety to the ways in which the idea of enclosure was taken up in local contexts (Edmonds 1999).

What the act of building meant, and how these places came to be used and understood could vary from one region, one valley and one generation to another. Much of life at the time may well have been ordered and understood at a regional scale. But these regions were not the bounded and stable entities that we sometimes assume. Nor were the monument categories that we routinely employ. In the dispersed social landscapes of the time, many social boundaries may have been recognized, some perhaps taking their inspiration from the line of a river, a watershed, or a ridge (Barnatt 1996; Tilley 1994). But these boundaries were not fixed. They could be worked and reworked as part of the playing out of links between communities, and between people, land, and the past. So could the ideas that lay behind the monuments that we study. Traditions overlapped with one another at varying scales of spatial and temporal resolution (Gosden 1999). It was through this tangle of relations and histories that ideas, artefacts, and people would have circulated, not as a tight and uniform "package", but as resources to be drawn upon in local discourse.

CONTEXT

If we are right to assign the Gardom's Edge enclosure to the Neolithic, what are we to make of this place? What was its context in the broader landscapes of the time? Compared to certain regions, evidence for the Neolithic in the Peak District is relatively sparse. As in other areas, lithic scatters provide our principal source of evidence for traditions of landscape occupation. Here though, the recent dominance of pasture and the persistence of moorland has placed constraints upon balanced recording. Against these scatters can be set the evidence of isolated stone axe finds, chambered tombs, long mounds, and the buildings identified at Lismore Fields (Barnatt 1996; Barnatt and Collis 1996; Garton 1991). These are complemented by pollen, albeit largely from the peat rich uplands (*e.g.* Hicks 1971; 1972).

Set in their topographic context, these data support a view of the region as a varied, patchwork landscape. This was a time when dense woodland was still a commonplace, particularly on the heavier soils of many valleys and in some uplands. Here, as in other areas, forests and clearings were a common context for routine experience; occupied and managed alongside the use of areas of more open country (Brown 1997; Evans *et al.* 1999). This was also a time when many people's lives unfolded across a series of places strung out along seasonal paths (Barnatt 1996). Much of the evidence would accord with a form of landscape occupation where limited cultivation took place alongside the husbandry of stock; the latter, along with other activities, involving cycles of periodic movement by dispersed communities.

There is no evidence to suggest that the common pattern of residence for much of the time was anything other than small scale; perhaps involving extended families and little more. These small communities may have divided and combined in various ways at different times of the year, their movements in step with the tasks that made up the seasonal round (Edmonds 1999; Pollard 1999; Whittle 1997). People's lives were stretched across summer and winter pastures, between higher and lower ground, and perhaps through different valley systems. Bound up in this pattern of living would have been a variety in the roll call of those who were present at particular places and times. Such a view is by no means incompatible with the evidence of the buildings excavated at Lismore Fields (Garton 1991).

These impressions are important. They move us away from the traditional vision of activities radiating out from a settled limestone "core" onto "marginal" gritstone uplands. In fact, the Peak District can be said to comprise a range of zones that were occupied and perhaps perceived in different ways (Barnatt 1996, 55). Distinctions can be drawn between the shale valleys and the lower limestone shelves; the higher reaches of the limestone plateau; the gritstone uplands of the east and southwest, and the higher ground of the northern and western uplands. Land for over-wintering; ground where the cattle grew fat; places visited from time to time; and areas in which others might be encountered more frequently. Under these conditions, the understandings that communities had of themselves, and of the land around them, involved a sense of tenure to be renewed rather than territory to be held. This would have been an open-ended and dynamic process, structured around the repetitive and probably cyclical use of places of practical, historic, and spiritual importance. And of course, these relations were far from static. Renewed over time, they might change from one year or from one generation to another.

We can catch glimpses of some of these themes in the available evidence. They were brought into focus in the customary use of specific sources of stone, such as the darker and finer cherts that outcrop in certain limestone valleys. Already worked for many generations, and thus important points of historical reference, these sources continued to be used in the Neolithic. Just how these places were visited and exploited remains difficult to determine. However, there is no reason to suppose that they were the exclusive preserve of a small community. They probably saw cyclical and persistent use by a more varied range of people, a pattern that brought with it a requirement to renew and redefine customary rights of access and broader social ties. Stone from these sources may have also moved from hand to hand through various forms of exchange, itself part of the process by which relations between people were reproduced over time. That process also extended to the acquisition of stone axes from distant upland sources, and of flint from the Trent Valley, the Wolds to the east and the boulder clays on the coast (Edmonds 1995). The presence of this material, and an apparent increase in the importance of Wolds flint during the period (Garton 1991), reminds us that scattered communities were caught up in broader webs of contact and communication.

Similar ideas may be useful for thinking about tombs (Barnatt and Collis 1996). Some, like Minninglow, dominate broad ridges which formed important seasonal pathways. Others are found in more low-lying locations, encountered on a path or viewed from a specific catchment. This variety indicates that it may not always have been the potential visibility of tombs that determined their location. Indeed, some, like Stoney Low may have drawn on the local topography so as to be purposefully hidden from the everyday eye. In others, it may have been the histories that certain places had already accrued that was more important. We get a sense of this at a site like the chambered tomb at Green Low, where activities prior to the foundation of the tomb stretched back into the Mesolithic (Manby 1965). It is simplistic to regard these monuments simply as territorial markers, signalling claims to land or other resources. That may have happened. But these were places that had their greatest significance for those who participated in acts of construction and embellishment, and in complex mortuary and ancestral rites. Visited at key junctures and seen or passed in the course of the seasonal round, tombs were a potent medium. Through them, people renewed their sense of tenure with particular places and their sense of community. Returning again and again, and adding to the fabric and the content of tombs, they grounded that attachment in the ancestral and genealogical past (Barrett 1994).

Whatever the location of tombs in the social geographies of the time, their histories were probably most clearly appreciated at a relatively local scale. Though there is much that is unclear, these may well have been locales that brought a limited number of lines together. Such events were crucial to the reproduction of a variety of relationships and may have even provided a basis for particular forms of authority. Where the ancestors were a powerful presence in the land, some standing would come from having their ear or speaking on their behalf. The point to stress here is that the range of the relations addressed at these places may have been relatively limited and this raises another question. To what extent did the communities of the time recognize themselves as part of something broader still? Though they moved from hand to hand, and through various forms of "embedded" procurement, the presence of non-local flint and stone artefacts attests to lines of contact that stretched beyond the local horizon. How was this possible? How were such understandings realized?

In one sense, such questions require no single answer. In the dispersed and fluid landscapes of the time, extensive webs of kinship, alliance and affiliation may have been carried forward in many ways; through marriage, trading partnerships, negotiations over access, and contact with others in many settings. However, the possibility remains that these more extensive social geographies were brought into focus at specific times and places and this returns us to the enclosure on Gardom's Edge. Given its character, scale and location, this may well have been a place at which different communities came together at certain times, perhaps in step with the movement of stock and perhaps for other reasons. Out of such moments may have come the recognition and redefinition of more extensive ties; the knot of relations that is captured in Isobel Smith's characterization of enclosures as "rallying points" (Smith 1971). It is unlikely that the Gardom's Edge enclosure was the only place to serve these purposes in the Peak District. A second smaller enclosure of possible Neolithic date has recently been identified some 11km to the southwest at Cratcliff Rocks (Makepeace 1999), and there may be others as yet unrecognized.

This returns us to parallels with other places. In talking about the purposes and interests that this enclosure served, it is difficult to avoid falling back on analogies with other sites which have, as yet, seen more extensive study. Multiple entrances and variations in the character of the bank along its line seem to echo the structure of other enclosures further to the south. Whether or not we follow specific arguments about the "gang-dug" character of working on sites with interrupted ditches, a basic link might be drawn (Bradley 1984). Parallels might also be sought where scarp or cliff edges formed part of the perimeter of specific enclosures, and in the ecotonal setting of many sites. And of course, the sense a of stone bank linking prominent natural outcrops echoes a pattern that can be detected elsewhere, perhaps reflecting the incorporation of features that had long held a historic and perhaps mythic significance (Bradley 1998a; Gosden and Lock 1998; Tilley 1996).

Such parallels are essentially superficial. They may help to bolster arguments about chronology, and they suggest the recognition of common themes. But it is unclear how far their value extends beyond this. It is certainly tempting to talk of episodes of consumption, and of the relations that were addressed when people came together. The boulder strewn nature of the interior and the presence of large exposed slabs at Gardom's Edge suggests a potential for use in "event-like" proceedings rather than persistent and extensive occupation; perhaps even the exposure of the dead. However, it may be unhelpful to simply fill in the gaps by extrapolating from those few sites in the south that have seen extensive excavation. To take this path would be to return to a superficial equation of form and function, treating the unique as typical (Harding 1991). Given the extraordinary variety of histories held within southern enclosures themselves, such an approach is clearly flawed. It might be better then, and certainly for the time being, to take a more cautious view. The enclosure at Gardom's Edge suggests an acquaintance with the idea of bounding specific places and times at which people could gather, but a recruitment of that idea in locally and historically specific ways.

CONCLUSION

For the moment, though a Neolithic date seems likely, there is much about the history of the Gardom's Edge enclosure that remains obscure. It is difficult to talk about the immediate conditions in which this place was made and the particular events it witnessed. There is certainly much more that can be made of the location of the site, and of the relationship between the bank and the local topography. There is also the build of the monument; the insight it offers into the act of construction and how that was played out over time. Hopefully, more work will add some depth to the image. Work elsewhere will also be crucial for establishing the context of the place. Beyond fieldwalking and environmental studies, this should include a thorough reappraisal of the status of several more enclosures in the region, amongst them Carl Wark and Cratcliff Rocks. Both may have roots that extend back beyond the Iron Age (Barnatt and Smith 1997; Makepeace 1999).

Our purpose in this paper has not been to argue for a wholesale shift of focus to local studies at the expense of broader perspectives. Quite the opposite. Enclosures themselves remind us that the world at that time was experienced and understood at a variety of scales, and one of our concerns should be how those scales were articulated (Bradley 1998b). What we have suggested here is that an understanding of the monument on Gardom's Edge cannot rest entirely on top-down analogies or simple extrapolation from enclosures identified and investigated elsewhere.

This problem may go well beyond the boundaries of enclosures, however we choose to define them (Last 1999, 95). We may be able to recognize the playing out of a common theme – an idea of enclosure that was taken up in different ways in different contexts. But some of the concerns that were brought into focus at these places may have also surfaced elsewhere. It may be that at least some of the purposes served by the building and use of an enclosure in one setting were also addressed at places that we currently classify in a completely different way – at stone sources or even cursus monuments. What we are interested in is the interplay between broader traditions and more localized histories. To explore that interplay, we have to keep a tension between our **categories** as well as between different **scales** of enquiry – local, regional, and even continental (Barrett and Kinnes 1988; Whittle 1995). Keeping that tension involves recognizing that important though they may have been, regional traditions were rather more blurred and fluid than we have tended to assume. That is part of the reason why we find such a variety in the character and history of different enclosures, and why we have such difficulty defining the category in a singular manner.

ACKNOWLEDGEMENTS

A number of people have made contributions to this paper in various ways. Initial survey of the area was undertaken with Stuart Ainsworth of the RCHME. Many aspects of the argument for a Neolithic date for the enclosure were thrashed out in the field with him. Since then, various people have assisted in more detailed survey and excavation: Kenny Aitchison, Anne Marie Heath, Guy Hopkinson, Mike Klemperer, Jamie Lund, Graham Robbins, and Jim Rylatt. We are particularly grateful to them, and to all those who have helped us in our work at Gardom's Edge over the past five years. A website for the Project can be viewed at:

http://www.shef.ac.uk/uni/projects/geap/index.html

BIBLIOGRAPHY

Ainsworth, S, and Barnatt, J, 1998, A scarp edge enclosure at Gardom's Edge, Baslow, Derbyshire. *Derbyshire Archaeological Journal*, 118, 5–23

Avery, M, 1982, The Neolithic causewayed enclosure, Abingdon. In H J Case and A W R Whittle (eds), *Settlement patterns in the Oxford region: excavations at the Abingdon causewayed enclosure and other sites* (= Council for British Archaeology Research Report 44). London. Council for British Archaeology. 10–50

Bamford, H, 1985, *Briar Hill. Excavation 1974–1978*. Northampton. Northampton Development Corporation

Barrett, J, 1994, *Fragments from antiquity*. Blackwell. Oxford

Barrett, J, 1999, Chronologies of landscape. In P Ucko and R Layton (eds), *The archaeology and anthropology of landscape*. London. Routledge. 21–30

Barrett, J C, and Kinnes, I A (eds), 1998, *The archaeology of context in the Neolithic and Bronze Age: recent trends*. Sheffield. Department of Archaeology and Prehistory, University of Sheffield

Barnatt, J, 1986, Bronze Age remains on the East Moors of the Peak District. *Derbyshire Archaeological Journal*, 106, 18–100

Barnatt, J, 1987, Bronze Age settlement on the gritstone East Moors of the Peak District of Derbyshire and South Yorkshire. *Proceedings of the Prehistoric Society*, 53, 393–418

Barnatt, J, 1996, Moving beyond the monuments: paths and people in the Neolithic landscapes of the Peak District. *Northern Archaeology*, 13/14 (Special edition), 43–60

Barnatt, J, 1999, Taming the land: Peak District farming and ritual in the Bronze Age. *Derbyshire Archaeological Journal*, 119, 19–71

Barnatt, J, Bevan, W, and Edmonds, M, 1995, *A prehistoric landscape at Gardom's Edge, Baslow, Derbyshire: excavations 1995. 1st interim report*. Sheffield. [Limited circulation printed report]

Barnatt, J, Bevan, W, and Edmonds, M, 1996, *A prehistoric landscape at Gardom's Edge, Baslow, Derbyshire: excavations 1996. 2nd interim report*. Sheffield. [Limited circulation printed report]

Barnatt, J, Bevan, W, and Edmonds, M, 1997, *A prehistoric landscape at Gardom's Edge, Baslow, Derbyshire: excavations 1997. 3rd interim report*. Sheffield. [Limited circulation printed report]

Barnatt, J, Bevan, W, and Edmonds, M, 1998, *A prehistoric landscape at Gardom's Edge, Baslow, Derbyshire: excavations 1998. 4th interim report*. Sheffield. [Limited circulation printed report]

Barnatt, J, Bevan, W, and Edmonds, M, 2000, *A prehistoric landscape at Gardom's Edge, Baslow, Derbyshire: excavations 1999 and 2000. 5th interim report*. Sheffield. [Limited circulation printed report]

Barnatt, J, and Collis, J (eds), 1996, *Barrows in the Peak District: recent research*. Sheffield. J R Collis Publications/Sheffield Academic Press

Barnatt, J, and Smith, K, 1991, The Peak District in the Bronze Age: recent research and changes in interpretation. In R Hodges and K Smith (eds), *Recent developments in the archaeology of the Peak District* (= Sheffield Archaeological Monographs 2). Sheffield. J R Collis Publications, Department of Prehistory and Archaeology, University of Sheffield.

Barnatt, J, and Smith, K, 1997, *The Peak District*. London. English Heritage and Batsford

Barrett, J, 1994, *Fragments from Antiquity*. Oxford. Blackwell

Bender, B, 1993, *Landscape, politics and perspectives*. Oxford. Berg

Beswick, P, and Merrills, D, 1983, L H Butcher's survey of early settlements and fields in the southern Pennines. *Transactions of the Hunter Archaeological Society*, 12, 16–50

Bevan, B, 1999, Northern exposure. In B Bevan (ed), *Northern exposure: interpretative devolution and the Iron Age in Britain* (= Leicester Archaeology Monographs 4). Leicester. Leicester University. 1–19

Bevan, B, 2000, Peak practice: whatever happened to the Iron Age in the southern Pennines? In J Harding and R Johnson (eds), *Northern Pasts* (= British Archaeological Report British Series 302). Oxford. Archaeopress. 141–56

Bradley, R, 1984, *The social foundations of prehistoric Britain*. London. Longman

Bradley, R, 1998a, Ruined buildings, ruined stones: enclosures, tombs and natural places in the Neolithic of south-west England. *World Archaeology*, 30.1, 13–22

Bradley, R, 1998b, *The significance of monuments*. London. Routledge

Brown, T, 1997, Clearances and clearings. Deforestation in the Mesolithic and Neolithic. *Oxford Journal of Archaeology*, 16.2, 133–146

Crawford, O G S, 1937, Causeway settlements. *Antiquity*, 11, 210–212

Crawford, O G S, and Keiller, A, 1928, *Wessex from the air*. Oxford. Clarendon Press

Cooney, G, 1997, Images of settlement and the landscape in the Neolithic. In P Topping (ed), *Neolithic landscapes* (= Neolithic Studies Group Seminar Papers 2). Oxford. Oxbow Books. 23–32

Curwen, E, 1930, Excavations in the Trundle. *Sussex Archaeological Collections*, 72, 100–130

Dixon, P, 1988, The Neolithic settlements on Crickley Hill. In C Burgess, P Topping, C Mordant, and M Maddison (eds), *Enclosures and defences in the Neolithic of western Europe* (= British Archaeological Reports International Series 403). Oxford. British Archaeological Reports. 75–78

Edmonds, M, 1993, Interpreting causewayed enclosures in the present and the past. In C Tilley (ed), *Interpretative archaeology*. Oxford. Berg. 99–142

Edmonds, M, 1995, *Stone tools and society*. London. Batsford

Edmonds, M, 1999, *Ancestral geographies of the Neolithic: landscapes, monuments and memory*. London. Routledge

Evans, C, 1988a, Monuments and analogy: the interpretation of Causewayed enclosures. In C Burgess, P Topping, C Mordant, and M Maddison (eds), *Enclosures and defences in the Neolithic of western Europe* (= British Archaeological Reports International Series 403). Oxford. British Archaeological Reports. 47–74

Evans, C, 1988b, Acts of enclosure: a consideration of concentrically organised causewayed enclosures. In J C Barrett and I A Kinnes (eds), *The archaeology of context in the Neolithic and Bronze Age: recent trends*. Sheffield. Department of Archaeology and Prehistory, University of Sheffield. 85–97

Evans, C, 1988c, Excavations at Haddenham, Cambridgeshire, a planned causewayed enclosure and its regional affinities. In C Burgess, P Topping, C Mordant, and M Maddison (eds), *Enclosures and defences in the Neolithic of western Europe* (= British Archaeological Reports International Series 403). Oxford. British Archaeological Reports. 127–49

Evans, C, Pollard, J, and Knight, M, 1999, Life in woods. *Oxford Journal of Archaeology*, 18.3, 241–254

Evans, J G, Rouse, A J, and Sharples, N, 1988, The landscape setting of causewayed camps: recent work on the Maiden Castle enclosure. In J C Barrett and I A Kinnes (eds), *The archaeology of context in the Neolithic and Bronze Age: recent trends*. Department of Archaeology and Prehistory, University of Sheffield. 73–84

Everson, P, 1989, Field survey by RCHME on the gritstone moorlands of the Derbyshire Peak District. In A Gibson (ed), *Midlands prehistory. Some recent and current researches into the prehistory of central England* (= British Archaeological Reports British Series 204). Oxford. British Archaeological Reports. 14–26

Fletcher, M, 1989, Stowe's Pound. In M Bowden, D Mackay, and P Topping (eds), *From Cornwall to Caithness. Some aspects of British field archaeology: papers presented to Norman V Quinell* (= British Archaeological Reports British Series 209). Oxford. British Archaeological Reports. 71–77

Garton, D, 1991, Neolithic settlement in the Peak District: perspectives and prospects. In R Hodges and K Smith (eds), *Recent developments in the archaeology of the Peak District* (= Sheffield Archaeological Monographs 2). Sheffield. J R Collis Publications, Department of Prehistory and Archaeology, University of Sheffield. 3–21

Gosden, C, and Lock, G, 1998, Prehistoric histories. *World Archaeology*, 30.1, 2–12

Harding, J, 1991, Using the unique as the typical: monuments and the ritual landscape. In P Garwood, R Skeates, and J Toms (eds), *Sacred and profane* (= Oxford Committee for Archaeology Monograph 32). Oxford. Oxford University Committee for Archaeology. 141–151

Hart, C, 1981, *The North Derbyshire Archaeological Survey*. Chesterfield. North Derbyshire Archaeological Trust

Hart, C, 1985, Gardom's Edge, Derbyshire: settlements, cairnfield, and hillfort. In D Spratt and C Burgess (eds), *Upland settlement in Britain* (= British Archaeological Reports British Series 143). Oxford. British Archaeological Reports. 71–76

Hicks, S P, 1971, Pollen analytical evidence for the effects of prehistoric agriculture on the vegetation of north Derbyshire. *New Phytologist*, 70, 647–667

Hicks, S P, 1972, The impact of man on the east Moor of Derbyshire from Mesolithic times. *Archaeological Journal*, 129, 1–21

Kendrick, T D, and Hawkes, C F C, 1932, *Archaeology in England and Wales, 1914–1931*. London. Methuen

Last, J, 1999, Out of line: cursuses and monument typology in eastern England. In A Barclay and J Harding (eds), *Pathways and ceremonies: the cursus monuments of Britain and Ireland* (= Neolithic Studies Group Seminar Papers 4). Oxford. Oxbow Books. 86–97

Long, D J, 1994, *Prehistoric fieldsystems and the vegetation development of the gritstone uplands of the Peak District*. [Unpublished PhD dissertation. Keele University]

Long, D J, Chambers, F M, and Barnatt, J, 1998, The palaeoenvironment and vegetational history of a later prehistoric fieldsystem at Stoke Flat on the gritstone uplands of the Peak District. *Journal of Archaeological Science*, 25.6, 505–20

Manby, T G, 1965, The excavation of Green Low chambered tomb. *Derbyshire Archaeological Journal*, 85, 1–24

Makepeace, G, 1999, Cratcliff Rocks – a forgotten hillfort. *Derbyshire Archaeological Journal*, 119, 12–18

Mercer, R J, 1981, Excavations at Carn Brea, Illogan, Cornwall, 1970–73. A Neolithic fortified complex of the third millennium bc. *Cornish Archaeology*, 20, 1–204

Mercer, R J, 1986, *Excavation of a Neolithic enclosure at Helman Tor, Lanlivery, Cornwall, 1986. Interim report* (= University of Edinburgh Project Paper 4). Edinburgh. Department of Archaeology, University of Edinburgh

Mercer, R J, 1988, Hambledon Hill, Dorset, England. In C Burgess, P Topping, C Mordant, and M Maddison (eds), *Enclosures and defences in the Neolithic of western Europe* (= British Archaeological Reports International Series 403). Oxford. British Archaeological Reports. 89–107

Mercer, R J, 1990, *Causewayed enclosures*. Princes Risborough. Shire Books

Palmer, R, 1976, Interrupted ditch enclosures in Britain: the use of aerial photography for comparative studies. *Proceedings of the Prehistoric Society*, 52, 161–86

Piggott, S, 1954, *The Neolithic cultures of the British Isles*. Cambridge. Cambridge University Press

Pollard, J, 1999, These places have their moments. Occupation practices in the British Neolithic. In J Bruck and M Goddman (eds), *Making places in the prehistoric world: themes in settlement archaeology*. London. UCL Press. 76–93

Pryor, F, 1988, Etton, near Maxey, Cambridgeshire: a causewayed enclosure on the Fen edge. In C Burgess, P Topping, C Mordant, and M Maddison (eds), *Enclosures and defences in the Neolithic of western Europe* (= British Archaeological Reports International Series 403). Oxford. British Archaeological Reports. 107–27

Pryor, F, 1998, *Etton: excavations at a Neolithic causewayed enclosure near Maxey, Cambridge-shire, 1982–7* (= English Heritage Archaeological Report 18). London. English Heritage

RCHME, 1987, *Gardom's Edge South, Derbyshire* (= National Monuments Record Nos. SK27 SE29: 161–66 and 175). [Limited circulation printed report]

RCHME and PPJPB, 1993, *An archaeological survey of the northern halves of Gardom's and Birchen Edges* (= National Monuments Record No. SK 27 SE 98). [Limited circulation printed report]

Russell, M, 1997, NEO-Realism: an alternative look at the Neolithic chalk database of Sussex. In P Topping (ed), *Neolithic landscapes* (= Neolithic Studies Group Seminar Papers 2). Oxford. Oxbow Books. 69–76

Smith, I F, 1966, Windmill Hill and its implications. *Palaeohistoria*, 12, 469–81

Smith, I F, 1971, Causewayed enclosures. In D D A Simpson (ed), *Economy and settlement in Neolithic and early Bronze Age Britain and Europe*. Leicester. Leicester University Press. 89–112

Thomas, K D, 1982, Neolithic enclosures and woodland habitats on the south downs in Sussex, England. In M Bell and S Limbrey (eds), *Archaeological aspects of woodland ecology* (= British Archaeological Reports International Series 146). Oxford. British Archaeological Reports. 147–70

Thomas, J, 1998, Towards a regional geography of the Neolithic. In M Edmonds and C Richards (eds), *Understanding the Neolithic of north-west Europe*. Glasgow. Cruithne Press. 37–60

Thomas, J, 1999, *Understanding the Neolithic*. London. Routledge

Thorpe, I J and Richards, C, 1984, The decline of ritual authority and the introduction of Beakers into Britain. In R J Bradley and J Gardiner (eds), *Neolithic Studies* (= British Archaeological Reports British Series 133). Oxford. British Archaeological Reports. 67–84

Tilley, C, 1994, *A phenomenology of landscape: places, paths and monuments*. Oxford. Berg

Tilley, C, 1996, The power of rocks: topography and monument construction on Bodmin Moor. *World Archaeology*, 28.2, 161–176

Ward, G H B, 1942, Ancient British defence works discovered near Baslow. *Sheffield Clarion Ramblers*, 1941–2, 76–81

Ward, G H B, 1943, Ancient British defence works discovered near Baslow. *Sheffield Clarion Ramblers*, 1942–3, 144–45

Whittle, A, 1977, *The earlier Neolithic of southern England and its continental background* (= British Archaeological Reports International Series 35). Oxford. British Archaeological Reports

Whittle, A, 1995, *Neolithic Europe. The creation of new worlds*. Cambridge. Cambridge University Press

Whittle, A, 1988, Contexts, activities, events – aspects of Neolithic and Copper Age enclosures in central and western Europe. In C Burgess, P Topping, C Mordant, and M Maddison (eds), *Enclosures and defences in the Neolithic of western Europe* (= British Archaeological Reports International Series 403). Oxford. British Archaeological Reports. 1–20

Whittle, A, 1997, Moving on and moving around: Neolithic settlement mobility. In P Topping (ed), *Neolithic landscapes* (= Neolithic Studies Group Seminar Papers 2). Oxford. Oxbow Books. 15–22

Whittle, A, and Pollard, J, 1998, Windmill Hill causewayed enclosure: a harmony of symbols. In M Edmonds and C Richards (eds), *Understanding the Neolithic of north-western Europe*. Glasgow. Cruithne Press. 231–247

Wilson, D R, 1975, Causewayed camps and interrupted ditch systems. *Antiquity*, 49, 178–186

Chapter 10

Neolithic enclosures: reflections on excavations in Wales and Scotland

Julian Thomas

INTRODUCTION

This contribution is concerned with three Neolithic enclosures, all of which the author has been involved in excavating over the past ten years. These three sites are all quite different from one another. One dates to the start of the Neolithic, while the other two are much later. One was defined by an interrupted ditch, one by a continuous ditch and bank, and one by rings of posts. And their locations vary too from the northwest tip of Wales to the southwest extremity of Scotland. Despite these contrasts of morphology and circumstance, it will be suggested that certain commonalities can be identified, and that these serve to illuminate the practice of building enclosures in Neolithic Britain.

One of our fundamental problems in discussing Neolithic enclosures, whether in Britain, Ireland, or on the continental mainland, arises from the legacy of culture-historic archaeology. It was a distinctive practice of culture history to reduce all customs and artefacts to equivalent markers of cultural affinity (*cf.* Childe 1956, 16). Where pottery styles, stone tools, funerary practices and domestic architecture were not well represented, or lacked the necessary diversity, ceremonial monuments could stand as cultural markers. For this reason, when Stuart Piggott set out to characterize the *Neolithic Cultures of the British Isles* (1954), his principal means of defining the earlier Neolithic culture groups of Britain (the Windmill Hill Culture and its successors) was on the basis of the presence of certain types of earthwork monuments (long barrows, causewayed camps, and flint mines). In this way, a means of categorization ultimately descended from Linnaean classification came to be applied to monumental structures. Simply because they have a formal (even, sometimes, "designed") lay-out, monuments have often proved more amenable to this kind of analysis than have other inhabited places, from settlements and extraction sites to cemeteries and rock-shelters. This encourages us to reduce enclosures to timeless plan views, which serve as a basis for comparison. However, like artefacts, sites have histories. The drawback of typology is that it requires us to define a particular moment in the monument's development as its point of maturity or completion. At this instant, the site is characteristic of a particular cultural identity, and certain of its attributes can be identified as being diagnostic. As well as objectifying monuments and rendering them static, this procedure has the effect of establishing a norm for each kind of site, so that a series of expectations are set up, against which new finds have to be judged.

These issues are raised here because they help to explain why ceremonial monuments have often been severed in our imaginations from the ebb and flow of prehistoric social life. While a perceived separation of "ritual" from the "everyday" has sometimes meant that enclosures, tombs, and shrines have been treated quite differently from other classes of archaeological evidence, it may be that more damage has been done by approaching them as **entities** as opposed to **projects** or **processes**. Each of the sites that are discussed in this Chapter is distinguished by the presence of a constructed boundary which defines a circular or oval area of space. But while these rings of posts or ditches are conventionally used as a means of identifying the place as being of a certain **kind**, detailed excavation has revealed that in all cases they represent only one of a complex series of transformations that have overtaken the site. The building of an enclosure need not inaugurate activity on a site, nor need it dictate an unchanging way in which the site will be used in future. Yet it may mark a significant shift in the way that a place is understood, and may provide an organization of space that has to be accommodated in subsequent developments.

BRYN CELLI WEN, ANGLESEY

The first of the sites that we will consider is Bryn Celli Wen, a causewayed enclosure in southern Anglesey. The site was located fortuitously in 1990, in the course of conducting a shovel-testing transect survey across the valley of the Afon Braint, centred on the chambered cairn of Bryn Celli Ddu, roughly 500m away (Edmonds and Thomas 1991a). This Project had been designed to investigate densities of chipped stone and prehistoric pottery held in the ploughsoil by excavating 1m by 0.5m pits through the topsoil on a grid basis. There was no hint of the enclosure's presence before the survey began. The site was later partially excavated by Mark Edmonds, Rick Peterson, and myself, between 1991 and 1993 (Edmonds and Thomas 1991b; 1992; 1993). Byrn Celli Wen lies on the end of a low spur overlooking the valley floor. Its eastern side is heavily eroded, while the western saddle of the hill is cloaked in colluvium. Accordingly, the archaeological visibility of the enclosure was low. The first indication of its presence came when a shovel-pit revealed a dark, burnt layer at the base of the ploughsoil, which contained flint flakes and crumbs of pottery. When a slightly larger trench was opened in order to assess this deposit, the butt-end of a shallow ditch was revealed, with evidence for repeated backfilling and recutting, as well as traces of burning. Subsequently, a magnetometer survey demonstrated that the ditch arced irregularly around the promontory.

The three seasons of excavation that followed succeeded in characterizing the enclosure as being single ditched, oval in plan, and roughly 200m by 120m in extent (Figure 10.1). The nature of the perimeter varied considerably around the circuit. On the eastern side the ditches were highly truncated, and many of the finds were recovered from the topsoil which had been removed in metre squares and sieved. In the 1991 trench, flint flakes, scrapers, and retouched pieces, and fragments of pottery all clustered along the line of the ditch. The pottery itself was extremely fragmentary, but at least one round-based bowl can be recognized, and the fabrics are entirely consistent with earlier Neolithic wares from elsewhere on the island (R Peterson pers. comm.). The ditch segments were all extremely shallow, but suggested very complex sequences of filling, which in most cases included the

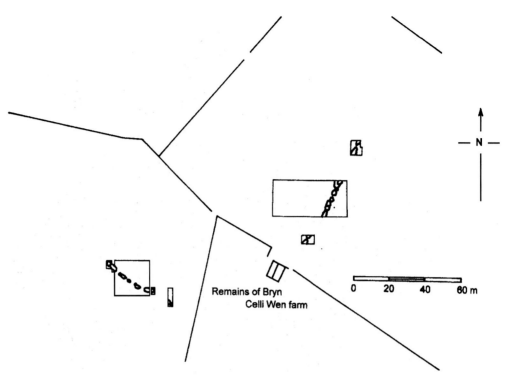

Figure 10.1: Bryn Celli Wen, Anglesey: plan of areas excavated 1990–3

introduction of large pieces of stone into the ditch. All of these ditches had been cut by multiple postholes and stakeholes. Stone deposits covered some of the posts, while one had evidently cut down beside a stone, so they were clearly not all contemporary.

This cutting of posts into the backfilled ditch deposits of causewayed enclosures finds parallels in the early levels at Crickley Hill, Gloucestershire (Dixon 1988), and in the inner and smallest of the three ditches at the newly excavated site at Chalk Hill, Ramsgate in Kent (Shand 1998). The posts or stakes were not sufficiently substantial or regularly set to have made up any kind of structure. It seems more likely that they represented markers of some kind, either locating significant deposits, or allowing the ephemeral traces of ditches to be relocated and subsequently redug. Concentric with the ditches was a line of smaller, slot-like features, which may indeed amount to a phase of recutting that went off-line at this point.

Most remarkable of all, though, was the linear stone cairn that formed part of the enclosure at one point. Given the degree of erosion to the subsoil, it remains a possibility that this material originally filled some kind of cut feature. When the stone was removed, it proved to have been piled over and around the broken remains of a large monolith, lying in a substantial pit. The shattered fragments resulting from its breaking were still in place, and a socket complete with packing stones was found in an extension to the trench. A very similar standing stone is still upright today, 1km away, on the far side of Bryn Celli Ddu.

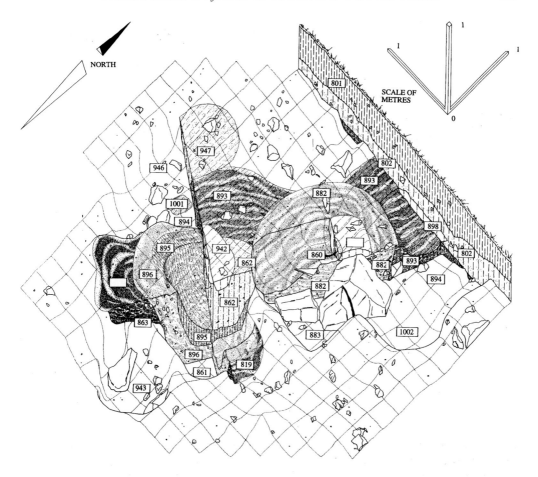

Figure 10.2: Bryn Celli Wen: isometric drawing of ditch section excavated in 1993, demonstrating the complexity of the sequence of recutting

Clearly, the monolith had been toppled to the ground and smashed, before being at once hidden and incorporated into the enclosure. Sherds from a single Mortlake vessel had been deposited in the cairn above the monolith.

On the western side of the hill the ditches were very much more substantial. One large ditch butt had been cut into bedrock, which had been split using fire, while another had been largely backfilled with rock fragments. In the 1993 season, five separate ditch segments were excavated beneath the colluvium. These were extremely variable in the character of their filling, but generally followed a sequence in which shallow primary cuts were followed by deep, conical recuts, and finally shallow bowl-shaped recuts with characteristic sandy fills (Figure 10.2). It was one of the deeper recuts which produced one of the finest artefacts recovered from the site, a complete polished flint axe.

Like many of the other sites that are discussed in this volume, Bryn Celli Wen challenges our expectations concerning Neolithic enclosures. Few of the ditch segments gave the impression of having been open for any long period of time, and their diminutive size suggests that the monument was not one that would have made a great visual impression. This was not a site that would have represented a continuous or dominating presence in the landscape. Few of these ditches give the impression of having been open for any amount of time, so it would not have represented a continuous monumental presence in the landscape. Rather, it was a location in which a series of constructional and depositional events took place, over a considerable period of time.

THE PICT'S KNOWE, DUMFRIES

Many of the details of Bryn Celli Wen contrast with our second site, the Pict's Knowe, a late Neolithic henge monument located immediately to the south of Dumfries in southwest Scotland (Figure 10.3). This site was investigated between 1994 and 1997 with the support of Historic Scotland (Thomas 1994; 1995; 1997). It was a low-lying monument, built on a small sand island in the Crooks Pow Valley, an area just inland from the Solway Firth, and which appears to have been saltmarsh throughout much of prehistory. Richards (1996) has pointed out the affinity between henge monuments and watery locations, and in this case it is possible that the users of the Pict's Knowe would have had to have passed over or through water in order to enter the site. The enclosure had been heavily damaged by rabbit burrowing, cattle trampling, field drainage, and root disturbance, with the effect that any internal features had been entirely destroyed. The ditches contained marbled and striated silts suggestive of deposition under wet conditions, a point that has been borne out by soil micromorphology (Crowther in Thomas forthcoming). These silts produced a sparse artefactual assemblage, including sherds from a single Grooved Ware vessel, and had stabilized long before a substantial phase of recutting in the Roman Iron Age, associated with the deposition of large quantities of wooden artefacts.

While the sandy surface of the interior had been entirely homogenized by rabbits, sieving of this material produced Ebbsfleet sherds, and an area around the entrance causeway had been preserved by a layer of peat lapping up out of the ditch. Here, numerous slots and stakeholes provided evidence of an ephemeral element of the henge architecture: presumably, temporary screens or fences which must have been renewed on numerous occasions. Further stakeholes were found revetting or screening the bank, and in a continuous distribution around the monument, becoming less dense with distance away from the site. Stakes were also identified **below** the bank, suggesting an activity which had been carried out over a long period, irrespective of the presence of the bank and ditch, an architecture which was continually in process.

Beneath the bank was a thin layer of peat, which had evidently formed swiftly, within 45 radiocarbon years (Tipping in Thomas forthcoming). Layers of burning at the top of the peat gave dates of between 2400 and 2030 BC at the 2 σ confidence level, and soil micromorphology suggests that the bank had been built immediately onto these layers. This indicates that the enclosure was contemporary with other late henges like Woodhenge, Condicote, Gorsey Bigbury, and Milfield North (Richards 1990, 260; Saville 1983; ApSimon *et al.* 1976, 158; Harding 1981).

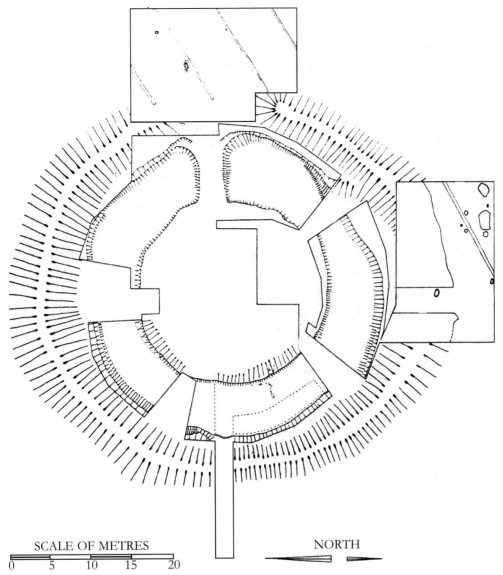

SCALE OF METRES   NORTH

0   5   10   15   20

Figure 10.3: The Pict's Knowe, Dumfries: excavations 1994–7

Interestingly, while the bank had clear terminals on either side of the entrance, a thin levelling layer contiguous with the bank carried on unbroken across the entrance. Beneath this layer were a series of remarkable pre-enclosure features. Two large postholes lay roughly in line with the ditch terminals. In each case the post had been withdrawn, and the socket covered with sand scooped up from the surface. Between the two posts was a small oval mound, its long axis anticipating the orientation of the later henge. The mound proved to cover a large pit, and its position inside the henge entrance perhaps finds a parallel with the mortuary enclosure at Maxey in East Anglia (Pryor and French 1985).

Finally, the removal of part of the bank on the southern side of the enclosure revealed a dense and bounded scatter of early Neolithic pottery and flintwork, together with a further pair of postholes. A little aside from this scatter was a very small pit, packed with sherds of six carinated vessels, lithics, and a flake from a polished stone axe. While the small sand island might have attracted activity over a long period for economic reasons, the character of this activity suggests instead that its repeated reuse can be attributed to its significance as a symbolically charged location.

DUNRAGIT, GALLOWAY

The final site to be considered here is the late Neolithic "palisaded" enclosure at Dunragit, near Stranraer in Galloway (Thomas 1999; 2000). While Bryn Celli Wen was located by accident and the Pict's Knowe constituted an upstanding earthwork, the Dunragit monument was discovered from the air by the Royal Commission on the Ancient and Historic Monument of Scotland in 1992. The air photographs show a series of structures, the most striking of which is made up of three concentric rings of posts, the largest in the order of 300m in diameter (Figure 10.4). This is bisected by the modern railway line. In addition, a number of smaller circles, ring-ditches, and alignments can also be recognized. The two innermost rings of the large enclosure are associated with an elaborate entrance structure, and it was partly this feature which originally suggested that the complex might have affinities with a group of later Neolithic palisaded enclosures, which include Forteviot and Meldon Bridge in Scotland (Gibson 1998; Burgess 1976), and sites such as West Kennet, Mount Pleasant, Ballynahatty, Walton, and Hindwell elsewhere in Britain and Ireland (Whittle 1997; Wainwright 1979; Hartwell 1998; Gibson 1998; 1999).

Interestingly, the entrance passageway at Dunragit is aligned southward toward a large mound at Droughduil, hitherto recorded as a motte, but with a profile that recalls prehistoric earthworks such as Silbury Hill. The immediate vicinity of the enclosure is rich in traces of prehistoric activity, from the Neolithic and Bronze Age occupation deposits in the dune systems of Luce Sands (McInnes 1964; Cowie 1996) to the chambered tombs at Mid Gleniron Farm, a little to the northeast (Corcoran 1963).

The two seasons of excavation which have taken place so far have concentrated on the two innermost rings of large postholes, in the area immediately to the north of the railway line. The trenches that have been opened have revealed an unexpected density and variety of features. The innermost ring of postholes was evidently composed of very large free-standing timbers, more a timber circle than a true palisade. The postholes were often ramped, and had been replaced on at least one occasion. In the western part of the area excavated in 1999–2000 the original postholes had all been recut, the soily fills of the secondary features contrasting with the gravelly packing of the primary sockets. Further to the east, the first and second phases of the inner ring diverged, forming separate sets of postholes. Several of the second-phase posts had been deliberately withdrawn, and significant deposits had been placed in the resulting crater. Into one, a deposit of greasy burnt soil had been tipped, containing numerous sherds of Grooved Ware, fragments of burnt bone, and flints, including a fine oblique arrowhead. Another contained the cremated remains of a woman and a sheep. Still another had been carefully cleaned out, and a

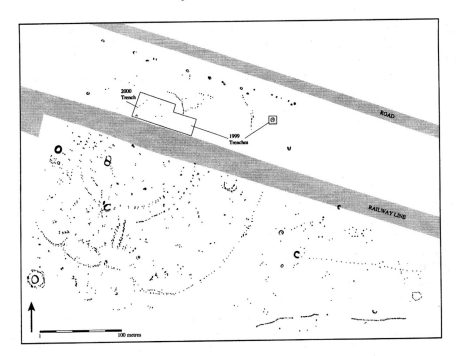

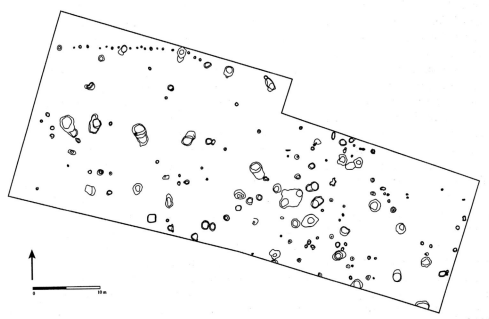

Figure 10.4: Dunragit, Galloway: air-photograph plot with areas excavated 1999–2000 (above) and 1999–2000 Trenches A and AA (below)

deposit of clean sand mounded up on its base. Onto this had been placed a mass of oak charcoal containing numerous small fragments of burnt bone. Provisionally, it is suggested that this material may represent pyre debris, possibly complementary to the cremated bones already described. After the funerary ceremony, the bones and ashes had presumably been carefully separated, and buried in holes created by the removal of two different posts.

The middle ring of posts contrast with the inner in a number of important ways. Finds of all sorts were far scarcer, and there was no trace of the complex depositional events represented in the inner ring. Rather than standing in isolation, the middle ring posts were interspersed by smaller uprights, forming a more complete barrier. The middle ring postholes were also generally smaller than those of the inner ring. This might indicate that the latter held larger timbers, but where postpipes survive there is little indication of such a contrast in size. Another possibility is that the inner ring features had been deliberately dug wider and deeper than required, conspicuously expending labour in the process. The middle ring postholes were perhaps more straightforwardly functional. This series of distinctions suggests that the roles of the two post-rings were quite different: the inner one a monumental focus for performative and depositional acts, the second simply a boundary or barrier containing these acts. Significantly, the middle post-ring has only one phase of construction, and this prompts the speculation that three concentric rings of the enclosure might not all have stood simultaneously. Quite possibly the outer ring replaced the middle, or vice versa. This argument is supported by the positioning of entrances in quite different places within the middle and outer post-rings.

In addition to the major post-rings, numerous other features were identified in the 1999–2000 trenches, not all of them visible on the air photographs of the site. A line of smaller, closely-spaced postholes with dark, charcoally fills crossed the arcs of the larger post-rings on a west-southwest to east-southeast axis. This can perhaps be interpreted as some form of subsidiary entrance structure associated with one or other phase of the main enclosure. The picture is complicated by two further arcs of postholes, which entered the northern side of the 1999 trench at much the same point as this alignment. These can perhaps be connected with an arc of posts of *c.* 40m diameter which is visible on the air-photograph plot immediately to the north of the excavated area.

Interestingly, this smaller post-ring is offset to the north of the late Neolithic enclosure, and the postholes that were excavated in 1999 produced large quantities of coarse Beaker pottery. A further arc of features (presumably posts) shows up from the air about 80m to the east of this ring, concentric with it and off line from the outer ring of the late Neolithic enclosure. It is possible, then, that the Beaker-associated monument had the same dual concentric structure as the two phases of the late Neolithic site. This implies that some conception of the architecture and the way in which it was to be used was maintained over a considerable period of time. Clearly, these arguments will have to be assessed in the course of future work.

CONCLUSION

Ostensibly, the three Neolithic enclosures described in this Chapter have little to connect them. However, they all illustrate the disadvantages of our habit of treating **places** as if they were **objects**. In all three cases it was the presence of an enclosing boundary (whether defined by ditch or by posts) that identified the location as a monument of a particular kind. However, at Bryn Celli Wen the ditch may only have been a temporary device, renewed on a number of occasions. At Dunragit only one of the rings of posts investigated so far has amounted to a continuous boundary, and what appears from the air to make up a coherent plan dissolves into a more complex and fragmented structural history on excavation. The ditch at the Pict's Knowe was permanent, but this could lead us into assuming unwisely that the henge had an unchanging spatial configuration. The temporary structures indicated by the slots and stakeholes imply that the interior of the enclosure may have been reconstructed on numerous occasions, perhaps altering the way in which the enclosure was used. All of these sites were reused and reworked over long periods, and at least two of them incorporated earlier monuments into their fabric. The Bryn Celli Wen monolith and the Pict's Knowe oval mound were erased, hidden, and absorbed, although the memory of their presence may have lent some significance to the later structures. Similarly, the essential configuration of the later Neolithic enclosure at Dunragit appears to have been reconstructed in the Beaker phase. Each of these sites can be seen as a project, or work in progress, in which contrasting or even conflicting materials and constructional devices were deployed in successive phases of building and deposition in order to transform the use and meaning of a location (or in order to establish continuity with the past). Our problem is that we tend to isolate particular diagnostic traits from within such sequences, and use them as the basis for a classification which flattens temporal variability.

ACKNOWLEDGEMENTS

I should like to thank all of those with whom I have worked on these three Projects, particularly Mark Edmonds, Rick Peterson, and Matt Leivers (who has been present on all three sites). I am also especially grateful to Ange Brennan, Chris Fowler, Jayne Gidlow, Erica Gittins, Sean Kingsley, Mark Johnson, Julia Roberts, Maggie Ronayne, Tim Whalley, and Lucy Wood for all of their assistance as staff. Historic Scotland should be warmly thanked for facilitating the investigations at the Pict's Knowe and Dunragit: Patrick Ashmore, Gordon Barclay, Deirdre Cameron, and Noel Fojut have given unflagging support for our work. A website for the Projects discussed in this paper can be viewed at:

http://www.arch.soton.ac.uk/Research/Dunragit/index.htm?blank.html

BIBLIOGRAPHY

ApSimon, A, Musgrave, J, Sheldon, J, Tratman, E K, and Wijngaaden-Bakker, L, 1976 Gorsey Bigbury, Cheddar, Somerset: radiocarbon dating, human and animal bones, charcoals and archaeological reassessment. *Proceedings of the University of Bristol Speleological Society*, 14, 155–183

Burgess, C B, 1976, Meldon Bridge: a Neolithic defended promontory complex near Peebles. In C Burgess and R Miket (eds), *Settlement and economy in the third and second millennia BC* (= British Archaeological Reports British Series 33). Oxford. British Archaeological Reports. 151–79

Childe, V G, 1956, *Piecing together the past: the interpretation of archaeological data.* London. Routledge and Kegan Paul

Cowie, T, 1996, Torrs Warren Sands, Galloway: a report on archaeological and palaeoecological investigations undertaken in 1977 and 1979. *Transactions of the Dumfriesshire and Galloway Natural History and Antiquarian Society*, 71, 11–105

Corcoran, J W X P, 1963, Excavation of a chambered cairn at Mid Gleniron Farm, Wigtownshire. *Transactions of the Dumfriesshire and Galloway Natural History and Antiquarian Society*, 41, 1–99–110

Dixon, P, 1988, The Neolithic settlements on Crickley Hill. In C Burgess, P Topping, C Mordant, and M Maddison (eds), *Enclosures and defences in the Neolithic of western Europe* (= British Archaeological Report International Series 403). Oxford. British Archaeological Reports. 75–88

Edmonds, M R, and Thomas, J S, 1991a, *Anglesey Archaeological Landscape Project: first interim report.* Lampeter. Saint David's University College

Edmonds, M R, and Thomas, J S, 1991b, *Anglesey Archaeological Landscape Project: second interim report.* Lampeter. Saint David's University College

Edmonds, M R, and Thomas, J S, 1992, *Anglesey Archaeological Landscape Project: third interim report.* Lampeter. Saint David's University College

Edmonds, M R, and Thomas, J S, 1993, *Anglesey Archaeological Landscape Project: fourth interim report.* Lampeter. Saint David's University College

Gibson, A, 1998, Hindwell and the Neolithic palisaded sites of Britain and Ireland. In A Gibson and D Simpson (eds), *Prehistoric ritual and religion. Essays in honour of Aubrey Burl*. Stroud. Sutton Publishing. 68–79

Gibson, A, 1999, *The Walton Basin Project: excavation and survey in a prehistoric landscape 1993–7* (= Council for British Archaeology Research Report 118). York. Council for British Archaeology

Harding, A, 1981, Excavations in the prehistoric ritual complex near Milfield, Northumberland. *Proceedings of the Prehistoric Society*, 47, 87–135

Hartwell, B, 1998, The Ballynahatty complex. In A Gibson and D Simpson (eds), *Prehistoric ritual and religion. Essays in honour of Aubrey Burl*. Stroud. Sutton Publishing. 32–44

McInnes, I J, 1964, The Neolithic and Bronze Age pottery from Luce Sands, Wigtownshire. *Proceedings of the Society of Antiquaries of Scotland*, 97, 40–81

Piggott, S, 1954, *Neolithic cultures of the British Isles.* Cambridge. Cambridge University Press

Pryor, F M M, and French, C A I, 1985, *The Fenland Project, No. 1: archaeology and environment in the lower Welland valley. Volume 1* (= East Anglian Archaeology 27). Cambridge. East Anglian Archaeology

Richards, C C, 1996, Henges and water: towards an elemental understanding of monumentality and landscape in late Neolithic Britain. *Journal of Material Culture*, 1, 313–36

Richards, J, 1990, *The Stonehenge Environs Project* (= Historic Buildings and Monuments Commission for England Archaeological Report 16). London. English Heritage

Saville, A, 1983, Excavations at Condicote henge monument, Gloucestershire, 1977. *Transactions of the Bristol and Gloucester Archaeological Society*, 101, 21–47

Shand, G, 1998, A Neolithic causewayed enclosure in Kent. *Past*, 29, 1

Thomas, J S, 1994, The Pict's Knowe, Dumfries, interim report 1994. *http://www.arch. soton.ac.uk/Research/Dunragit/index.htm?blank.html*

Thomas, J S, 1995, The Pict's Knowe, Dumfries, interim report 1995. *http://www.arch. soton.ac.uk/Research/Dunragit/index.htm?blank.html*

Thomas, J S, 1997, The Pict's Knowe, Dumfries, interim report 1996–7. *http://www.arch. soton.ac.uk/Research/Dunragit/index.htm?blank.html*

Thomas, J S, 1999, Excavations at Dunragit, Dumfries and Galloway, 1999. *http://www.arch. soton.ac.uk/Research/Dunragit/index.htm?blank.html*

Thomas, J S, 2000, Excavations at Dunragit, Dumfries and Galloway, 2000. *http://www.arch. soton.ac.uk/Research/Dunragit /index.htm?blank.html*

Thomas, J S, forthcoming, *Place and memory: excavations at the Pict's Knowe, Holywood and Holm Farm, Dumfries, 1994–8*

Wainwright, G J, 1979, *Mount Pleasant, Dorset: excavations 1970–71* (= Reports of the Research Committee of the Society of Antiquaries of London 37). London. Society of Antiquaries

Whittle, A W R, 1997, *Sacred Mound, Holy Rings. Silbury Hill and the West Kennet palisade enclosures: a later Neolithic complex in north Wiltshire* (= Oxbow Monograph 74). Oxford. Oxbow Books

Chapter 11

Neolithic enclosures in Scotland

Gordon Barclay

INTRODUCTION

This brief and admittedly selective survey of a little-explored area – Neolithic enclosures in Scotland – was put together at the organizers' invitation to provide fuller geographical coverage. Although both henges and cursus monuments are enclosures of a sort, no detailed consideration of them in Scotland is included; both have received fair coverage in recent years (Barclay and Harding 1999; Barclay 1988; 1999a; Brophy 1999; Clare 1986; 1987; Harding 1987).

I have written elsewhere (Barclay 1992; 1995; 1997b; 1999b) about the late start of serious aerial photography in Scotland and how the last 25 years of flying have so radically changed the face of lowland Scotland's archaeology – cursus monuments for example – where the distribution has grown from one to over 50. To some extent the same is true of other forms of enclosure, which I describe here, but the picture is still far from clear.

In preparing this paper I began to appreciate just how different the interpretative traditions of early and middle Neolithic archaeology are in northern Britain, precisely because we have no causewayed camp tradition (*e.g.* Ashmore 1996). To the outside observer that tradition seems to lie at the very core of the way in which the Neolithic of midland and especially southern England is perceived and interpreted (*e.g.* Parker Pearson 1993). In the north we have erected an interpretative structure that has no such obvious "central places" (if I might use that term) in the middle part of the Neolithic, unless we are to see some of the cursus monuments fulfilling this role (*cf.* Brophy 1999). This has clearly affected the way in which the origin of henges has been considered; for example, the view was expressed widely until about a decade ago that henges developed from the causewayed camp tradition (Harding 1987), but as radiocarbon dating increasingly suggests an origin, or at least one origin, for henges in the north, this relationship has become less sustainable (Parker Pearson 1993).

How do we explain this missing element? Perhaps the lack of a tradition of early and middle Neolithic enclosures may reflect real differences in social structure and economy. For example, we have heard much in recent years about a mobile early Neolithic (Barrett 1994; Edmonds 1995; Parker Pearson 1993; Thomas 1991). However, some workers outside southern England argue vigorously that while this may be relevant for some parts of the British Isles, it appears not to be, or at least has not been demonstrated, in others (Barclay 1997a; 2000; Cooney 1997). Could it be though that the causewayed camp tradition does indeed relate, initially at least, to a more mobile pastoral tradition, leading in time to a more settled pastoral economy of the kind that must surely be represented by the defensive enclosures and vast cattle bone assemblages at Hambledon Hill (Mercer 1989a; 1989b)? Or could it be that a northern equivalent of the causewayed camp tradition lies as yet unidentified in the vast range of miscellaneous enclosures thrown up by the 25 years of aerial reconnaissance in Scotland?

TWO EXCAVATED NEOLITHIC ENCLOSURES

In Scotland there is a handful of excavated enclosures with associated Neolithic dates or which may reasonably be inferred to be Neolithic. The two most striking are Meldon Bridge, excavated over twenty years ago (Burgess 1976), and Blackshouse Burn, excavated over ten years ago (Figures 11.1 and 11.2). Both saw final publication only recently (Lelong and Pollard 1998; Speak and Burgess 1999). Perhaps these delays in publication have helped to restrict the integration of an enclosure tradition, beyond the henges and cursus monuments, into interpretations of Scotland's various regional Neolithics.

Meldon Bridge

The enclosure at Meldon Bridge had not fully emerged on aerial photographs when parts of it were threatened first by road realignment and then by the construction of a pipeline. An interim interpretation was published shortly after the excavation (Burgess 1976). Fortunately, the final report has now been published (Speak and Burgess 1999), and an up-to-date sequence can be proposed.

In rescue excavations carried out from 1974 to 1977 several episodes of activity were revealed, separated by protracted periods not represented in the archaeological record. Intensive use is attested only from the early to mid fourth millennium BC. At this date there began a long Neolithic use indicated by widely-scattered groups of pits, containing much impressed pottery in a local style. The calibrated radiocarbon dates for this activity range from 3800–2900 BC(4676±180 BP, SRR–643) to 2880–2460 BC (4082±80 BP, SRR–645). The pits were lined with broken and burnt pottery and other materials, and then sealed. At the time of the excavation this was inevitably interpreted as "refuse disposal" and seen as a clear marker for domestic activity. However, this "structured deposition" is now commonplace on sites which later saw the erection of major ceremonial monuments. What is perhaps unusual here is the inclusion of later Neolithic impressed wares, rather than the simple earlier Neolithic bowls which are more often found in this sort of context in Scotland (*e.g.*

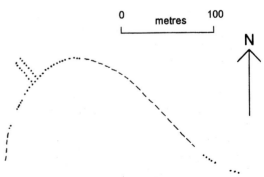

Figure 11.1: The palisaded enclosure at Meldon Bridge, Peeblesshire (After Burgess 1976)

Barclay and Russell-White 1993). The number of dates for these local impressed styles is limited, and their currency is generally taken to be very much in the later part of the span of calibrated dates from Meldon Bridge – that is the mid third millennium BC. However, given our very limited data set, we cannot dismiss at this time an origin in the earlier part of the calibrated spans, in the fourth millennium BC.

The later part of the pit-digging may have overlapped with the construction of a massive timber wall, 600m long and up to 4m high, shutting off the 8ha promontory between the Lyne Water and Meldon Burn. The radiocarbon determinations for the wall are not very helpful: 3100–2550 BC (4280±80 BP, HAR-790) and 3050–2250 BC (4100±130 BP, HAR-797) are available to play with.

A timber avenue entrance, of a kind that has since become familiar from many parts of Britain (Whittle 1997), led into the enclosure on the northwest, unfortunately not in the area excavated, and standing posts, standing stones, and settings of posts and stakes were erected. Cremation burials were also deposited in the interior.

No cultural material can certainly be associated with the enclosure. A disturbed cist burial, yielding a jet bead, slug-knife and sherds of Beaker or Food Vessel, was inserted into the area and there was further activity in the mid to late second millennium BC, when the site was used as an extensive cremation cemetery. This phase involved erecting rows of posts, some standing in pits containing cremations. There was also a burial in a rough cist, and two cremations were deposited in Cordoned Urns. There is no evidence for further activity until the Roman period.

Blackshouse Burn

Limited excavations were undertaken on two enclosures at Blackshouse Burn, by Peter Hill, in 1985 and 1986. The smaller of the two enclosures lay on the edge of a bog, and the larger contained within it the heads of two streams. An excavation report has been prepared by Olivia Lelong and Tony Pollard (1998), and the description that follows is adapted from that report.

The larger enclosure measures about 300m in diameter, defined by a low bank 8m to 14m across (Figure 11.2). The bank is nowhere more than 1.5m high, and is less than 1m high in places, although it seems to have been extensively robbed for stone – a late 18th century description notes stone robbers coming across urned cremations. There are possible entrances, although two may relate to later paths. Excavation revealed traces of pre-bank activity – the erection of light structures and a hearth. The bank appears to be made up of linked, fairly straight segments. It had been built by erecting a double row of timber posts and piling a stony bank between the two rows. The bases of the preserved waterlogged posts were recovered. The bank was later elaborated, with stones pitched around the standing posts and, in a final stage in some parts, the bank was capped once the posts had decayed. One of the posts was dated to 2900–2350 BC (4035±55 BP, GU–1983), suggesting that the enclosure was built in the early to mid third millennium BC. The bank was built in bays defined by stones set on edge, but these would not have been visible on completion. This, and the segmentation of the bank, offers the possibility of prolonged rather than unitary construction. There are 19 stony mounds in the interior, all less than 5m in diameter and under 0.3m high. Two were sectioned during the excavation but provided little clue as to their function.

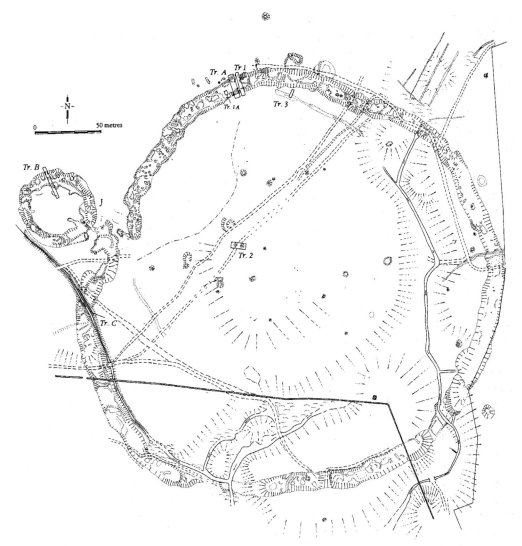

Figure 11.2: Excavation plan of the embanked enclosure at Blackshouse Burn, Lanarkshire. (After Lelong and Pollard 1998)

The smaller enclosure, about 40m in diameter, was also sectioned. A number of pits had been dug into the peat, perhaps to act as sumps to drain the peat to some extent. The stony bank was erected past the edges of these pits. Other features in the interior hinted at a timber structure of some sort.

The two enclosures lie in a landscape densely populated by archaeological features. Pollard and Lelong have drawn attention to the way in which the double heads of the burn are contained within the enclosure, and the choice of a site on the edge of a bog. This was seen as a feature paralleling what had been found at Meldon Bridge, not far to the east. It was noted that the enclosure lay hidden from view from the valley below. Pollard and Lelong argue in their report for a ceremonial use associated with transhumance.

OTHER EXCAVATED SITES

Several sites investigated through small-scale excavations give hints of other Neolithic enclosure-building activity.

In the 1970s salvage excavation was undertaken at Kinloch Farm in Fife (Figure 11.3: Barber 1982). This enclosure did not appear clearly on aerial photographs until after excavation had begun. It appeared to be about 35m in diameter within two roughly concentric ditches. The inner ditch was some 3.8m wide and 0.25m deep. The outer ditch was about 3m across and 0.2m deep. An incoherent pattern of features was located within the excavation trench. A small assemblage of pottery of a kind comparable to later Neolithic impressed wares was recovered from some of the features. A sample of charcoal floated from the fill of the inner ditch, and therefore taphonomically unreliable, produced a radiocarbon determination of 3640–3360 BC (4725±70 BP, GU-1375). Taking doubts about the stated errors of early radiocarbon determinations into account, this would suggest a date of *c.* 3800–3100 BC, similar to the earliest range for the pit digging at Meldon Bridge. It has been suggested that this site might represent an enclosed settlement tradition.

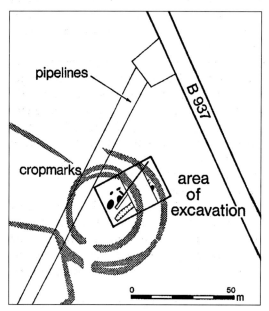

Figure 11.3: Excavation plan of the enclosure at Kinloch Farm, Collessie, Fife. (After Barber 1982, fig 1)

At North Mains, Strathallan in Perthshire a small research excavation (Barclay and Tolan 1990) was carried out on a bivallate enclosure cutting off the corner of a river terrace a couple of hundred metres from the henge and massive round barrow on the same farm (Barclay 1983). The outer ditch had a pattern of postholes not only along its inner edge but also round the ditch butt and along the outer edge, perhaps suggesting a barrier of un-familiar type. After the 2m deep inner ditch had filled, a stone platform was built and a charcoal sample from its surface produced a radiocarbon deter-mination of 1740–1310 BC (3250 ±80 BP, GU–2682). While relatively late, the large ditch may have taken a considerable time to fill completely, and a construction date within the earlier Bronze Age or even the late Neolithic is not impossible. However, a charcoal sample from a feature in the interior produced a clear Iron Age date and the sequence and nature of the site remains obscure.

Further possible Neolithic features may have turned up under a hillfort in the west, at Carwinning Hill in Ayrshire, where Cowie (1978) found shallow causewayed ditches: Neolithic pottery was also found on the hilltop. It is hoped that final publication of this site will not now be long delayed.

There have also been deliberate attempts to find Neolithic causewayed camps within known monuments. Roger Mercer excavated a crop-mark causewayed enclosure at Spott Dod in East Lothian, only to prove hillfort builders also used causewayed ditches in the Iron Age (Mercer 1984). It has been suggested that the multi-vallate and multi-entrance enclosures at Brown Caterthun and Barmekin of Echt might be of Neolithic date (Barclay 1997a), but excavations at the Brown Caterthun have comprehensively proved the proposition wrong, at least for that site (Dunwell and Strachan 1997).

AERIAL PHOTOGRAPHIC EVIDENCE

It is within the aerial photographic record in Scotland that our best chances for detecting Neolithic enclosures now lie. Serious locally-based aerial photography where the results could be accessed in Scotland has only been under way for 25 years. Areas hitherto seen as having a sparse distribution of monuments now have dense spreads of sites of all periods, which we have barely begun to explore (Barclay 1992; Hanson and Macinnes 1991). The category of "enclosure" is large and within it may lurk unsuspected Neolithic surprises. The selection presented here is based on my own trawls through the National Monuments Record for Scotland and on suggestions by Stratford Halliday and Richard Strathie. There is a distinct bias to Eastern Scotland and the Scottish Borders – other possibilities no doubt remain to be identified elsewhere.

Whittle (1997), in setting his excavated sites at West Kennett in context, has usefully provided a valuable overview of known and suspected enclosures of possibly similar type. The clear timber-post lined passage first noted at Meldon Bridge has become a regularly occurring feature – found at Walton (Powys), Forteviot (Figure 11.4 upper), Leadketty (Figure 11.5) (both Perthshire), and Dunragit (Wigtownshire) (Figure 11.4 lower; RCAHMS 1996). Although an obvious explanation is as an entrance, the Meldon Bridge enclosure seemed to have another formal entrance in the excavated area (Speak and Burgess forthcoming). The Dunragit pit complex has certain similarities, although not close, to Meldon Bridge, particularly in the possible "passage" feature.

The Forteviot complex is closer still, and contains a range of hengiform or barrow features (Whittle 1997). Close by at Leadketty there is a further Meldon Bridge type enclosure, with its passage feature, that has not yet been fully plotted, but it lies immediately next to what is generally considered the best candidate for a causewayed camp in Scotland – at Leadketty (Barclay 1998). Arable fieldwalking over the two enclosures has produced Neolithic worked flint.

Looking beyond Leadketty in Strathearn there are interesting large enclosures, with irregular ditches of a kind familiar from Neolithic sites elsewhere in Perthshire, which may be considered as potential candidates: Inverdunning, Pittentian, Loanleaven (Figure 11.6), and Millhaugh.

Gordon Barclay

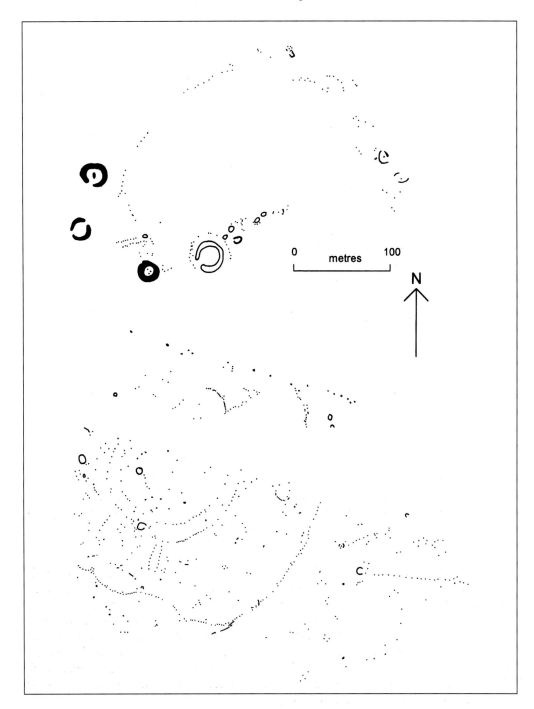

Figure 11.4: Enclosure complexes at (upper) Forteviot, Perthshire, and (lower) Dunragit, Wigtownshire. (Based on crop-mark plots prepared by RCAHMS)

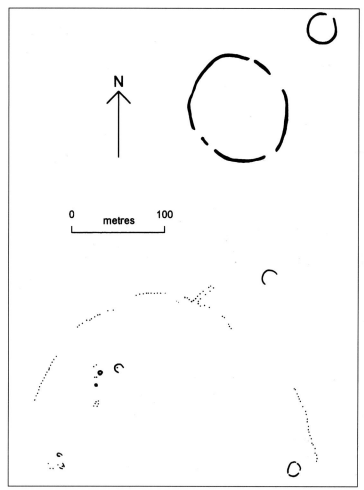

Figure 11.5: Complex of ditched and pit-defined enclosures at Leadketty, Perthshire. (Based on crop-mark plots prepared by RCAHMS with additional sketch plotting)

The possible massive timber enclosure a few miles to the east, at Huntingtower, which has only appeared on one aerial photograph (Barclay 1982), has to some extent been lost from the literature as a possible further later Neolithic post-defined enclosure.

If we consider that the North Mains terrace edge enclosure mentioned above was an early Bronze Age or Neolithic possibility, then there are further sites in Strathearn of the same morphology, at South Mains, Innerpeffray, and Craig Shot. I am grateful to Richard Strathie for bringing to my attention 13 "cliff-edge" enclosures in the catchment of the River Tweed, which may include early sites, but it would perhaps be premature to suggest any similarity of date on mere morphology.

In the Scottish Borders the enclosure at Whitmuirhaugh (Figure 11.7), adjacent to an impressive early historic settlement complex, may be worth further investigation.

Figure 11.6: The enclosure at Loanleven, Perthshire. (Photograph by RCAHMS. Crown Copyright reserved)

Figure 11.7: The enclosure at Whitmuirhaugh, Sprouston, Roxburghshire. (Photograph by RCAHMS. Crown Copyright reserved)

CONCLUSION

It is clear then there are enclosure traditions in the various Neolithics of Scotland but they are barely explored and, as we can see from Blackshouse Burn and Meldon Bridge, hardly absorbed into mainstream explanatory models. The publication of Blackshouse Burn and particularly Meldon Bridge is an important step, but what is needed is more excavation to identify and characterize the range of material present. That we have a late Neolithic timber palisade tradition is clear; that that tradition may be analogous to traditions elsewhere in Britain is likely. And we can see a relationship of some sort between the henges lying within the Forteviot enclosure. But whether there is an early to middle Neolithic tradition is unresolved. The proximity of the ditched enclosure and Meldon Bridge type enclosure at Leadketty is intriguing, and the sites offer some interesting possibilities. In another ten years perhaps we will have a fuller story to tell.

BIBLIOGRAPHY

Ashmore, P J, 1996, *Neolithic and Bronze Age Scotland*. London. Batsford

Barber, J W, 1982, The investigation of some plough-truncated features at Kinloch Farm, Collessie in Fife. *Proceedings of the Society of Antiquaries of Scotland*, 112, 524–533

Barclay, A, and Harding, J, 1999, *Pathways and ceremonies. The cursus monuments of Britain and Ireland* (= Neolithic Studies Group Seminar Papers 4). Oxford. Oxbow Books

Barclay, G J, 1982, The excavation of two crop-marks at Huntingtower, Perthshire. *Proceedings of the Society of Antiquaries of Scotland*, 112, 580–583

Barclay, G J, 1983, Sites of the third millennium bc to the first millennium ad at North mains, Strathallan, Perthshire. *Proceedings of the Society of Antiquaries of Scotland*, 113, 122–281

Barclay, G J, 1988, Review of "Henge monuments and related sites of Great Britain" by A F Harding. *Proceedings of the Prehistoric Society*, 54, 343–344

Barclay, G J, 1992, The Scottish gravels: a neglected resource? In M Fulford and E Nichols (eds), *Developing landscapes of lowland Britain. The archaeology of the British gravels: a review*. London. Society of Antiquaries of London. 106–124

Barclay, G J, 1995, What's new in Scottish prehistory? *Scottish Archaeological Review*, 9/10, 3–14

Barclay, G J, 1997a, The Neolithic. In K J Edwards and I B M Ralston (eds), *Scotland: environment and archaeology, 8000 BC – AD 1000*. Chichester. Wiley. 127–149

Barclay, G J (ed), 1997b, *State-funded Rescue Archaeology in Scotland: past, present and future*. Edinburgh. Historic Scotland

Barclay, G J, 1998, *Farmers, temples and tombs: Scotland in the Neolithic and early Bronze Age*. Edinburgh. Canongate

Barclay, G J, 1999a, Cairnpapple revisited: 1948–1998. *Proceedings of the Prehistoric Society*, 65, 17–46

Barclay, G J, 1999b, A hidden landscape: the Neolithic of Tayside. In A F Harding (ed), *Experiment and Design*. Oxford. Oxbow. 20–9

Barclay, G J, 2000, Between Orkney and Wessex: the search for the regional Neolithics of Britain. In A Ritchie (ed), *Neolithic Orkney in its European context: conference proceedings*. Cambridge. McDonald Institute for Archaeological Research. 275–85

Barclay, G J, and Russell-White, C J (eds), 1993, Excavations in the ceremonial complex of the fourth to second millennium BC at Balfarg/Balbirnie, Glenrothes, Fife. *Proceedings of the Society of Antiquaries of Scotland*, 123, 43–210

Barclay, G J, and Tolan, M, 1990, Trial excavation of a terrace-edge enclosure at North Mains, Strathallan, Perthshire. *Proceedings of the Society of Antiquaries of Scotland*, 120, 45–53

Barrett, J, 1994, *Fragments from antiquity*. Oxford. Blackwell

Brophy, K, 1999, The cursus monuments of Scotland. In A Barclay and J Harding (eds), *Pathways and ceremonies. The cursus monuments of Britain and Ireland* (= Neolithic Studies Group Seminar Papers 4). Oxford. Oxbow Books. 119–129

Burgess, C, 1976, Meldon Bridge: a Neolithic defended promontory complex near Peebles. In C Burgess and R Miket (eds), *Settlement and economy in the third and second millennia BC* (= British Archaeological Reports British Series 33). Oxford. British Archaeological Reports. 151–179

Clare, T, 1986, Towards a reappraisal of henge monuments. *Proceedings of the Prehistoric Society*, 52, 281–316

Clare, T, 1987, Towards a reappraisal of henge monuments: origins, evolution and hierarchies. *Proceedings of the Prehistoric Society*, 53, 457–477

Cooney, G, 1997, Images of settlement and the landscape in the Neolithic. In P Topping (ed), *Neolithic Landscapes* (= Neolithic Studies Group Seminar Papers 2). Oxford. Oxbow Books. 23–31

Cowie, T G, 1978. *Preliminary report on excavations at Carwinning Hill, Dalry, Ayrshire*. [Limited circulation printed report]

Dunwell, A J, and Strachan, R, 1997, Brown Caterthun. *Discovery and Excavation in Scotland 1996*, 13–14

Edmonds, M, 1995, *Stone tools and society*. London. Batsford

Hanson, W S, and Macinnes, L, 1991, The archaeology of the Scottish Lowlands: problems and potential. In W S Hanson and E A Slater (eds), *Scottish archaeology: new perceptions*. Aberdeen. Aberdeen University Press. 153–166

Harding, A F, 1987, *Henge monuments and related sites of Great Britain* (= British Archaeological Reports British Series 175). Oxford. British Archaeological Reports

Lelong, O and Pollard, T, 1998, The excavation and survey of prehistoric enclosures at Blackshouse Burn, Lanarkshire. *Proceedings of the Society of Antiquaries of Scotland*, 128, 13–54

Mercer, R J, 1984, Spott Dod: crop-mark enclosure. *Discovery and Excavation, in Scotland 1983*, 19

Mercer, R J, 1989a, The earliest defences in western Europe: part 1: warfare in the Neolithic. *Fortress*, 2, 16–22

Mercer, R J, 1989b, The earliest defences in western Europe: part 2: the archaeological evidence. *Fortress*, 3, 2–11

Parker Pearson, M, 1993, *Bronze Age Britain*. London. Batsford and English Heritage

RCAHMS, 1996, *Catalogue of aerial photographs 1992*. Edinburgh. RCAHMS

Speak, S, and Burgess, C, 1999, Meldon Bridge: a centre of the third millennium BC in Peeblesshire. *Proceedings of the Society of Antiquaries of Scotland*, 129, 1–118

Thomas, J, 1991, *Rethinking the Neolithic*. Cambridge. Cambridge University Press

Whittle, A, 1997, *Sacred Mound, Holy Rings. Silbury Hill and the West Kennet palisaded enclosures: a later Neolithic complex in north Wiltshire* (= Oxbow Monograph 74). Oxford. Oxbow Books

Chapter 12

Neolithic enclosures in the Isle of Man

Timothy Darvill

INTRODUCTION

Situated in the middle of the Irish Sea more or less mid-way between Scotland, Ireland, England, and Wales, the Isle of Man has long been known for its ensemble of megalithic tombs (Megaw 1938; Daniel 1950, 179–81; Henshall 1978), the late Neolithic house at Ronaldsway (Bruce *et al.* 1947), and a scatter of late Neolithic cremation cemeteries associated with earthfast jars (Bersu 1947). Recent research has provided a more secure context for some of these familiar elements by setting them alongside a broader range of Neolithic cultural assemblages in the Island and within the Irish Sea region generally (Moffatt 1978; Burrow 1997). In 1995, as part of an extensive research programme of investigations and surveys, a series of ditched enclosures was discovered at the Billown Quarry Site near Castletown in the southern part of the Island. This discovery served to broaden still further the range of Neolithic monuments and structures known on the Island. It also introduced further lines of inquiry about the cultural connections of those communities living on the Island between the fifth and third millennia BC, and raised the question as to whether other contemporary enclosures could be recognized elsewhere on the Island.

This short review is divided into three main parts. First, by way of background, there is a very brief summary of the Manx Neolithic and the nature of the Billown Neolithic Landscape Project. This is followed by a discussion of the enclosures at Billown and their wider relationships. Finally, consideration is given to a small number of other sites on the Island that may be considered as potential Neolithic enclosures. Figure 12.1 shows the distribution of key sites in the Isle of Man referred to below.

THE MANX NEOLITHIC AND THE BILLOWN PROJECT

The Isle of Man is a small but geographically varied island of about 570 square kilometres. It lies in the middle of the Irish Sea, variously influenced and culturally connected to coastal and inland communities living around the Irish Sea basin. Tidal flows and currents within the Irish Sea favoured two directions of movement through historic and prehistoric times (Bowen 1970; Davies 1946, 41). South to north movements from Cornwall, southeast

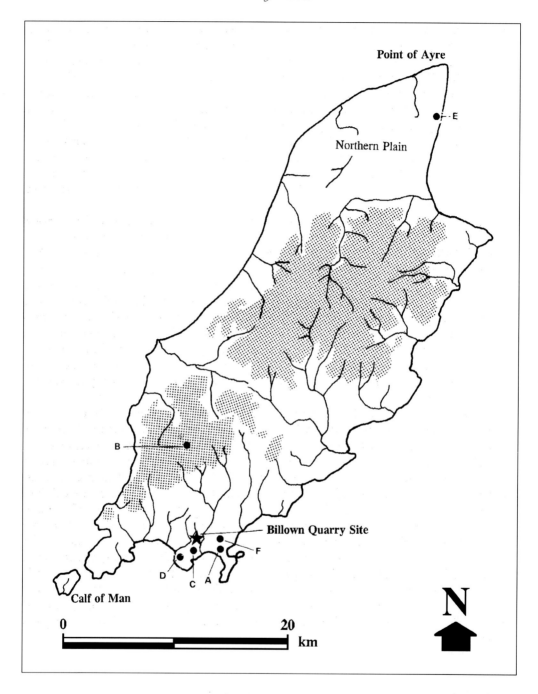

Figure 12.1: The Isle of Man showing the position of the Billown Quarry Site and other key places on the Island mentioned in the text. A: Ronaldsway; B: South Barrule; C: Skibrick Hill; D: Balladoole; E: Phurt; F: The Broog. Land over 150m ASL stippled

Ireland, and the west coast of Wales relate to the southeastern shores of Mann, but north to south influences from Antrim and Galloway relate to the northwestern coastlands.

The Neolithic period in the Island divides into two main cultural-historical phases (Darvill 2000). The earlier Neolithic spans the later fifth and fourth millennia BC, and is conventionally characterized by round-bottomed pottery of Mull-Hill tradition (Piggott 1932) together with long barrows and passage graves that allow links to be proposed with the more widespread Clyde-Carlingford traditions (Clark 1935, 75–81; Piggott 1954, 157; Burrow 1997, 11–17). The later Neolithic, broadly the third millennium BC, is distinctive to the Isle of Man and was defined as the Ronaldsway Culture by Basil Megaw following the excavation of a Neolithic house at Ronaldsway Airport in 1943 and a cemetery at Ballateare in 1946 (Bruce *et al.* 1947; Bersu 1947; Piggott 1954, 346–51; Moffatt 1978; Burrow 1997, 19–31; Burrow and Darvill 1997).

Billown is situated in the southern part of the Isle of Man, approximately 2.5km north of Castletown and 1.2km west of Ballasalla, in the parish of Malew, sheading of Rushen (Figure 12.1). The Billown Quarry Site is centred on NGR SC 268702 and occupies slightly elevated ground (*c.* 40m OD) within a generally undulating plain. It lies on a narrow interfluve between the Silver Burn to the east and a stream from Chibbyr Unjin to the west. Both watercourses run southwards, emptying into the Irish Sea at Castletown and Poyll Vaaish respectively. On a clear day there are good views from the site. To the north is upland, dominated by South Barrule with its hillfort crowned summit at 483m above sea level. To the northwest and west are further hills, many rising to over 200m above sea level, while to the southwest it is possible to see the coast with the Irish Sea beyond. Views south and east are more restricted, but in general look out over the coastal plain and the valley of the Silver Burn.

The Billown Neolithic Landscape Project is a joint venture by Bournemouth University's School of Conservation Science in association with Manx National Heritage. It began in the summer of 1995 following the discovery, two years earlier, of pits, postholes, and gullies containing early and middle Neolithic pottery and flintwork within an area of land identified for stone quarrying. The rationale of the Project involves three main strands: "rescue" excavation of an extensive site prior to its destruction by quarrying; research into the evolution and development of a tract of land and the communities who inhabited it during a critical period in the early occupation of the Island, namely the later Mesolithic through to the later Bronze Age; and training and the provision of opportunities for students and the general public to participate in the process of archaeological excavation and survey. Between 1995 and 1998 open area excavations have examined 0.5ha while geophysical and geochemical surveys of the surrounding landscape provide information for an area of about 1 square kilometre. Annual interim reports have been published (Darvill 1996a; 1997; 1998; 1999a; 2000) together with general overviews of progress (Darvill 1996b; 1999b).

THE BILLOWN QUARRY SITE ENCLOSURES

Geophysical surveys in 1995 revealed a series of anomalies provisionally identified as the braided course of a curved causewayed ditch. No trace of the boundary was visible on the ground surface as an earthwork or soil-mark. The geophysical anomaly was evaluated in the same season and confirmed as a series of intercutting Neolithic ditches (Darvill 1996a). Excavations in subsequent seasons, especially between 1996 and 1998, allowed the detailed investigation of a 45m length of the main enclosure boundary together with associated features and antenna ditches connected to the main boundary. Geophysical surveys over the same period allow a provisional interpretation of the surviving portion of the enclosure and its boundaries, although this is based on the identification of what are currently considered contiguous anomalies; parts of the circuit have yet to be tested through excavation.

Surveys and the main enclosure

As currently understood the main enclosure is D-shaped in plan, at least 240m north to south and more than 220m east west with an area in excess of 4ha (Figure 12.2). The flat face, in fact slightly concave, opens to the west, and may have had an entrance more or less in the centre. A large white quartz standing stone, The Boolievane Stone, stands about 40m west of the enclosure, more or less central to the western boundary. The eastern part of the enclosure has been partly cut away by quarrying over the last few centuries.[1] Geophysical surveys suggest the presence of a small penannular enclosure about 14m in diameter and with an entrance to the southeast immediately inside the enclosure about mid-way along the west face (Darvill 1998, 25–6). As a whole the enclosure occupies all of a low gently rounded hilltop; the internal penannular enclosure stands on the highest ground within the bounded area. The ground outside the enclosure to the west, around the Boolievane Stone is notably poor in geophysical anomalies and on this basis may be considered to have been fairly open ground.

Excavations

Excavation of the enclosure has been confined to the northern boundary, part of the interior on the north side, and a substantial area immediately outside the enclosure. At least two main phases are represented, in some cases involving sufficient remodelling as to suggest a succession of enclosures on more or less the same area (Figure 12.3).

The earliest phase is represented as a continuous linear ditch about 1m wide and up to 0.5m deep running on a northeast to southwest alignment for a distance of about 25m (F14/F28) before turning sharply northwest and continuing in a generally westward curving course for a distance of about 90m (F17/F272/F297/F400). This line is broken by two wide gaps, one of which contains a mini-henge structure. This northward projecting arm of ditch probably continues into areas yet to be explored, and forms what is currently referred to as the northern annexe. In due course it may be shown that these ditches in fact form a northern enclosure. About 1.5m south of the sharp corner already referred to is a second continuous ditch (F68) which continues the general line of first ditch in a southwesterly direction. The gap between the two ditches is interpreted as an entrance allowing communication between the interior of the main enclosure and the area to the north. All of these ditches show some evidence of recutting, and the fills contain Neolithic pottery and numerous complete leaf-shaped arrowheads. Whether the ditches were ever flanked by a bank is not known; certainly none survives within the excavated areas. For

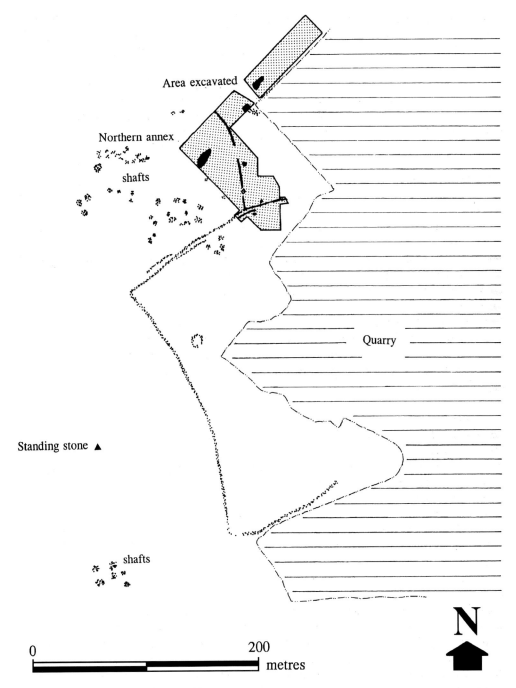

Area excavated

Northern annex

shafts

Standing stone ▲

shafts

Quarry

N

0   200
                                           metres

Figure 12.2: Provisional plan of the enclosures at the Billown Quarry Site as revealed through excavations (1995–1998) and geophysical survey

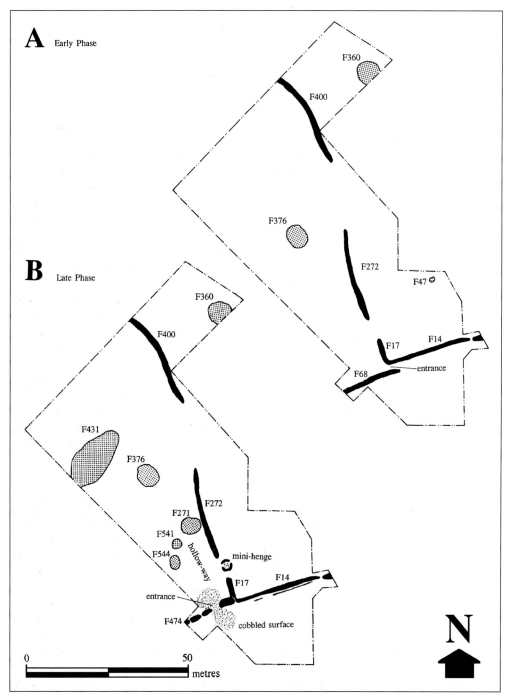

Figure 12.3: Plans showing the principal features provisionally assigned to the early and late phase of the Neolithic enclosure sequence on the Billown Quarry Site from excavations between 1995 and 1998

much of its course, especially north of the sharp turn northwards, the ditch profile is asymmetrical, with a steeper northern side and a more shallow southern side.

The southerly of these early ditches, F68, appears to have been deliberately in-filled fairly soon after being dug. It was sealed by a layer of stones packed into its upper fill. This fill was in turn overlaid by a thin layer of soil, possibly the result of excavating a new line of ditches some 1.5m to the north. This new line was causewayed in form. One segment (F127) joined (and stratigraphically cut) the corner of ditch F17/F28 while others (F281 and F474) continued the line. Overall, the alignment of the causewayed ditch extends the line of the non-causewayed ditch F28/F14 southwestwards.

The gap between segments F127 and F281 in the causewayed ditch is about 2.5m wide and appears to have formed an entrance, presumably replacing the one that had been in-filled and covered when the ditches were remodelled. A sequence of three postholes on the east side and six on the west side suggests some elaboration and periodic reconstruction. A cobbled stone surface extending for over 7m either side of the entrance, sealing the earlier ditch F68, is further evidence that this entrance received heavy usage. Moreover, the natural surface north of the entrance appears to have been eroded in the form of a slight hollow-way leading into the centre of the space (?annexe) defined by the ditches west of F272 and south of F400.

The causewayed ditch segments were recut on at least three occasions. In its last phase, the most easterly, F127, had a narrow slot cut along its southern edge. Stone slabs were set upright in the slot, a large granite erratic being set in the slot adjacent to the entrance (Figure 12.4). A second similar stone may have been set on the other side of the entrance, perhaps as a final replacement for the earlier wooden setting, but only the stone socket survived at the time this area was excavated. The ditch fills contained small amounts of bowl-style Neolithic pottery, flintwork including numerous leaf-shaped arrowheads, and white quartz pebbles that seem to have mainly been placed on or near the bottom of the ditch segments. Small quantities of carbonized plant remains, including cereals, have been recovered from the ditch fills. Bone is not preserved on the site so it is not known whether animal or human body parts were also included in the ditch fills.

Internal and associated features
The area excavated within the main enclosure revealed few features: a small stone cairn (Darvill 1996a, 20), a series of undated postholes, a short length of gully (F222), a scoop (F233), and a narrow gully (F231) running parallel to the main ditch F14. The topsoil in this area is rather deeper than to the north of the ditch system, suggesting perhaps that the areas either side of this boundary were subject to differential land-use at some stage.

North and northwest of the main enclosure, in the area tentatively identified as the northern annexe/enclosure, and beyond, is a series of scoops, pits, and shafts. Some of these features are extremely large and most preserve evidence for occasional visits that involved lighting fires and perhaps cooking and eating. F376, for example, was a large pit in the bottom of which was a shaft. The pit was about 6m in diameter with gently sloping sides. In the upper fill was a hearth in which lay the remains of three early Neolithic bowls (Darvill 1998, 17); charred plant remains include cereals and hazlenut shells. Under the hearth was what turned out to be the burnt remains of a series of planks. A radiocarbon date on the charcoal from one of these timbers suggests that the tree from which the plank

was made was cut down about 4950–4590 BC (5910±70 BP, Beta-110691)). Below the planks was the top of a circular shaft extending downwards from the bottom of the pit for a distance of 2.5m. By contrast, F431 was an extensive scoop, 25m long and up to 15m wide, probably dug in a series of episodes with pits dug in the bottom of the scoop. Charcoal from a hearth in the central part of the scoop, at a depth of about 1.2m below the ground surface, provided a radiocarbon date of 2920–2490 BC (4170±90 BP, Beta-129019). Fourteen pits, scoops and shafts of Neolithic date have so far been excavated; geophysical survey suggests that these are part of a scatter of perhaps 70 such structures, all but three or four situated outside the main enclosure (see Darvill 1999a, 71).

Access, movement and vistas
All these scoops, pits, and shafts were accessible from the entrance through the northern boundary of the main enclosure, and as already noted a hollow-way had formed

immediately north of the cobbled area in the entranceway suggesting fairly heavy usage. In passing through the northern entrance in a northerly direction the field of view is dominated by one of the highest mountain on the Island, South Barrule, which rises to 483m above sea level.[2] Its top is 5.7km from the Billown Quarry Site, and it is capped by a clearly visible round stone cairn of unknown date (Megaw 1938, 237).

Dating and sequence
The northern entrance to the main enclosure appears to coincide with a scatter of flintwork of the heavy blade industries traditionally assigned to the later Mesolithic of the Island (Woodman 1978). Charcoal from pre-enclosure pit F526 has been dated to 4680–4390 BC (5680±40 BP, Beta-125767), the earliest ditch fill (F69) to 4770–4520 BC (5780±40 BP, Beta-125768), and the latest ditch recut, which includes the stone setting referred to above (F127), to 2120–1770 BC (3590±40 BP, Beta-125766). This provisional dating is broadly confirmed by the range of cultural material recovered, and shows that the use of the site spans what is conventionally regarded as the earlier and later Neolithic.

Discussion and analogies
The Billown Quarry Site enclosures extend the distribution of recorded causewayed enclosures into new territory; they are also the first to be found on any of the small islands within the British Isles archipelago. In summary, current interpretations suggest that the focus of the site was a large D-shaped enclosure that underwent several phases of reconstruction, each with episodes of boundary recutting, over a period of up to 2000 years. Throughout its history there was an entrance in the north side of the enclosure boundary giving access to an area of pit/shaft digging, possibly within a smaller northern enclosure or annexe, or at least in an area subdivided by ditches connected to the main enclosure boundary. Available radiocarbon dates suggest that construction of the first enclosure lies well back in the mid fifth millennium BC making it amongst the earliest in the British Isles.[3]

Although the outline of the Billown main enclosure must be regarded as provisional pending further investigations and verification of the detail, the emergent plan is not without parallels, especially in western, central, and eastern England (Figure 12.5). Haddenham, Cambridgeshire, for example, has an outline that is very similar in plan and scale (8.5ha) to Billown. Here too there is a curved west-facing "front" with an oval enclosure behind (Evans 1988a; 1998b). D-shaped plans to Neolithic monuments are fairly widely known, and can be seen also in the form of the inner ditch at Windmill Hill, Wiltshire (Smith 1965), and at a much smaller scale at the Grendon Barrow, Northampton-shire (Gibson 1985). Mention may also be made of the undated ditched enclosure that appears to pre-date the massive stone circle known as Long Meg and Her Daughters, Cumbria (Soffe and Clare 1988). Although slightly more irregular in plan than either Haddenham or Billown appears to be, there is a south facing slightly concave "front" with a centrally placed main entrance and the standing stone of Long Meg directly in front of the entrance at a distance of about 100m. The apparently later stone circle fits between the enclosure and the standing stone (Figure 12.5C).

The complexity of the Neolithic boundary works at Billown, the final recut slot containing carefully packed stones dating to the early second millennium BC, and the

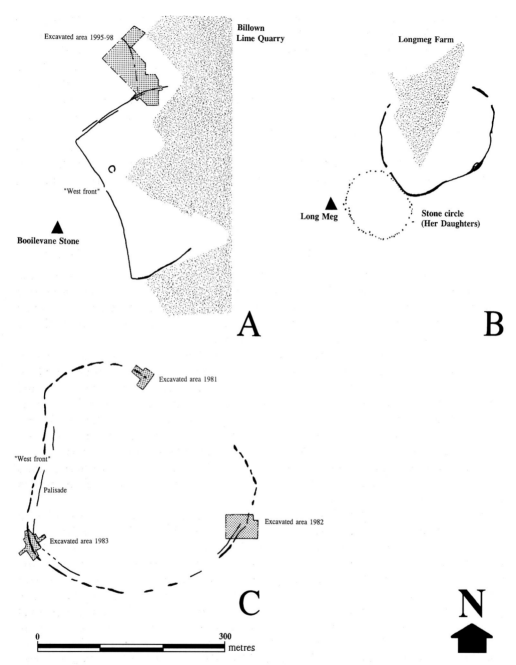

Figure 12.5: Comparative ground plans of Neolithic enclosures. A: Billown, Isle of Man; B: Haddenham, Cambridgeshire; C: Long Meg and Her Daughters, Cumbria. (B after Evans 1988, fig 7.5; C after Soffe and Clare 1988, fig 1)

abundance of arrowheads, allows parallels to be drawn with the complex at Hambledon Hill, Dorset (Mercer 1980; 1988). The presence of human crania on the floor of the enclosure ditches at the main enclosure at Hambledon Hill also has certain similarities with the placement of white quartz pebbles on the ditch floors at Billown (*cf.* Mercer 1980, 32). Other comparisons may be made with enclosures in southern and especially southwestern England including the presence of pits outside the boundary on the north side of Robin Hood's Ball, Wiltshire, (Richards 1990, 61–5) and the relatively high proportion of leaf-shaped arrowheads in assemblages from Carn Brae, Cornwall (Saville in Mercer 1981,124), Hembury, Devon (Liddell 1935, 162), and Crickley Hill, Gloucestershire (Dixon 1988, 83) amongst other sites. To what extent some of these similarities can be attributed to connections facilitated by maritime links along the western seaways is a matter deserving further investigation.

OTHER POSSIBLE NEOLITHIC ENCLOSURES IN THE ISLE OF MAN

The enclosures at Billown Quarry Site have no surface earthwork traces, and even the material recovered from fieldwalking is not especially distinctive. The site was discovered through a combination of field evaluation carried out during the first phase of quarry expansion and extensive geophysical survey. It is highly likely, therefore that other similar and contemporary enclosures exist on the Isle of Man.

Geophysical surveys on Skibrick Hill to the south of Billown revealed a massive oval ditched enclosure some 170m by 120m overall, bounded by four broadly concentric lines of ditches with an internal area 75m by 85m. There were simple entrances to the east and west, the eastern entrance having a quartz standing stone set to one side of the entrance corridor (Laughlin in Darvill 1997, 38–41). Although promising as a Neolithic enclosure, evaluative excavations in 1998 showed that the main use of the site dated to the later Bronze Age, broadly 800 BC to 400 BC (Russell and Darvill 1998). It remains possible that the initial cutting of at least some of the ditches was in fact earlier, with reuse in later times as at Thwing, East Riding of Yorkshire (Manby 1980), but further dating would be needed to substantiate such a proposition.

The possibility that the Ronaldsway Neolithic house site (Bruce *et al.* 1947) lay within an enclosure was also investigated within the context of the Billown Neolithic Landscape Project. Access here is difficult because the area in which the Neolithic site lies in cut by the main runway and the northern taxiway of the Island's international airport. In the autumn and winter of 1998, however, the entire northeastern part of the airport and adjacent land was surveyed in advance of plans being developed to modify the taxiway system. Extensive geophysical surveys were carried out, and two test-pits excavated (Darvill *et al.* 1999). Several curved linear boundary works were identified and one is tentatively dated to the later Neolithic on the basis of charcoal from the fill which yielded an AMS radiocarbon determination that calibrates to 2140–1770 BC (3600±60 BP, Beta-125769). It is unlikely, however, that this ditch forms part of an enclosure as such; more likely it is some kind of land boundary with a house or structure set beside it to the north in a pattern rather reminiscent of the Storey's Bar Road site at Fengate with its field boundaries and later Neolithic occupation partly obscured in this case by a later ring-ditch (Pryor 1978, 58–68).

Southwest of the Billown Quarry Site, overlooking the coast at Bay ny Carrickey, is the hilltop enclosure on Chapel Hill, Balladoole. This site has been investigated through excavation on several occasions, notably by Gerhard Bersu in the winter of 1944–5. This work revealed a Viking ship burial, lintel grave cemetery, and what was believed to be a later prehistoric defended enclosure (Bersu and Wilson 1966; Bersu 1974). A reassessment of the 20th century excavations together with extensive geophysical and geochemical surveys in 1999 confirms the complexity of occupation and long-lived use of the hilltop, but also raises fundamental questions about some of Bersu's interpretations of the earlier material (Madden 2000). There was certainly extensive Mesolithic and Neolithic activity on the hilltop and what is described as "a habitation layer, probably of Neolithic date" (Bersu and Wilson 1966, 1). There is very little evidence to date the enclosure to the later prehistoric period, and the possibility that it is Neolithic in origin must be seriously entertained given its cultural layer, position, and morphological similarity with sites such as Carn Brea, Cornwall (Mercer 1981), Clegyr Boia, Pembrokeshire (Chapter 6) and Green How, Cumbria (Horne *et al.* 2001).

Perhaps rather surprisingly there are no substantial traces of possible enclosure boundaries accidentally discovered during disturbances prompted by development or in the course of investigating sites of other periods. Stephen Burrow, in his review of the Manx Neolithic (1997), provides no firm examples despite the vigilance of archaeologists working on the Island and the vast amount of fieldwalking and surface collection carried out by Alan Skillan and others, especially on the Northern Plain. Perhaps some flint-scatters will eventually prove to represent traces of enclosed sites and in this regard there is a need to systematically sample a selection of sites to see what exactly they do represent. A good starting place, and a site that has all the hallmarks of being an enclosure except the boundary itself, is at Purt on the northeast coast. Since 1983, large quantities of pottery and flintwork have been eroding from the cliff section, and there are visible features including pits, postholes, and hearths. Finds include a saddle quern and the butt of a Group VI axe (Burrow 1997, 43).

Aerial photography is another approach that has contributed much to the recognition of Neolithic enclosures in many parts of the British Isles in recent decades, but which has yet to make much impact in the Isle of Man. Surveys by Nick Higham and Barri Jones between 1980 and 1983 (Higham and Jones 1982; 1984) together with a single period of reconnaissance by Bob Bewley in July 1995 (Bewley 1999), serve to complement existing commercial and military coverage and illustrate the potential. No obviously Neolithic enclosures were recognized, but one site deserving of further attention as a possible candidate is The Broog north of Ronaldsway (Higham and Jones 1982, 9).

CONCLUSION

The discovery of the enclosures at the Billown Quarry Site opens up many new and exciting possibilities not only for work in the Isle of Man but also for the all the lands fringing the Irish Sea. The possibility that the Billown enclosures are early in date and draw heavily on cultural influences from the southern part of the western seaways suggests that some rethinking of the way the west of Britain is viewed in the Neolithic may be necessary. Rather than seeing these lands are the edge of Europe and somehow at the end of the line for the transference of ideas by land perhaps it is more appropriate to develop models based on rapid maritime interactions.

More practically, the recognition and definition of Neolithic sites in general, and enclosure sites in particular, in the west of Britain needs the development and adaption of available techniques of survey and excavation. At Billown, the best results in terms of prospection and the definition of landscape arrangements at different periods have come through extensive use of geophysics and geochemistry. With these results to hand, targeted excavation is all the more effective. Neolithic enclosures are large structures, however, and finding them requires the application of archaeological techniques on a large scale.

NOTES

1   Quarrying at Billown is believed to extend back to at least the 12th century AD when limestone as extracted to build the keep of the castle in Castletown.

2   Sadly, the placename does not provide any clues to the special character of this hill. The name "South Barrule" is interpreted by Gelling (1970, 131) as being a survival from the Norse language and meaning the southern "watch fell" meaning a place from which a lookout was kept.

3   Support for an early date can be found in evidence for an elm decline at 4250–3990 (5313±38 BP, UB-3555) in the Dhoo Valley, Glen Vine, in the central part of the Island (Innes 1995).

ACKNOWLEDGEMENTS

The surveys and excavations connected with the Billown Neolithic Landscape Project involve many individuals and organizations, all of whom are acknowledged in the relevant annual reports. In preparing this summary paper, special thanks to Miles Russell and Roger Doonan of Bournemouth University; Andrew Foxon and Andrew Johnson of Manx National Heritage; and Robert Farrar, Robert Middleton, Alan Skillan, and Alan Kelly who work so hard collecting together information about the distribution of Neolithic sites in the Isle of Man. An internet site about the Billown Neolithic Landscape Project can be viewed at:

http://csweb.bournemouth.ac.uk/consci/billown/index/htm

BIBLIOGRAPHY

Bersu, G, 1947, A cemetery of the Ronaldsway Culture at Ballateare, Jurby, Isle of Man. **Proceedings of the Prehistoric Society**, 13, 161–169

Bersu, G, 1974, Chapel Hill – A prehistoric, early Christian and Viking site at Balladoole, Kirk Arbory, Isle of Man. *Proceedings of the Isle of Man Natural History and Antiquarian Society*, 7.4 (1970–2), 632–65

Bersu, G, and Wilson, D, 1966, *Three Viking graves in the Isle of Man* (= Society of Medieval Archaeology Monograph 1). London. Society for Medieval Archaeology

Bewley, R, 1999, Aerial photography in the Isle of Man. In P J Davey (ed), *Recent archaeological research on the Isle of Man* (= British Archaeological Reports British Series 278). Oxford. Archaeopress. 315–320

Bowen, E G, 1970, Britain and the British Seas. In D Moore (ed), *The Irish Sea Province in archaeology and history*. Cardiff. Cambrian Archaeological Association. 13–28

Bruce, J R, Megaw, E M, and Megaw, B R S, 1947, A Neolithic site at Ronaldsway, Isle of Man. *Proceedings of the Prehistoric Society*, 13, 139–160

Burrow, S, 1997, *The Neolithic culture of the Isle of Man. A study of sites and pottery* (= British Archaeological Reports British Series 263). Oxford. Archaeopress

Burrow, S, and Darvill, T, 1997, AMS dating of the Ronaldsway Culture of the Isle of Man. *Antiquity*, 71, 412–19

Clark, G, 1935, The prehistory of the Isle of Man. *Proceedings of the Prehistoric Society*, 1, 70–92

Daniel, G E, 1950, *The prehistoric chamber tombs of England and Wales*. Cambridge. Cambridge University Press

Darvill, T, 1996a, *Billown Neolithic Landscape Project, Isle of Man, 1995* (= School of Conservation Sciences Research Report 1). Bournemouth and Douglas. Bournemouth University and Manx National Heritage

Darvill, T, 1996b, Billown, Isle of Man. *Current Archaeology*, 13.6 (Number 150), 232–37

Darvill, T, 1997, *Billown Neolithic Landscape Project, Isle of Man, 1996* (= School of Conservation Sciences Research Report 3). Bournemouth and Douglas. Bournemouth University and Manx National Heritage

Darvill, T, 1998, *Billown Neolithic Landscape Project, Isle of Man. Third report: 1997* (= School of Conservation Science, Research Report 4). Bournemouth and Douglas. Bournemouth University and Manx National Heritage

Darvill, T, 1999a, *Billown Neolithic Landscape Project, Isle of Man. Fourth report: 1998* (= School of Conservation Science, Research Report 5). Bournemouth and Douglas. Bournemouth University and Manx National Heritage

Darvill, T, 1999b, Billown Neolithic Landscape Project 1995–1997. In P J Davey (ed), *Recent archaeological research on the Isle of Man* (= British Archaeological Reports British Series 278). Oxford. Archaeopress. 13–26

Darvill, T, 2000, *Billown Neolithic Landscape Project, Isle of Man. Fifth report: 1999* (= School of Conservation Science, Research Report 7). Bournemouth and Douglas. Bournemouth University and Manx National Heritage

Darvill, T, forthcoming, Neolithic Mann in context. In A Ritchie (ed), *Neolithic Orkney in its European context*. Cambridge. McDonald Institute Monographs

Darvill, T, Cheetham, P, Hopper, M, Lannigan, K, Madden, C, Portet, S, Smith, S, and Stocks, A, 1999, Ronaldsway Airport: field evaluation. In T Darvill, *Billown Neolithic Landscape Project, Isle of Man. Fourth Report: 1998* (= School of Conservation Science, Research Report 5). Bournemouth and Douglas. Bournemouth University and Manx National Heritage. 40–53

Davies, M, 1946, The diffusion and distribution pattern of the megalithic monuments of the Irish Sea and North Channel coastlands. *Antiquaries Journal*, 26, 38–60

Dixon, P, 1988, The Neolithic settlements on Crickley Hill, Gloucestershire. In C Burgess, P Topping, C Mordant, and M Maddison (eds), *Enclosures and defences in the Neolithic of western Europe* (= British Archaeological Reports International Series 403). Oxford. British Archaeological Reports. 75–88

Evans, C, 1988a, Excavations at Haddenham, Cambridgeshire: a "planned" enclosure and its regional affinities. In C Burgess, P Topping, C Mordant, and M Maddison (eds), *Enclosures and defences in the Neolithic of western Europe* (= British Archaeological Reports International Series 403). Oxford. British Archaeological Reports. 127–148

Evans, C, 1988b, Acts of enclosure: a consideration of concentrically organised causewayed enclosures. In J C Barrett and I A Kinnes (eds), *The archaeology of context in the Neolithic and Bronze Age: recent trends*. Sheffield. Department of Archaeology and Prehistory, University of Sheffield. 85–97

Gelling, M, 1970, The place-names of the Isle of Man. *Journal of the Manx Museum*, 7 (Number 86), 130–39

Gibson, A, 1985, A Neolithic enclosure at Grendon, Northamptonshire. *Antiquity*, 49, 213–9

Henshall, A, 1978, Manx Megaliths again: An attempt at structural analysis. In P J Davey (ed), *Man and Environment in the Isle of Man* (= British Archaeological Reports British Series 54). Oxford. British Archaeological Reports. 171–176

Higham, N, and Jones, B, 1982, Manx archaeology from the air. *Popular Archaeology*, 3.9 (March 1982), 8–13

Higham, N, and Jones, B, 1984, From Ronaldsway to Ramsey. Air photography in the Isle of Man. *Popular Archaeology*, 5.8 (February 1984), 7–13

Horne, P D, MacLeod, D, and Oswald, A, 2001, A probable Neolithic causewayed enclosure in northern England. *Antiquity*, 75, 17–18

Innes, J B, 1995, *The Dhoo Valley, Isle of Man: a palaeo-environmental assessment* (= Centre for Manx Studies Research Report 2). Douglas. Centre for Manx Studies

Liddell, D M, 1935, Report on the excavations at Hembury Fort (1934 and 1935). *Proceedings of the Devon Archaeological Exploration Society*, 2.3, 135–75

Madden, C, 2000, Chapel Hill, Balladoole, Arbory. In T Darvill *Billown Neolithic Landscape Project, Isle of Man. Fifth Report: 1999* (= School of Conservation Science, Research Report 7). Bournemouth and Douglas. Bournemouth University and Manx National Heritage. 54–67

Manby, T, 1980, Bronze Age settlement in eastern Yorkshire. In J Barrett and R Bradley (eds), *Settlement and society in the British later Bronze Age* (= British Archaeological Reports British Series 83). Oxford. British Archaeological Reports. 307–370

Megaw, B R S, 1938, Manx megaliths and their ancestry. *Proceedings of the Isle of Man Natural History and Antiquarian Society*, 4.2, 219–39

Mercer, R J, 1980, *Hambledon Hill. A Neolithic landscape*. Edinburgh. Edinburgh University Press

Mercer, R J, 1981, Excavations at Carn Brea, Illogan, Cornwall, 1970–73. A Neolithic fortified complex of the third millennium bc. *Cornish Archaeology*, 20, 1–204

Mercer, R J, 1988, Hambledon Hill, Dorset, England. In C Burgess, P Topping, C Mordant, and M Maddison (eds), *Enclosures and defences in the Neolithic of western Europe* (= British Archaeological Reports International Series 403). Oxford. British Archaeological Reports. 89–106

Moffatt, P J, 1978, The Ronaldsway Culture: A review. In P J Davey (ed), *Man and environment in the Isle of Man* (= British Archaeological Reports British Series 54). Oxford. British Archaeological Reports. 177–215

Piggott, S, 1932, The Mull Hill Circle, Isle of Man, and its pottery. *Antiquaries Journal*, 12, 146–157

Piggott, S, 1954, *Neolithic cultures of the British Isles*. Cambridge. Cambridge University Press

Pryor, F, 1978, **Excavation at Fengate, Peterborough, England: the second report** (= Royal Ontario
  Museum Archaeology Monograph 5). Toronto. Royal Ontario Museum

Richards, J, 1990, **The Stonehenge Environs Project** (= Historic Buildings and Monuments
  Commission for England Archaeological Report 16). London. English Heritage

Russell, M, and Darvill, T, 1999, Excavations at the multi-ditched enclosure on Skibrick Hill. In T
  Darvill, **Billown Neolithic Landscape Project, Isle of Man. Fourth Report: 1998** (= School of
  Conservation Science, Research Report 5). Bournemouth and Douglas. Bournemouth
  University and Manx National Heritage. 30–39

Smith, I F, 1965, **Windmill Hill and Avebury. Excavations by Alexander Keiller 1925–1939**.
  Oxford. Clarendon Press

Soffe, G and Clare, T, 1988, New evidence of ritual monuments at Long Meg and Her Daughters,
  Cumbria. **Antiquity**, 62, 552–557

Woodman, P, 1978, A re-appraisal of the Manx Mesolithic. In P J Davey (ed), **Man and environment
  in the Isle of Man** (= British Archaeological Reports British Series 54). Oxford. British
  Archaeological Reports. 119–140

Chapter 13

Donegore Hill and other Irish Neolithic enclosures: a view from outside

Alison Sheridan

INTRODUCTION

The discovery and partial excavation of a large early Neolithic palisaded enclosure at Thornhill near Derry in the summer and autumn of 2000 is the latest addition to the growing, if bewilderingly diverse, population of Irish Neolithic enclosures. Like many others, it is known from just a small exposed area, but there is scope for eventual larger-scale exploration. Quantities of undecorated carinated bowl style pottery have been recovered from primary contexts (Logue pers. comm.; Anon. 2000), and so an early fourth millennium BC date appears likely, contemporary with – or perhaps even slightly predating – the palisaded enclosure at Knowth, Co. Meath (Eogan 1984) and the causewayed and palisaded enclosure at Donegore Hill, Co. Antrim (Mallory and Hartwell 1984; Mallory 1993).

This brief contribution attempts to present no more than a rapid survey of the evidence for enclosures in Neolithic Ireland, with particular emphasis on the period 4000–3500 BC, when Ireland's only "classic" causewayed enclosure at Donegore Hill was in use(*cf.* Cooney forthcoming). Others – notably Alex Gibson (1998a), Tom Condit and Derek Simpson (1998), Gabriel Cooney (2000), Jim Mallory (1993), and Barrie Hartwell (1998) – have already eloquently discussed groups of enclosures or specific sites, and no doubt the picture will continue to change as dramatic new discoveries emerge, and as undated enclosures are explored.

The locations of the sites mentioned in the text are given in Figure 13.1.

EARLY NEOLITHIC ENCLOSURES

Donegore Hill, County Antrim

This site was discovered through fieldwalking, excavation, and aerial survey led by Jim Mallory of the Queen's University of Belfast in the early 1980s (Mallory and Hartwell 1984; Mallory 1993). The final excavation report is due for publication in 2001. An area of 4ha on the top of Donegore Hill had been enclosed by two roughly concentric sets of interrupted, partly rock-cut ditches and palisades; the outer set measures 219m by 175m (Figure 13.2). The ditches do not appear to have been primarily defensive in nature: they are broad but shallow, around 3m wide and 1m deep, and do not consistently follow the

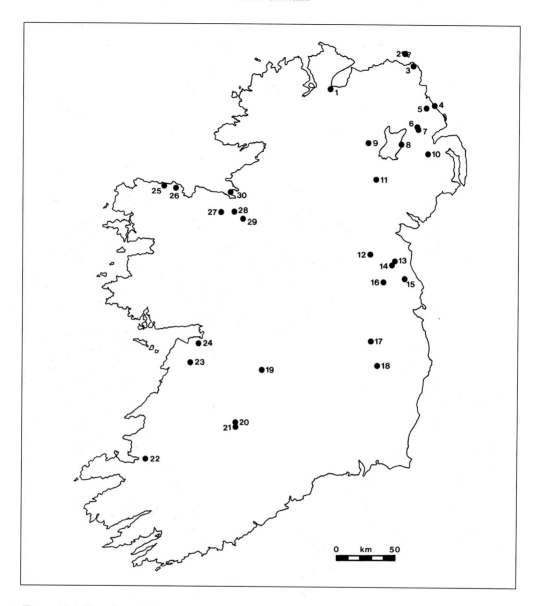

Figure 13.1: Locations of the sites mentioned in the text. Key: 1: Thornhill, Co. Derry; 2: "Shandragh", Rathlin Island; 3: Goodland; 4: Ballygalley; 5: Linford site 4; 6: Donegore Hill; 7: Lyles Hill; 8: Langford Lodge (2–8 all Co. Antrim); 9: Tullywiggan, Co. Tyrone; 10: Ballynahatty, Co. Down; 11: Scotch Street, Armagh, Co. Armagh; 12: Raffin, Co. Meath; 13: Townleyhall I, Co. Louth; 14: Boyne Valley (Newgrange, Knowth etc.); 15: Fourknocks; 16: Tara (14–16 all Co. Meath); 17: Dún Ailinne (Knockaulin Hill), Co. Kildare; 18: Baltinglass Hill, Co. Wicklow; 19: Ashleypark, Co. Tipperary; 20: Lough Gur, Co. Limerick; 21: Red Bog, Ballynagallagh, Co. Limerick; 22: Lee Valley, Co. Kerry; 23: Roughan Hill, Co. Clare; 24: Turlough Hill, Co. Clare; 25: Céide Fields, Co. Mayo; 26: Rathlackan, Co. Mayo; 27: Knocknashee; 28: Rathdooney Beg; 29: Keash; 30: Knocknarea (27–30 all Co. Sligo)

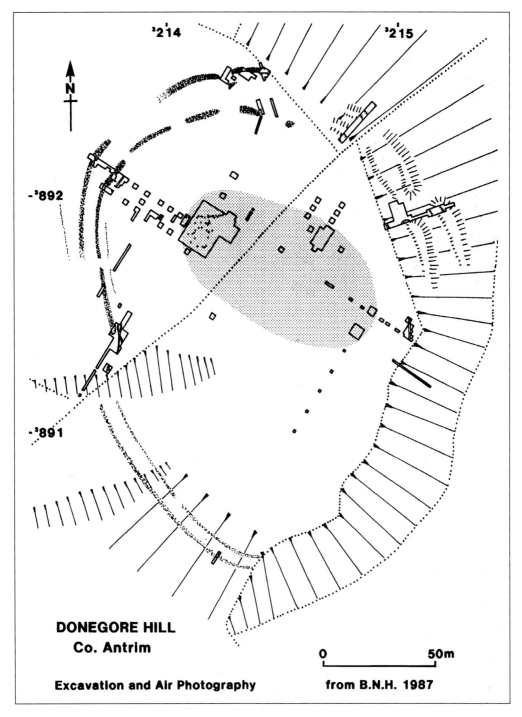

Figure 13.2: Donegore Hill causewayed enclosure. (Reproduced by courtesy of Professor J P Mallory)

contours of the hill. They would have sufficed to define an enclosed area and hinder ready access to the interior. Similarly, the palisades are more like fences than stockades, with an estimated maximum height of only 1.5m (Gibson 1998a). The dating evidence for the ditches and palisades, comprising eleven dates including a couple of problematic ones, will be discussed in detail in the final excavation report. It appears that both the inner and outer ditches could have been dug at roughly the same time, between 4000–3400 BC (quite possibly between 4000–3700 BC). The palisades may have a slightly more complex history. The outer one may slightly pre-date the ditches, and the inner one may have involved more than one period of palisade building, with the earliest phase coeval with the digging of the inner ditch.

The interior had been badly damaged by ploughing, and most of the substantial artefactual assemblage (mainly comprising some 49,000 sherds of pottery) was found in disturbed ploughsoil. Nevertheless, several hundred postholes, pits, hearths, and other features were found. Some of these clearly post-date the initial, early Neolithic use of the hilltop: for example, a pit containing two Grooved Ware pots has been dated to 2870–2470 BC (4085 ± 45 BP, GrN-15959; Brindley 1999), and a penannular post-built structure on the summit produced a late Bronze Age date of 800–410 BC (2518 ± 60 BP, UB-3069; Mallory pers. comm.). Many features, however, do relate to the causewayed enclosure and four have produced dates ranging from *c.* 3950–3600 BC; a fifth is dated to 3700–3100 BC (4705 ± 85 BP, UB-2664).

Artefactual finds comprise the aforementioned vast amount of pottery, representing 1500 vessels at the very least, together with a much smaller amount of flint (occurring both as finished artefacts and as debitage); stone axeheads including examples of porcellanite, imported from over 35km away; and serpentine beads, also imported but from an unknown distance. Organic material survives as fragments of burnt bone, and carbonized hazelnuts, barley grains, and seeds of several wild plant species. No definitely human bone was found, nor were there features which could convincingly be interpreted as being funerary in function. Indeed, the round cairn just across the valley of Six Mile Water, on the summit of Lyles Hill, offers the nearest, albeit contested, evidence for contemporary funerary practices (Evans 1953). This will be returned to below.

The pottery has been examined by Anna Brindley, who places it within the tradition of early Neolithic ceramics which is variously labelled "Western Neolithic", "carinated bowl", or even "Grimston-Lyles Hill ware". In 1985 and 1995 the present author argued that the Donegore and Lyles Hill plainware (*i.e.* carinated/shouldered bowls and uncarinated bowls and cups, some of it with rippled burnishing) represented a very early and minor deviation from the earliest, widespread version of carinated bowl pottery (as seen, for example, at Biggar Common, South Lanarkshire: Sheridan 1997). Anna Brindley, who has had access to far more of the Donegore pottery, disagrees and regards the Donegore and Lyles Hill material as falling within the "traditional carinated bowl" canon. Examination of the pre-publication Donegore drawings, kindly made available by Anna Brindley, confirms the present author's view that there **are** differences from "traditional carinated bowl", but that these are indeed minor, are those of degree, and their significance should not be over-stated. Some of the rims are slightly flatter, heavier, or more angular, and some of the carinations are slightly more angular and shoulder-like, for example, but the repertoire of vessel shapes is basically the same. During the early currency of this ceramic tradition, such variation is to be expected; an analogous example is Audrey Henshall's North-eastern Style of carinated bowl pottery in northeast Scotland, distinguished by the liberal use of ripple burnishing and fingertip fluting (Henshall 1984; *cf.* some of the Lyles Hill material). There is basic accord between Brindley's view and this author's view that the Donegore pottery is early Neolithic in date, and is part of (or stems from) a tradition which seems to have been established over large areas of Britain and Ireland around 4000–3800 BC (*cf.* Herne 1988). That it was probably not the earliest carinated bowl pottery to have been used in Ireland is perhaps given some support from the phytolith evidence, which indicates that the enclosure was established in an already partly-deforested landscape (Mallory 1993).

The question of how to interpret the evidence for activities at Donegore is as fraught as it is for any causewayed enclosure. The radiocarbon evidence could be read in various ways, but the marked homogeneity of the artefactual finds favours a short timescale for activities, with the construction and principal use of the enclosure spanning no more than 300–400 years, and probably substantially less time than this. The paucity of scrapers (132) and arrowheads (49 complete, broken or preform) has been interpreted by Mallory as indicating very short term or intermittent occupation. The contrasting abundance of pottery need not contradict this view: a smashing time may indeed have been enjoyed by all!

The construction of the ditches and palisades, and the moderate number of arrowheads, suggest that Donegore, unlike some other causewayed enclosures (*e.g.* Crickley Hill, Hambledon Hill), was neither heavily fortified nor subjected to attack. Indeed, neighbourly relations (if such they were) with people at Lyles Hill involved the sharing of a very similar material culture, down to their serpentine beads. And although not everyone accepts Aubrey Burl's contention (1984) that the hilltop cairn on Lyles Hill belongs to the early Neolithic tradition of communal cremation under non-megalithic round mounds as seen in parts of Britain (*cf.* Kinnes 1979 and *cf.* Knockiveagh, Co. Down: Collins 1957), this does remain a distinct possibility. If this was the case, then might the users of Donegore have cremated and monumentalized some of their dead at Lyles Hill – or at least looked across to that monument?

The comparability between the Donegore area and parts of early Neolithic Britain, in terms of ceramic tradition and possibly funerary tradition, has already been noted; other instances could be added. There is, of course, a more obvious point of similarity in the fact that Donegore exists as a causewayed enclosure, closely comparable to many from southern England. There is a paradox, however: while most of the ceramic and funerary comparanda are to be found in northern and eastern Britain, the distribution of British causewayed enclosures remains markedly southern in bias, notwithstanding a few northern candidates such as Leadketty in Perthshire (RCAHMS 1994, 40), as other contributors to this volume have pointed out. Furthermore, by and large the kind of pottery associated with these enclosures tends not to be carinated bowl (see, for example, the Mildenhall and later pottery from Etton, Cambridgeshire: Kinnes 1998). How significant is this, and how is it to be explained?

The answer to this is inextricably connected with the thorny question of how the Mesolithic-Neolithic transition occurred in Britain and Ireland. The view, which has been fashionable in some quarters, that the process was primarily one of gradual adoption of a new economy and new lifestyles by indigenous gatherer-hunter-fishers (*e.g.* Thomas 1991) is unconvincing – at least so far as northern Britain and Ireland are concerned. The alternative view, that some population movement (small-scale and multi-origin) was probably the agent for the rapid and widespread appearance of domesticates and novel lifestyles, is also problematic but is more plausible. Schulting's recent re-evaluation of the dating evidence for the Mesolithic-Neolithic transition in Scotland and southern England supports the idea of the rapid widespread appearance of a "Neolithic Package[s]" (Schulting 2000), while recent discoveries in northern France underline the similarities between non-megalithic funerary monuments there and in parts of Britain (*e.g.* Colombiers-sur-Seulles: Chancerel and Desloges 1988). Another French connection, this time along the Atlantic façade to Scotland, has recently been posited by the present author (Sheridan 2000). A convincing point of departure for users of carinated bowl pottery remains elusive, however, despite the attractiveness of the idea that these people represent small pioneering communities of emigrant farmers and their descendants – the "cowboy" scenario.

Returning to the Donegore causewayed enclosure paradox, it may be that there are many more causewayed enclosures awaiting discovery in areas of carinated bowl use in eastern and northern Britain. Alternatively, the idea of enclosure building may have been part of the cultural tradition of the users of carinated bowl pottery, as a way of creating and maintaining a community's identity, but may not have been practised – or not, at least, in the form of causewayed enclosures – throughout the areas where carinated bowl pottery was used.

That other kinds of enclosure existed during the first half of the fourth millennium BC in Ireland is discussed below.

Palisaded enclosures

There are two definite examples, from Thornhill, Co. Derry, and Knowth, Co. Meath, and two sites which have previously been claimed as Neolithic palisaded enclosures – Lyles Hill, Co. Antrim, and Tara, Co. Meath – but which have proved to be problematic.

Thornhill, Co. Derry: As excavations are still in progress, these remarks are necessarily provisional; I am grateful to the excavator, Paul Logue, for providing them. Exploratory excavation in advance of building work at Thornhill School, a few kilometres north of Derry City, has revealed the existence of a palisaded enclosure up to 100m across, with rectangular timber houses and outhouses within. Finds include a stone axehead imported from Great Langdale (Anon. 2000). The site is located on a low ridge on the banks of the River Foyle, around 36m OD. Two rows of palisades appear to be present, and there is evidence suggesting their destruction by burning. Several flint arrowheads have been found in the vicinity of the palisades, suggesting an attack. Quantities of traditional carinated bowl have been found in primary contexts, so there is every reason to suspect an early fourth millennium BC date. Whether the two palisades represent different periods of construction (*i.e.* enlargement or reduction in size of the enclosed area) remains to be determined.

Knowth, Co. Meath: Two roughly parallel arcs of palisade trench from what appears to be an early Neolithic enclosure (Figure 13.3) were discovered during Professor George Eogan's excavations in the 1960s and 1970s (Eogan 1984, 219; Eogan and Roche 1997, 44–5). The palisades consisted of close-set posts averaging 0.25m in diameter and with an

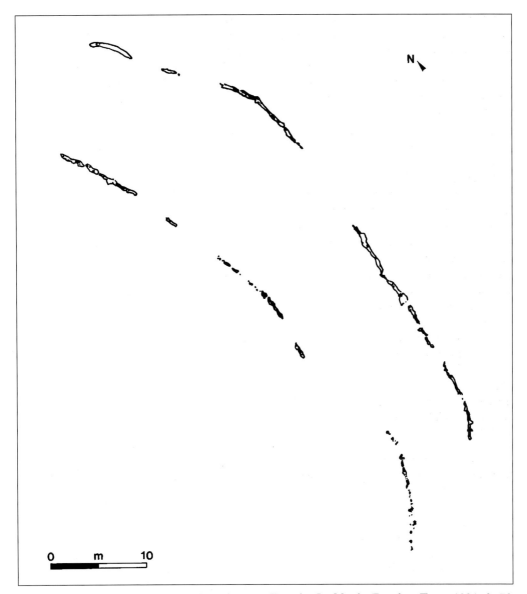

Figure 13.3: The palisade trenches of the enclosure at Knowth, Co. Meath. (Based on Eogan 1984, fig 78. Other features which may or may not be contemporary have been omitted)

estimated height of 1.5m; as with the Donegore palisades, Alex Gibson has described them as "fencing" (1998a, 73). A pebbled gap in the inner palisade arc appears to be an entrance, and the fact that the gap is not echoed in the outer arc may indicate that the two are not contemporaneous. The overall extent of the area assumed to be enclosed by the inner and outer palisades has been estimated at *c.* 70m and *c.* 100m respectively (Eogan and

Roche 1997, 44). The site is positioned at the western end of the ridge overlooking the Bend of the Boyne, close to the summit of a localized rise. It was not the earliest Neolithic structure in the area: it overlay a subrectangular house, which in turn post-dated other Neolithic houses and habitation debris. The pottery associated with the palisades (and the subrectangular house) could be described as modified carinated bowl, whose minor deviations from the traditional canon are similar to those noted for Donegore. There are no dates directly associated with the palisades, but charcoal from a pit inside the subrectangular house produced a date of 3790–3380 BC (4852±71 BP, BM-1076). Dates from a subsequent period of occupation and passage tomb building nearby have large standard deviations and are uninformative as *termini ante quos*, but a date for the palisaded structure between 3800–3500 BC seems plausible (*cf.* Grogan 1997).

Tara, Co. Meath: Geophysical survey within the Ráith na Ríg enclosure on the Hill of Tara during the 1990s revealed traces of what appeared to be a large enclosure, defined by two roughly concentric palisades, the outermost one extending 150m east to west by 180m north to south (Newman 1997, 75, 146–7, fig. 31). It was initially suspected that a short stretch of ditch found under the Duma nan nGiall (Mound of the Hostages) passage tomb during excavations in the late 1950s (de Valera 1961, 28) might be part of this, and so the site was considered as a possible early Neolithic double palisaded enclosure. However, more recent geophysical work, and new information on the sub-passage tomb ditch, has occasioned a re-evaluation of the evidence (Newman pers. comm.; Fenwick and Newman forthcoming). Firstly, the inner of the two palisades was found to mirror the ground-plan of the palisade which runs inside the Iron Age bank and ditch of Ráith na Ríg. An Iron Age date for this therefore seems likely. Secondly, it has emerged that the genuinely Neolithic sub-passage tomb ditch runs in the opposite direction from that of the putative outer palisade, and it appears to belong to a small enclosure of some kind. A radiocarbon date of 3100–2100 BC (4080±160 BP, D-42) was obtained from charcoal within this ditch. Finally, the putative outer palisade provided only a weak geophysical signal, and there is now no reason to suspect that it represents a Neolithic enclosure. The one definite Neolithic enclosure that was identified during the 1998–9 geophysical survey – a hengiform site of suspected late Neolithic date – will be discussed below.

Lyles Hill, Co. Antrim: Often discussed as evidence for a palisaded hilltop enclosure, the two parallel rows of palisade trenches excavated in 1988 by Derek Simpson and Alex Gibson (Figure 13.4; Simpson and Gibson 1989) are not without their interpretative problems. Having established that the embanked enclosure around Lyles Hill is of Bronze Age and Iron Age rather than Neolithic date, as the original excavator had assumed (Evans 1953), the team discovered the palisade trenches some 40m inside the bank in the southeastern area, not far from the summit cairn. Both had unweathered pottery of modified carinated bowl type within them, but the inner palisade produced a date of 3340–2910 BC (4433±40 BP, UB-3074) while the outer one was dated to 2620–2300 BC (3974±50 BP, UB-3062), both from charcoal. Furthermore, a nearby hearth associated with the same kind of pottery produced a date of 3950–3050 BC (4765±125 BP, UB-3063). This last date (large standard deviation notwithstanding) is the only one remotely comparable with Donegore dates for similar pottery. With such a small area exposed, these palisades pose more questions than answers. If they were genuinely part of a palisaded

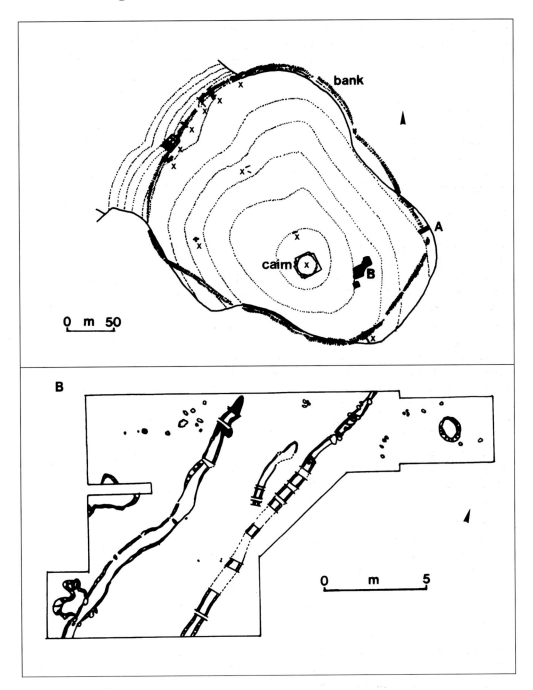

Figure 13.4: Lyles Hill, showing the Bronze Age and later banked enclosure, the cairn, the position of the 1936–7 trenches ("x") and the 1987–8 trenches ("A, B"). Inset: the palisade trenches and other features in part of B. (Reproduced courtesy of Derek Simpson)

enclosure, perhaps running parallel to the embanked enclosure, they clearly did not encompass the full extent of Neolithic activity on the hill. Significant numbers of Neolithic artefacts have been found outside the putatively enclosed area. During the conference that gave rise to this volume, one of the excavators (AG) suggested that the palisades may have been from a different kind of structure altogether. Once more, only further excavation is likely to advance our understanding.

Other kinds of enclosure
Several other kinds of enclosure are known from the first half of the fourth millennium BC. The walls which enclose individual farmsteads and which form part of a larger landscape division at Céide Fields, Co. Mayo (Caulfield 1988; Caulfield *et al.* 1998) may reflect concerns with land ownership at the level of the individual household. Although these households formed part of the broader community, and the extensive landscape divisions were the product of this community, nevertheless these enclosures are qualitatively different from the ones discussed previously. The Céide Fields system appears to have been established around 3700–3500 BC. The later Neolithic/early Bronze Age landscape divisions excavated by Carleton Jones at Roughan Hill, Co. Clare (Jones 1998) and those of probable Neolithic/Bronze Age date explored by Gretta Byrne (1994) at Rathlackan, Co. Mayo (both illustrated in Cooney 2000, fig. 2.7), are other examples of the same basic phenomenon.

Different again, but hard to interpret due to extensive later disturbance, is the roughly circular ditch enclosing an area of 20.5m by 23.5m on the summit of Knockaulin Hill, Co. Kildare (Wailes 1990; Johnston 1990). The presence of lithics including a leaf-shaped arrowhead within the ditch, and of modified carinated bowl pottery in the vicinity, suggest that it may be of early to middle Neolithic date; but its nature and function remain unclear.

At Rathdooney Beg, Co. Sligo, a broad, deep annular ditch surrounding a large, kerbed, presumably funerary mound, produced an intriguingly early date for initial ditch fill of 3940–3510 BC (4990±40, 4940±40 and 4840±50 BP, Beta-110614 and 109607–8; Mount 1998; 1999). The ditch is likely to have provided the material for the mound, which stands 6.1m high and 24.5m across, and is located on the summit of a drumlin. The mound is comparable in size – if not in construction – with some large passage tombs in the area, but the date from the ditch would seem to this author to be too early for a large passage tomb (*cf.* Sheridan 1986). Once more, further excavation is needed to clarify matters.

MIDDLE AND LATE NEOLITHIC ENCLOSURES
A similar diversity of enclosure types is evidenced for the period *c.* 3500–2500 BC.

Henges and hengiform sites, palisaded enclosures, and timber/pit circles
The evidence for henges and hengiform sites of demonstrably or presumably late Neolithic date has recently been reviewed by Tom Condit and Derek Simpson (1998), so will not be repeated here, except to comment that their survey revealed a wide range of candidates, over a large part of Ireland. Most, of course, remain undated. Some may well turn out to be post-Neolithic, and some show the elasticity of the term "hengiform"; but the study

usefully highlighted the fact that many of these were constructed in areas of pre-existing Neolithic activity, particularly of a funerary nature (*e.g.* in and around the Boyne Valley). The work of Michael Connolly and Tom Condit in the Lee Valley, Co. Kerry (Connolly and Condit 1998) amplifies the evidence for one such complex.

Barrie Hartwell's work at Ballynahatty, Co. Down (Hartwell 1998) has provided sound dating evidence (*c.* 3000–2500 BC) and Grooved Ware associations for part of another such complex (Figure 13.5). The oval, double-ringed enclosure of substantial timbers enclosing a smaller circular timber structure (Figure 13.6) lies within an area of ceremonial activity spanning most or all of the Neolithic period. The near-identity and contemporaneity between the smaller structure and that at Knowth, Co. Meath (Eogan and Roche 1999) need not be rehearsed here; nor is it necessary to dwell on the evidence for other Grooved Ware associated timber enclosures, at Fourknocks and Newgrange, Co. Meath (Brindley 1999; O'Kelly *et al.* 1993; Sweetman 1985; 1987; 1997; Eogan and Roche 1999, 104–5). Alex Gibson has already discussed British comparanda for later Neolithic palisaded enclosures and timber circles (Gibson 1998a; 1998b; 1999).

Finally, as indicated above, recent geophysical survey on the Hill of Tara has revealed clear evidence for a large, oval hengiform enclosure (Newman 1999; Fenwick and Newman forthcoming). It consists of a ditch surrounded by two rows of regularly spaced pits or postholes, and is 210m by 175m in extent. It is cut by (and therefore pre-dates) the Iron Age Ráith na Ríg enclosure, and it appears deliberately to encompass the Duma nan nGiall (Mound of the Hostages) passage tomb. Fuller details are about to be published by Joe Fenwick and Conor Newman.

Enclosures definitely or probably associated with settlement sites
The enclosures integrated within broader landscape divisions at Rathlackan and Roughan Hill have already been mentioned above. Other enclosures, featuring individual homesteads, can be identified at a few sites. At Townleyhall I, Co. Louth (Liversage 1960), a penannular bank with an external ditch *c.* 18m in maximum diameter surrounded a stakehole structure and pit associated with middle Neolithic-type pottery. An approximate date bracket of 3650–3350 BC has been estimated for such pottery (Sheridan 1995). This putative house seems to have been rebuilt several times, and then subsequently sealed with a low mound of clay. The cremated remains of two or three people – one associated with a bowl of the same type of pottery – were deposited at or after the time of sealing. Perhaps these were the former occupants, and this was an act of final closure.

On the slopes of Knocknarea, Co. Sligo, some of the 25 hut sites identified so far consist of small enclosed structures (Bergh 2000). Two have produced numerous Neolithic artefacts and dates of 3030–2580 BC (4250±75 BP, Lu-1947) and 3550–2650 BC (4440±140 BP, St-9030). One consists of an insubstantial, subrectangular post-built structure surrounded by a penannular bank and exterior ditch 13m across (Bengtsson and Bergh 1984).

Another penannular ditch which may originally have enclosed a house was found during rescue excavations at Scotch Street, Armagh (Lynn 1988). Interior structures may well have been obliterated by subsequent occupation. The V-shaped ditch was around 1m in both width and depth, and was 12m in internal diameter; it is thought to have silted up rapidly, over a period of a few years. Sherds of several plain and decorated Neolithic pots

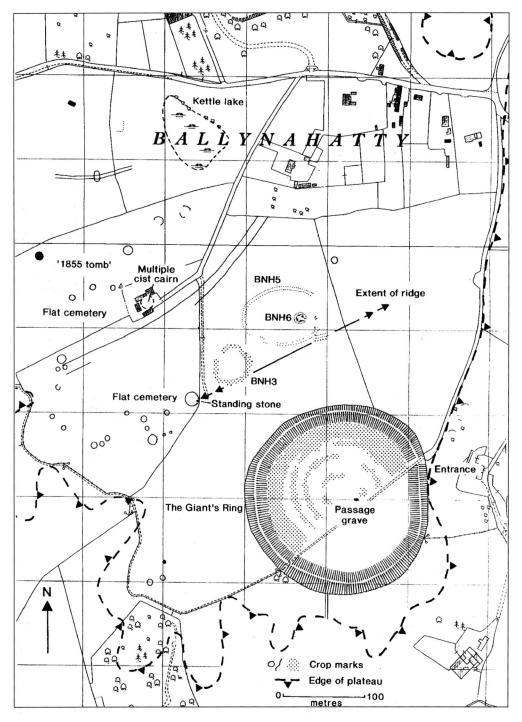

Figure 13.5: The Ballynahatty complex: overall plan. (Reproduced by courtesy of Barrie Hartwell)

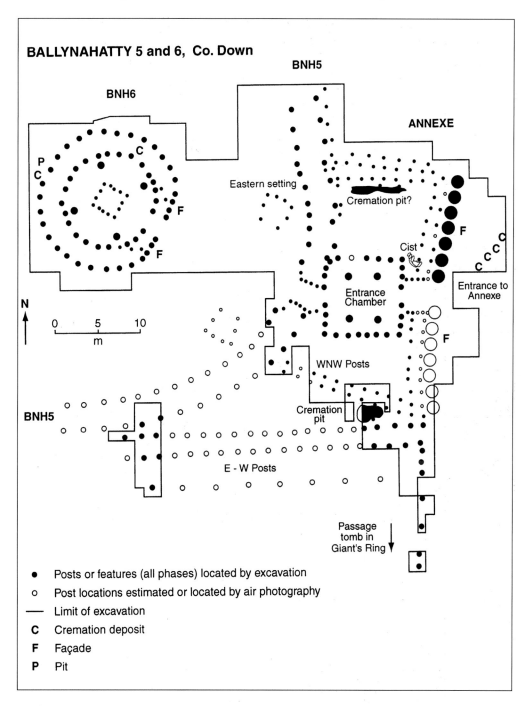

Figure 13.6: The Ballynahatty complex: detail of the entrance to the enclosure BNH5 in relation to timber circle BNH6. (Reproduced by courtesy of Barrie Hartwell)

were found in its fill (Sheridan 1985), along with flint items and animal teeth. Some sets of sherds from individual pots were associated with spreads of charcoal which may represent hearth sweepings; one such spread in the upper fill produced dates of 3100–2880 BC (4340±50 BP, UB-2379) and 2900–2300 BC (4090±105 BP, UB-2380).

Several penannular enclosures have been identified within a village-like cluster at Lough Gur, Co. Limerick (Grogan and Eogan 1987). Some 25–30m in external diameter, these wall-enclosed homesteads are believed to date to the later Neolithic or Beaker period, and they overlie earlier traces of unenclosed houses.

Ditched or embanked enclosures around funerary sites

A few passage tombs appear to have had ditches or banks encircling them. Although it is not always possible to demonstrate a Neolithic date for the latter, this was certainly the case with site K at Newgrange, Co. Meath (O'Kelly *et al.* 1978; Cooney 2000, 153–6). Here a tomb was initially surrounded by a penannular ditch, and was subsequently remodelled and enlarged. A ditch excavated around the top of the larger mound may recall the original version. On Knocknarea, Co. Sligo, a cruciform passage tomb is enclosed by an annular stone bank some 5m away from the cairn, and the massive Miosgán Meadhbha (Queen Maeve's Cairn) is enclosed by a clay bank, its form respecting low cairns which project from the main cairn (Bergh 1995, 236–40, 244, 246). Stefan Bergh has argued that these were part of the original design of the monuments, and if this is so, this is reminiscent of the ditch and stone wall surrounding the passage tomb at Maes Howe, Orkney (Renfrew 1979; Historic Scotland 1999, 16).

The passage tomb-related site at Fourknocks II, Co. Meath, includes a penannular ditch edging its mound, and here contemporaneity with the construction of a cremation trench and lintelled passage seems likely (Hartnett 1971; see Cooney 2000, 106, for a discussion of the complex construction sequence).

At Ashleypark, Co. Tipperary, double encircling banks and ditches added monumental emphasis to a Linkardstown-type cist (Manning 1985; Cooney 2000, 97–9).

Other enclosures

Raffin, Co. Meath: Part of a ditched, sub-rectangular hilltop enclosure was excavated between 1989 and 1993 (Newman 1995; 1997, 147). The V-sectioned ditch was 3m wide and 1.8m deep, and appeared to enclose an area *c.* 20m by 30m; no trace of a bank was found. No artefactual material other than debitage from pressure-flaking of flint was found in it, but charcoal from mid-way up the hill produced a date of 3330–2910 BC (4411±43 BP, UB-3681), thereby providing a *terminus ante quem* for its creation (Newman, pers. comm.). Post-dating this, but pre-dating a building dated to 810–560 BC (2565±22 BP, UB-3712), was a timber circle consisting of at least five concentric circles, grading down in height towards the centre; whether this was a Neolithic site remains to be seen.

Linford, Co. Antrim (site 4): A gully with a line of pits along its interior may be part of a late Neolithic subrectangular enclosure, in an area of pre-existing Neolithic activity (Doyle and Moore 1997; Moore and Williams forthcoming). The dimensions of the putative enclosure are at least 14m by 10m. A few sherds of plain and decorated pottery were found in the gully, and these are comparable with pottery from a nearby feature which has been dated to 3550–2900 BC (4545±77 BP, UB-3551).

Goodland, Co. Antrim: This slightly enigmatic site, located on a surface outcrop of flint, features an irregular, possibly subrectangular segmented "enclosure" ditch around 12m across; numerous pits; and a scatter of postholes and stakeholes (Case 1973). Structured deposition of sherds and other material appears to have occurred in pits and in depressions left by the removal of flint nodules. Several phases of middle Neolithic activity were involved, the whole dated rather unsatisfactorily by a *terminus ante quem* of 3400–2100 BC (4150±200 BP, D-46) and a date from a pit of 3650–2900 BC (4575±135 BP, UB-230E). Some of the pottery is closely comparable to that found at the roughly contemporary site at Linford (see above) and at "Shandragh" on Rathlin Island (see below). Humphrey Case (1973, 178) has interpreted the site thus:

> "... we have here a ritual site of those camping in the ridge or nearby over many seasons in the summer, and engaged in digging and gathering flint (and to some extent quartz) and breaking it up into suitable pieces to carry off to permanent settlements."

If this attractive interpretation is correct, then the ritual – *i.e.* the careful placing of sherds and other material – may indicate acts of respect for a source of an everyday necessity, flint.

Knocknarea, Co. Sligo: Recent survey work by Stefan Bergh has identified stretches of bank following the 260–250m contour line, and apparently forming part of a large enclosure encompassing the summit with its passage tomb cemetery (Bergh 2000; Bengtsson and Bergh 1984). In places the enclosure consists of multiple, segmented banks. Finds of numerous Neolithic artefacts immediately inside the banks and overlying them demonstrate that the banks are of Neolithic date, probably broadly contemporary with the aforementioned huts which lie within. Bergh has suggested that the enclosure was constructed to define a ritual space, and has cited Knocknashee and Keash in Co. Sligo, and Baltinglass Hill, Co. Wicklow, as likely parallels, all on hills crowned by passage tombs. Baltinglass Hill has, however, been discussed by John Waddell (1998) as a bivallate hillfort in an area of multivallate hillforts, of later prehistoric date.

POSSIBLE NEOLITHIC ENCLOSURES AND SOME RED HERRINGS

Various potential candidates have been proposed in addition to those already mentioned, but these are either undated, or too incomplete to be identified positively as enclosures. Undated sites include a large hilltop enclosure constructed with segmented stone walling at Turlough Hill, Co. Clare. It contains numerous hut circles and, whilst undated, it differs in design from the numerous later stone forts in the area (Cotter pers. comm.). Only excavation will shed light on its date.

Neolithic settlement sites where only short and uninformative stretches of ditch have been recovered include Langford Lodge, Co. Antrim (Waterman 1963); Ballygalley, Co. Antrim (Simpson *et al.* 1995), "Shandragh" (Knockans), Rathlin Island, Co. Antrim (Conway 1995), and Tullywiggan, Co. Tyrone (Bamford 1971).

Red herrings in this context include the inner of two banks and ditches enclosing Cathedral Hill, Downpatrick, Co. Down (Proudfoot 1954). Three sherds of carinated bowl pottery were found in the ditch, but these must have been residual, as a large quantity of flat-rimmed ware was also found in the ditch and under its associated bank. This pottery points to a late Bronze Age date for the enclosure and makes the site comparable with those such as Haughey's Fort, Co. Armagh (Mallory 1995). Also of Bronze Age date is a large (140m by 100m) oval banked enclosure with internal palisades at Red Bog, Ballynagallagh, Co. Limerick (Cleary 1997 and pers. comm.).

CONCLUSION

Despite the emergence of some patterning amidst the diversity of Neolithic enclosures, it is clear that many sites require further investigation and tighter dating before the picture becomes clearer. What is evident, and indeed unsurprising, is that various different traditions of enclosure existed, with variations in function as well as in construction and size. And while this paper has necessarily focused on enclosures, the way to understand them better is to consider all the evidence available for Neolithic landscape use together. If the next two decades provide as many surprises as the previous two, the future of Irish Neolithic studies is set to be lively.

ACKNOWLEDGEMENTS

The springboard for this paper was Professor Gabriel Cooney's contribution to the English Heritage/Prehistoric Society *Causewayed Enclosures in Europe* conference entitled "From Lilliput to Brobdignag: the traditions of enclosure in the Irish Neolithic", and his support is gratefully acknowledged. Opinions and any errors, however, are the author's. Thanks are also due to Paul Logue, Professor Jim Mallory, Anna Brindley, Conor Newman, Brian Williams, Dermot Moore, and Malachy Conway for sharing their unpublished information, to Charles Mount for advice on Rathdooney Beg, to Claire Cotter for information on Turlough Hill, to Gerry McCormac for dating advice, to Barrie Hartwell and Professor George Eogan for permission to reproduce their Ballynahatty and Knowth illustrations, and finally to Professor Derek Simpson for permission to reproduce the Lyles Hill illustration and for bringing the Thornhill site to my attention.

BIBLIOGRAPHY

Anon., 2000, Spectacular evidence for Neolithic at Derry development site. *Archaeology Ireland*, 14.3, 5

Bamford, H, 1971, Tullywiggan. *Excavations 1971*, 24–5

Bengtsson, H, and Bergh, S, 1984, The hut sites at Knocknarea North, Co. Sligo. In G Burenhult, *The archaeology of Carrowmore* (= Theses and Papers in North-European Archaeology 14). Stockholm. University of Stockholm. 216–318

Bergh, S, 1995, *Landscape of the monuments: a study of the passage tombs in the Cúil Irra Region, Co. Sligo, Ireland* (= Arkeologiska Undersökningar Skrifter 6). Stockholm. Riksantikvarieämbetet

Bergh, S, 2000, Transforming Knocknarea – the archaeology of a mountain. ***Archaeology Ireland***, 14.2, 14–18

Brindley, A, 1999, Irish Grooved Ware. In R Cleal and A MacSween (eds), ***Grooved Ware in Britain and Ireland*** (= Neolithic Studies Group Seminar Papers 3). Oxford. Oxbow Books. 23–35

Burl, H A W, 1984, Report on the excavation of a Neolithic mound at Boghead, Speymouth Forest, Fochabers, Moray, 1972 and 1974. ***Proceedings of the Society of Antiquaries of Scotland***, 114, 35–73, fiche 1: A2–C10

Byrne, G, 1994, Rathlackan. ***Excavations 1993***, 61–2

Case, H J, 1973, A ritual site in north-east Ireland, In G Daniel and P Kjaerum (eds), ***Megalithic graves and ritual***. Copenhagen. Jutland Archaeological Society. 173–96

Caulfield, S, 1988, ***Céide Fields and Belderrig Guide***. Killala. Morrigan Book Company

Caulfield, S, O'Donnell, R G, and Mitchell, P I, 1998, Radiocarbon dating of a Neolithic field system at Céide Fields, County Mayo, Ireland. ***Radiocarbon***, 40, 629–40

Chancerel, A, and Desloges, J, 1988, Les sépultures pré-mégalithiques de Basse Normandie. In J Guilaine (ed), ***Sépultures d'Occident et Genèse des Mégalithismes***. Paris. Editions Errance. 91–106

Cleary, R M, 1997, Red Bog, Ballynagallagh. ***Excavations 1996***, 66

Collins, A E P, 1957, Trial excavations in a round cairn on Knockiveagh, Co. Down. ***Ulster Journal of Archaeology***, 20, 8–28

Condit, T, and Simpson, D D A, 1998, Irish hengiform enclosures and related monuments: a review. In A Gibson and D Simpson (eds), ***Prehistoric ritual and religion. Essays in honour of Aubrey Burl***. Stroud. Sutton Publishing. 45–61

Connolly, M, and Condit, T, 1998, Ritual enclosures in the Lee Valley, Co. Kerry. ***Archaeology Ireland***, 12.4, 8–12

Conway, M, 1995, "Shandragh", Knockans South, Rathlin Island. ***Excavations 1994***, 6

Cooney, G, 2000, ***Landscapes of Neolithic Ireland***. London. Routledge

Cooney, G, forthcoming, From Lilliput to Brobdingnag: the traditions of enclosure in the Irish Neolithic. In ***Proceedings of the Causewayed Enclosures in Europe Conference***.

de Valera, R, 1961, Excavation of the Mound of the Hostages: supplementary note. In S P Ó Ríordáin, ***Tara: the monuments on the hill*** (1961 edition). Dundalk

Doyle, L, and Moore, D, 1997, ***Antrim coasts and glens: a preliminary assessment of the archaeology***. Belfast. The Queen's University of Belfast and Environment and Heritage Service DOENI

Eogan, G, 1984, ***Excavations at Knowth, 1***. Dublin. Royal Irish Academy

Eogan, G, and Roche, H, 1997, ***Excavations at Knowth, 2: settlement and ritual sites of the fourth and third millennia BC***. Dublin. Royal Irish Academy

Eogan, G, and Roche, H, 1999, Grooved Ware from Brugh na Bóinne and its wider context. In R Cleal and A MacSween (eds), ***Grooved Ware in Britain and Ireland*** (= Neolithic Studies Group Seminar Papers 3). Oxford. Oxbow Books. 98–111

Evans, E E, 1953, ***Lyles Hill: a late Neolithic site in County Antrim***. Belfast. HMSO

Fenwick, J, and Newman, C, forthcoming, Geomagnetic survey on the Hill of Tara, County Meath – 1998/99. In ***Discovery Programme Reports 6***. Dublin. Royal Irish Academy/Discovery Programme

Gibson, A, 1998a, Hindwell and the Neolithic palisaded sites of Britain and Ireland. In A Gibson and D D A Simpson (eds), ***Prehistoric ritual and religion. Essays in honour of Aubrey Burl***. Stroud. Sutton Publishing. 68–79

Gibson, A, 1998b, ***Stonehenge and timber circles***. Stroud. Tempus Publishing Limited

Gibson, A, 1999, Grooved Ware and timber circles. In R Cleal and A MacSween (eds), *Grooved Ware in Britain and Ireland* (= Neolithic Studies Group Seminar Papers 3). Oxford. Oxbow Books. 78–82

Grogan, E, 1997, From houses to henges – the prehistoric sequence at Brú na Bóinne. *Archaeology Ireland (Brú na Bóinne Special Supplement)*, 11.3, 30–1

Grogan, E, and Eogan, G, 1987, Lough Gur excavations by Seán P Ó'Ríordáin: further Neolithic and beaker habitations on Knockadoon. *Proceedings of the Royal Irish Academy*, 87C, 299–506

Hartnett, P J, 1971, The excavation of two tumuli at Fourknocks (sites II and III), Co. Meath. *Proceedings of the Royal Irish Academy*, 71C, 35–89

Hartwell, B, 1998, The Ballynahatty complex. In A Gibson and D Simpson (eds), *Prehistoric ritual and religion. Essays in honour of Aubrey Burl*. Stroud. Sutton Publishing. 32–44

Henshall, A S, 1984, The pottery. In H A W Burl, Report on the excavation of a Neolithic mound at Boghead, Speymouth Forest, Fochabers, Moray, 1972 and 1974. *Proceedings of the Society of Antiquaries of Scotland*, 114, 59–66

Herne, A, 1988, A time and a place for the Grimston Bowl. In J Barrett and I A Kinnes (eds), *The archaeology of context in the Neolithic and Bronze Age: recent trends*. Sheffield. Department of Archaeology and Prehistory, University of Sheffield. 9–29

Historic Scotland, 1999, *Nomination of the heart of Neolithic Orkney for inclusion in the World Heritage List*. Edinburgh. Historic Scotland

Johnston, S A, 1990, The Neolithic and Bronze Age activity at Dún Ailinne, Co. Kildare. *Emania*, 7, 26–31

Jones, C, 1998, The discovery and dating of the prehistoric landscape of Roughan Hill in Co. Clare. *Journal of Irish Archaeology*, 9, 27–44

Kinnes, I A, 1979, *Round barrows and ring-ditches in the British Neolithic* (= British Museum Occasional Paper 7). London. British Museum

Kinnes, I A, 1998, The pottery. In F Pryor, *Etton: excavations at a Neolithic causewayed enclosure near Maxey, Cambridge, 1982–7* (= English Heritage Archaeological Report 18). London. English Heritage. 161–214

Liversage, D, 1960, A Neolithic site at Townleyhall, Co. Louth. *Journal of the Royal Society of Antiquaries of Ireland*, 90, 49–60

Lynn, C J, 1988, Armagh in 3000 BC: 39–41 Scotch Street, Armagh. In A Hamlin and C J Lynn (eds), *Pieces of the past*. Belfast. HMSO. 8–10

Mallory, J P, 1993, A Neolithic ditched enclosure in Northern Ireland. In J Pavúk (ed), *Actes du XIIᵉ Congrès International des Sciences Préhistoriques et Protohistoriques*. Bratislava. UISPP. 415–8

Mallory, J P, 1995, Haughey's Fort and the Navan complex in the late Bronze Age. In J Waddell and E Shee Twohig (eds), *Ireland in the Bronze Age: Proceedings of the Dublin Conference, April 1995*. Dublin. The Stationery Office. 73–86

Mallory, J P, and Hartwell, B, 1984, Donegore. *Current Archaeology*, 8.9 (Number 92), 271–5

Manning, C, 1985, A Neolithic burial mound at Ashleypark, Co. Tipperary. *Proceedings of the Royal Irish Academy*, 85C, 61–100

Moore, D G, and Williams, B B, forthcoming, Excavations in Linford Townland, County Antrim, 1990–1991. *Ulster Journal of Archaeology*

Mount, C, 1998, Ritual, landscape and continuity in prehistoric County Sligo. *Archaeology Ireland*, 12.3, 18–21

Mount, C, 1999, Excavation and environmental analysis of a Neolithic mound and Iron Age barrow cemetery at Rathdooney Beg, County Sligo, Ireland. *Proceedings of the Prehistoric Society*, 65, 337–71

Newman, C, 1995, Raffin Fort, Co. Meath: Neolithic and bronze age activity. In E Gorgan and C Mount (eds), *Annus Archaeologiae. Proceedings of the OIA Winter Conference 1993*. Dublin. The Office of Public Works. 55–65

Newman, C, 1997, *Tara: an archaeological survey* (= Discovery Programme Monographs 2). Dublin. Royal Irish Academy/Discovery Programme

Newman, C, 1999, Astonishing new monument at Tara. *Past*, 33, 1

O'Kelly, M J, Cleary, R M, and Lehane, D, 1993, *Newgrange, Co. Meath, Ireland: the late Neolithic/Beaker period settlement* (= British Archaeological Reports International Series 190). Oxford. British Archaeological Reports

O'Kelly, M J, Lynch, F, and O'Kelly, C, 1978, Three passage graves at Newgrange, Co. Meath. *Proceedings of the Royal Irish Academy*, 78C, 249–352

Proudfoot, B, 1954, Excavations at Cathedral Hill, Downpatrick, Co. Down: preliminary report on excavations in 1953. *Ulster Journal of Archaeology*, 17, 97–102

RCAHMS, 1994, *South-East Perth: an archaeological landscape*. Edinburgh. Royal Commission on the Ancient and Historical Monuments of Scotland

Renfrew, A C, 1979, *Investigations in Orkney* (= Reports of the Research Committee of the Society of Antiquaries of London 38). London. Society of Antiquaries of London

Schulting, R, 2000, New AMS dates from the Lambourn long barrow and the question of the earliest Neolithic in southern England: repacking the Neolithic package? *Oxford Journal of Archaeology*, 19.1, 25–35

Sheridan, J A, 1985, *The role of exchange studies in "Social Archaeology", with special reference to the prehistory of Ireland from the fourth to the early second millennium b.c.* [Unpublished PhD dissertation. University of Cambridge]

Sheridan, J A, 1986, Megaliths and megalomania: an account, and interpretation, of the development of passage tombs in Ireland. *Journal of Irish Archaeology*, 3 (1985/6), 17–30

Sheridan, J A, 1995, Irish Neolithic pottery: the story in 1995. In I A Kinnes and G Varndell (eds), *'Unbaked Urns of Rudely Shape': essays on British and Irish pottery for Ian Longworth* (= Oxbow Monograph 55). Oxford. Oxbow Books. 3–21

Sheridan, J A, 1997, Pottery. In D A Johnston, Biggar Common, 1987–93: an early prehistoric funerary and domestic landscape in Clydesdale, South Lanarkshire. *Proceedings of the Society of Antiquaries of Scotland*, 127, 202–23

Sheridan, J A, 2000, Achnacreebeag and its French Connections: vive the 'Auld Alliance. In J C Henderson (ed), *The prehistory and early history of Atlantic Europe* (= British Archaeological Reports International Series 861). Oxford. Archaeopress. 1–15

Simpson, D D A, Conway, M, and Moore, D G, 1995, Ballygalley (Croft Manor). *Excavations 1994*, 2–4

Simpson, D D A, and Gibson, A, 1989, Lyles Hill. *Current Archaeology*, 10.7 (Number 114), 214–5

Sweetman, D, 1985, A late Neolithic/early Bronze Age pit circle at Newgrange, Co. Meath. *Proceedings of the Royal Irish Academy*, 85C, 195–221

Sweetman, D, 1987, Excavation of a late Neolithic/early Bronze Age site at Newgrange, Co. Meath. *Proceedings of the Royal Irish Academy*, 87C, 283–98

Sweetman, D, 1997, The Newgrange pit circle. *Archaeology Ireland (Brú na Bóinne Special Supplement)*, 11.3, 24–5

Thomas, J, 1991, *Rethinking the Neolithic*. Cambridge. Cambridge University Press

Waddell, J, 1998, *The prehistoric archaeology of Ireland*. Galway. Galway University Press

Wailes, B, 1990, Dún Ailinne: a summary excavation report. *Emania*, 7, 10–21

Waterman, D, 1963, A Neolithic and dark age site at Langford Lodge, Co. Antrim. *Ulster Journal of Archaeology,* 26, 43–54

Chapter 14

Danish causewayed enclosures – temporary monuments?

I J N Thorpe

INTRODUCTION

The history of causewayed enclosures in Denmark in a sense begins with Arne Pedersen, a farmer on the island of Fyn (Andersen 1997, 15). In 1967 he decided to grow carrots on a sandy promontory at Sarup, a few miles from the coast in the southwestern part of the island, and ploughed his fields slightly deeper than usual. Like most farmers in Denmark, he was fully aware of the importance of any archaeological discovery, and so he reported the dark patches with plentiful prehistoric artefacts, which the ploughing had revealed, to his local museum. Excavations determined that this was a rich middle Neolithic Funnel Beaker (TRB) site and a major project commenced. By 1972, the director of excavations, Niels Andersen, had realized that Sarup was a causewayed enclosure, like the recently discovered site at Büdelsdorf in Holstein (Hingst 1970), not far south of the border with Germany.

Since that time the number of causewayed enclosures in Denmark has risen dramatically, sometimes from new work, in other cases through reinterpretation of old excavations. Some two dozen examples are now known in Denmark (Andersen 1997, 135 and Appendix).

DISTRIBUTION

The distribution of Neolithic enclosures in Denmark is widespread, with examples from Jutland, Fyn, Als, Langeland, Zealand (see Figure 14.1) and Bornholm. The island of Bornholm in the Baltic and the Vasagård and Ringborgen enclosures (Nielsen 1996) are not dealt with further in this article – not only are they so remote from the remainder of Denmark, but also they appear to be slightly later in date than other Danish enclosures and are enclosed solely by palisades. All major areas of Denmark appear to contain enclosures, with the exception of western Jutland and the southern islands of Lolland and Falster.

Some enclosures occur in close proximity to one another. At Bjerggård and Toftum, Jutland, the enclosures are only 3.5km apart, and are inter-visible (Madsen 1988) – they may form a pair, although it is possible that the Toftum enclosure had been abandoned before that at Bjerggård was constructed. Most recently a possible companion to the Sarup

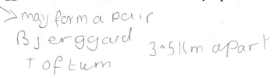

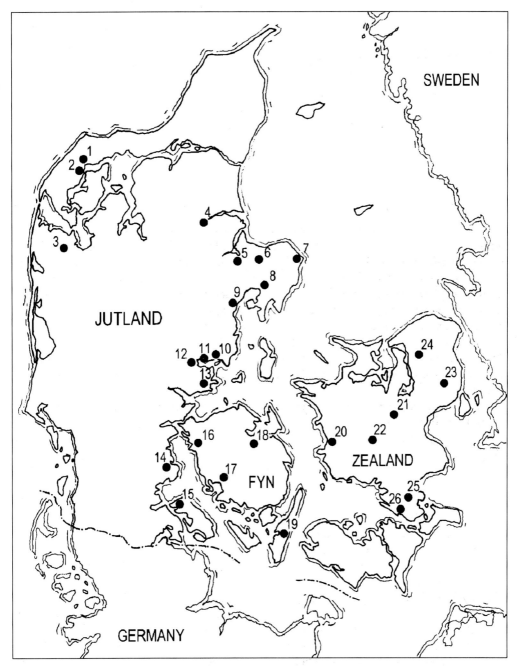

Figure 14.1: Distribution of recorded causewayed enclosures in Denmark. 1: Liselund; 2: Vilsund; 3. Mølbjerg; 4: Lokes Hede; 5: Store Brokhøj; 6: Kongsager; 7: Blakbjerg (Grenå); 8: Ballegård; 9: Voldbæk; 10: Toftum; 11: Bjerggård; 12: Årupgård [possible]; 13: As Vig; 14: Lønt; 15: Bundsø; 16: Hygind; 17: Sarup; 18: Åsum Enggård; 19: Troldebjerg; 20: Trelleborg; 21: Søndergårde [possible]; 22: Sigersted; 23: Knardrup Galgebakke; 24: Skævinge Boldbaner; 25: Markildegård (Bårse); 26: Ellerødgård [possible]

26 recorded causewayed
enclosers,

possible companion
enclosure.

enclosure has been discovered only some 500m away, consisting of a length of palisade similar to that uncovered at Sarup I.

Gaps in the distribution of enclosures may well be more apparent than real, as methods of discovery have tended to be reliant on chance; for example, reconnaissance along the line of motorways and pipelines, which of course have an uneven distribution themselves. Aerial photography has only become a significant factor in site discovery in the 1990s, but will certainly remain so for some time.

RECORDED SETTLEMENTS AND ENCLOSURES

The realization that causewayed enclosures existed in Denmark has prompted the re-evaluation of several already known sites, hitherto interpreted as major settlements. Thus Eriksen and Madsen (1984) suggested that the sites at Knardrup Galgebakke on Zealand and Troldebjerg on Langeland were better interpreted as causewayed enclosures. The three claimed houses at Knardrup (Larsen 1957) are fairly unconvincing, but Eriksen and Madsen's reinterpretation of the houses as ditches seems equally speculative at present; the site is located on a clear promontory, as are many Danish causewayed enclosures (see below), but it is surely premature to assume that any major site in such a topographic situation must be an enclosure. There is certainly no *a priori* reason why major unenclosed sites could not have existed too.

At Troldebjerg some 25 houses were argued by the excavator to exist within an area 250m by 100 m (Winther 1935, 6–13). The two features of the site which aroused Eriksen and Madsen's suspicions were its location on a ridge between two areas of boggy land and the main longhouse discovered by Winther. This was apparently a strange composite construction with a continuous bedding trench 71m long forming one side and arcs of postholes the other. Re-excavation of the site resulted in Winther's bedding trench being reinterpreted as a palisade with a row of posts outside (Eriksen and Madsen 1984; Madsen 1988). Inside the area enclosed by this palisade would then be a settlement of middle Neolithic date with a series of small huts and a rich cultural layer which runs up to the claimed palisade. The relationship between the palisade and the cultural layer has been disputed (Midgley 1992, 326–7), but the most plausible reconstruction (Madsen 1988) is that the settlement material built up at a time when the palisade and post-setting were standing, either still in use or starting to decay (Thorpe 1996, 125). While there are questions concerning their alternative interpretations, the overall thrust of Eriksen and Madsen's reconsideration of the evidence is entirely reasonable: at the time the sites concerned were excavated there was a strong expectation that the normal house form in the TRB would be the longhouse, while the alternative interpretation of sites as enclosures was not yet possible.

Other sites such as Trelleborg on Zealand (Andersen 1982) have been reinterpreted on the basis of the existence of Neolithic ditch segments, uncovered here during the excavation of the famous Viking fortress and confirmed by subsequent reinvestigation. Many other sites may fall into this category, such as As Vig in Jutland (Davidsen 1978), where elongated pits, one surrounded by posts (thus resembling Sarup – see below), produced middle Neolithic finds (Andersen 1997, 270).

LOCATION, LAY-OUT, AND CONSTRUCTION

There are common features to the location and lay-out of the Danish enclosures (Madsen 1988; Midgley 1992, 341–43). The vast majority are on promontories surrounded by wetland or open water, although some sites not naturally circumscribed are now coming to light. Even here, as at Bjerggård (Madsen 1988), the enclosures are situated on the tops of hills, so still isolated to some extent.

The lay-out of enclosures is known only in a minority of cases, primarily the result of small-scale excavations and the lack of geophysical and aerial photographic survey in Denmark (see Figure 14.2). In particular, this may lead to an underestimate of the number of ditch circuits and a concentration on the inner area of enclosures. Where known, the ditch lay-out is mostly a single circuit, or sometimes double lines, with the ditches separated by causeways. The Danish enclosures therefore seem to consist of relatively shallow spaces compared to those in Britain (Evans 1988) or Büdelsdorf in Holstein (Hingst 1970), with five circuits of ditches.

This relatively open barrier either cuts off a promontory or forms a boundary around the whole site. In general, the lay-out of the sites is fairly simple, with the notable exception of Sarup (Andersen 1997, 27–63). Here, in the Fuchsberg phase promontory enclosure (Sarup I) of 8.5ha, there were two lines of ditches, with individual ditch segments fenced off, fencelines and a palisade (2–3m high) forming further barriers inside the ditches and a series of small enclosures tacked on to the outside of the palisade. There was a single narrow entrance into the enclosure (other entrances only gave access to fenced areas), reached by a fenced corridor nearly 30m long, and screened by another fence so that outsiders could not see easily into the enclosure (Figure 14.3). Sarup therefore appears to be quite untypical of Danish enclosures as a whole, in that entry to the enclosure could have been quite tightly controlled. Aerial photographic evidence and excavations at Toftum and Bjerggård suggest that elsewhere access to the interior of enclosures was relatively free, as in Britain.

Enclosure size is highly variable (Andersen 1997, 271): it ranges from 12ha to 20ha at Lokes Hede in Jutland (Birkedahl 1994), with other sites in the same range such as Årupgård and Lønt (Madsen 1988) also in Jutland, down to Bjerggård (Madsen 1988) at 1.6ha (negative excavation results make the discovery here of outer ditches highly unlikely), with several other sites enclosing less than 5ha. As before, the incomplete mapping of many enclosures means that more subtle patterns of variation in size on a geographical or chronological basis cannot be discerned.

Despite this, it is possible to produce estimates of the effort involved in the creation of enclosures in some cases. These are considerable. Thus an analysis of Sarup I ditch-digging, tree-felling, and palisade construction led to the conclusion that some 100,000 work hours would have been expended on building the enclosure (Andersen 1988b). Those for larger enclosures with complete ditch circuits could be even higher.

DEPOSITION AND OTHER ACTIVITIES

The question of the activities carried out at causewayed enclosures can best be approached through Sarup, as it is by far the most intensively explored of the enclosures, having seen

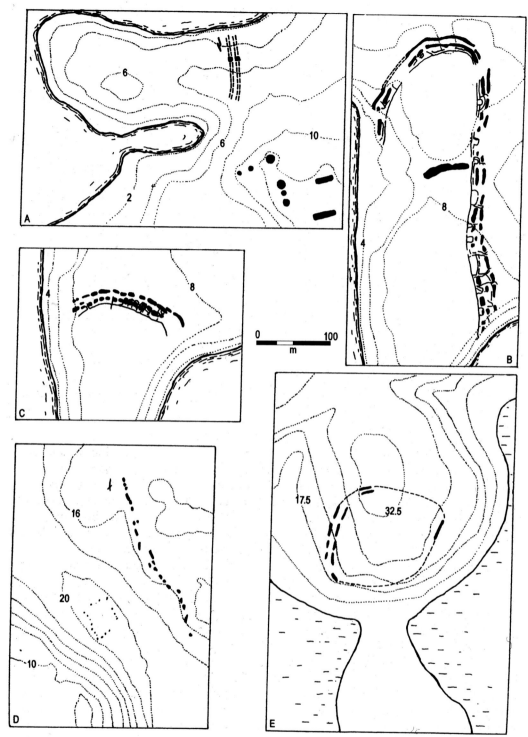

Figure 14.2: Plans of causewayed enclosures in Denmark. Contours in metres. A: Lønt; B: Sarup I; C: Sarup II; D: Markildegård; E: Toftum

Figure 14.3: Reconstruction view of the screened entrance to Sarup I. (Drawing by Phil Marter, based on Andersen 1988c)

almost total excavation. By far the most clear-cut activity is the deposition of material, singly and in groups – deliberately placed deposits are a clear feature of both enclosures, although they are far more numerous in Sarup I (Andersen 1997, 27–63). At the base of ditches Fuchsberg pottery, including two complete funnel beakers, flintwork, human adult (probably male) and child jaws and skulls, and occasional animal bones (little bone survived in the acid soil) had been placed. In four ditch segments stone settings near the ditch base were revealed, with pottery, animal bones, and charcoal in and below the stones and layers of charcoal and burnt soil, suggesting that the charcoal was sometimes still smouldering when it was buried in the ditch. The volume of finds higher-up in the ditch was far greater, but included less of the obviously "special" deposits. However, even the more mundane potsherds and flintwork from the ditch fill are interpreted as deliberate deposits rather than settlement debris, as small sherds and flint waste from tool manufacture were largely absent (Andersen 1988b).

Some evidence has been published relating to differences between ditch segments, seen to be highly important for British enclosures (Thorpe 1996, 176). The numbers of finds from different ditch segments ranges from three objects per cubic metre to 320 per cubic metre, but it is not clear how far there was variation in the nature of finds in individual ditch segments. However, the flint tools were examined for microwear traces, which showed that they had mainly been used to work wood, but also hide and bone, and that tools used to work different materials tended to be found in different ditch segments. It seems clear from stratigraphic observations that individual ditch segments had quite different histories: while some appeared to have been left after backfilling, others were recut on several occasions. What the relationship may be between recutting and deposition is not established, but the possibility certainly exists that different ditches or groups of ditches were maintained by particular family or clan groups (Thorpe 1996, 172; Andersen 1997, 324).

On a broader scale, there is a clear difference between the northern and southern areas of the ditch circuits, with nine times more material recovered from the base of the northern than the southern ditches (Andersen 1997, 54). The proportions of find material and type are also different, with roughly equal amounts of pottery and flintwork in the northern area, but almost no flint (and only a single tool) from the southern. This may be related to the later history of these ditch segments, as the northern ones were more heavily reworked.

The palisade trench contained considerable amounts of pottery, far more than in lower parts of the ditches or in the interior of the enclosure; it appears that complete vessels were placed along the palisade at some parts; some areas also have concentrations of burnt flint and bones, but flintwork is generally rare. Neither the ditches nor the palisade are believed to have been in use for long (Andersen 1988a), the ditches for a single year before they were deliberately backfilled and the palisade also for as little as a single year, but in any case rotting within a generation and not being replaced. Even in the case of recut ditch segments activity is thought to have ended within a few years of their original cutting.

Inside the enclosure were nearly 100 features, most of them small postholes and pits, but about a dozen are larger and are interpreted as offering pits (Andersen 1997, 56). Nine of these contain complete vessels; one large vessel contained two smaller pots and a large quantity of carbonized emmer wheat with a tiny amount of barley and no weed seeds (Jørgensen 1976), perhaps itself offered as a sacrifice, with the burning rendering it unusable (Jensen 1994, 100). Nearby was another pit containing burnt wheat grains, together with sherds from one of the same pots as in the other pit. Two pits held axes, one of flint, the other a small greenstone axe perforated to make it an amulet. Other pits produced flint tools but only a little flint waste, for example, one contained ten scrapers used for scraping wood and only seven pieces of waste. From the purity of the flint and plant assemblages Andersen (1988b) has concluded that the flint was brought into the site and only selected grain was buried. The ratio of flint tools to waste is very high compared with the contemporary Skaghorn settlement, while emmer wheat is found almost exclusively at Sarup I compared with equal amounts of emmer and barley at Skaghorn. Andersen also argues that the pits may have been for burial, possibly of children – alternatively, they could have held human bodies temporarily before deposition in the ditch or removal elsewhere, as suggested for Hambledon Hill (Thorpe 1984).

The smaller Sarup II enclosure (Andersen 1997, 63–87), cut off some 3.5ha of the promontory, partly overlapping with the Sarup I enclosure. It was constructed in the Klintebakke or middle Neolithic AIa phase, so within only a short time of the abandonment of Sarup I. It comprises a double line of ditch segments with a palisade behind. This palisade was a fairly insubstantial barrier of stakes probably no more than a metre high. Two narrow entrances allowed access through the stake line to the interior, but did not allow a clear line of sight from the outside. Several of the segments of the inner ditch themselves lay within fenced enclosures (fencing also surrounded a tree on this line), which if completed by wattlework would mean that only by peering over the fence (again probably only a metre high) could the contents of the ditch segment be seen. Overall Sarup II is a far smaller undertaking than Sarup I, estimated at some 18,000 work hours compared with *c*. 100,000 for its predecessor.

The ditches of this enclosure were also far less productive than those of Sarup I, with only some 130 finds in the primary layers. Although there were no layers of stone or charcoal at the base of these ditch segments, there were some special finds, such as the conjoining sherds from a single bowl found in three ditch segments and four pits inside the enclosure, a burnt flint axe and the skull of a domestic pig surrounded by stones. Despite this, many of the ditch segments were recut several times, so they still had a continuing importance. The Sarup II palisade was equally devoid of finds, with only two small sherds recovered from the stakeholes.

There were, however, more pits in the interior of Sarup II in less than half the area. Of the 144 pits, slightly less than half were interpreted as postholes, several as being for storage and some 25 as ritual offering pits (double the number in Sarup I). Most contained pottery, primarily funnel-necked vessels, but there were also two complete flint axes in one pit and a fine battle-axe of banded sandstone in another. A four-post setting set inside a ring-ditch at the southern end of the enclosure produced burnt adult human bones (possibly from the same individual) from the fill of two postholes. Another activity represented on the site seems to have been potting, as one pit contained both unworked clay and sausages of rolled clay ready for use. There was, however, remarkably little grain from this phase of activity, indeed less burnt grains than apple pips were recovered. It certainly seems to be the case that in Sarup II the interior was of greater significance than the ditches. This may relate to the continuing visibility of the ditches of Sarup I, which would themselves have marked the area within which Sarup II was constructed as a special space.

Other sites have produced similar evidence of placed deposits of various kinds (Andersen 1993; 1997). The bases of ditches at many sites contained deliberate deposits, including whole pots at Bjerggård, Lønt, Liselund in Jutland, Markildegård on Zealand (placed on birch bark mats), Store Brokhøj in Jutland and Toftum; a pile of flint tools at Bjerggård, heaps of animal bone, sometimes with human skulls, as at Bundsø on Als, Hygind on Fyn and at Bjerggård; other parts of human bodies at Ballegård in Jutland, at Hygind, at Troldebjerg and at Åsum Enggård on Fyn. Traces of fire were noted in the ditches at Bjerggård and Toftum. Another activity undertaken in enclosure ditches appears to have been pottery manufacture. At Store Brokhøj (Madsen and Fiedel 1987) one of the ditch segments contained parts of Fuchsberg style pots and nearly complete vessels, heavily burnt clay daub with wattle impressions, a group of large rounded stones, and a massive charred tree trunk. The stones and the tree trunk made up a construction which ran below the area of pottery and daub, and is interpreted as a pottery kiln; nearby ditch segments contained large amounts of pottery and daub which are believed to be the remnants of unsuccessful firings. The significance of this activity being carried out at an enclosure is difficult to gauge, as so little of the enclosure has been excavated. Similar activities were, however, carried out at Sarup, although at a rather later date (see above).

Relatively few sites have seen the exploration of large areas of the interior of the enclosure, but some have produced offering pits as at Sarup (Madsen 1988). At the large

Lønt enclosure, many pits have been found, some including complete vessels; at Årupgard, also in Jutland, pits have produced complete pots and a well-known hoard of eight copper ornaments and 271 amber beads found in a pot placed in a pit inside this probable enclosure (Sylvest and Sylvest 1960). The Liselund enclosure has so far produced pits containing deposits of axes and grain (Westphal 1996). Similar deposits appear to have taken place at Lokes Hede and at Sigersted on Zealand. There are also apparently deliberate deposits related to buildings at enclosure sites, as at Troldebjerg, where thin-butted axes and small funnel beakers were buried in foundation trenches and in pits inside structures (Skaarup 1990).

At Toftum (Madsen 1977) the site was constructed and abandoned within the Fuchsberg pottery phase, but the ditches show a series of activities involving natural and deliberate infilling, recutting and final backfilling. Some backfilling (which mainly took place in the inner ditch) included the deposition of complete vessels, but other areas of the ditches were backfilled with cultural debris including heaps of shells, flintwork and potsherds. Toftum is the only definite enclosure with a faunal assemblage worth discussing – dominated by pigs with smaller numbers of cattle, deer and sheep. Madsen has argued that the sheer volume of this material must imply the presence on the site of a settlement, with an economy based on pig breeding, but an alternative would be to interpret it as a mass of feasting debris. The pig remains may relate to ceremonial meals (for which pig are eminently suitable, as they can be killed off and bred back up to former numbers again much more quickly than cattle). If Troldebjerg is accepted as an enclosure then a rather different picture emerges from the much larger assemblage excavated there (Nyegaard in Skaarup 1985), with pig slightly out-numbering cattle and smaller numbers of sheep/goat. However, at Troldebjerg we have to bear in mind the possibility that some of this material relates to a settlement post-dating (even if only slightly) the palisade enclosure. The Skaghorn settlement site near Sarup (contemporary with Sarup I) has a different faunal assemblage again, with mostly cattle and a few pigs (Andersen 1997, 93)

Unlike Britain, Danish causewayed enclosures were constructed during a relatively short period from c. 3400 to 3150 BC. Moreover, in a number of cases, including Sarup and Toftum, activity at the sites occurred over an even shorter time span, with intensive bursts of construction followed by the deposition of considerable amounts of material ranging from human bones to battle-axes, perhaps within a generation.

This clearly suggests that causewayed enclosures in Denmark can be seen as temporary monuments, at least in their initial phase of enclosure and deposition. The effort expended was therefore even more impressive given the short duration of maintenance of the resulting enclosures. Unlike some "temporary" monumental sites in Britain, Danish enclosures were not constantly being extended, but were reworked for a short time before their character underwent a significant transformation.

GENERAL MODELS OF THE MIDDLE NEOLITHIC

A model of the development of these major enclosures has been put forward by Madsen (1988). He argues that around 3500 BC there was increased forest clearance, denoting a growing population, and greater rivalry between communities who occupied large territories with a system of shifting agriculture. This was coped with by an increasing ritualization of society, providing a peaceful framework for both competition and cooperation within and between groups, ensuring social stability. Two aspects of ritual were particularly important: the rituals of the dead, and the shared investment of labour in building enclosures. The idea of enclosures already existed in other Neolithic communities outside Denmark, and was drawn upon at this crucial time. The enclosures were not neutral, shared by all-comers, but belonged to specific groups, who brought in members of other communities to participate in the construction and subsequent rituals — the success of the enclosure thus reflected the importance and strength of the group itself. However, the continued growth in settlements led to greater permanency in occupation sites, which then rendered the enclosures unnecessary to resolve tensions, and the over-investment in ritual and ceremonial was abandoned with relief.

The initial observations of increased forest clearance (Iversen's *Landnam*) on which Madsen's case was founded are soundly based, and have been confirmed by later pollen analysis. Ard marks also first occur at the end of the early Neolithic (Thrane 1989). These developments could in turn lead to an increase in the perceived value of land (Andersen 1997, 312–313). It is also the case that settlements appear to grow in size during this period (a few large settlements do occur earlier – Thorpe 1996, 128), although as Madsen himself notes, the intensity of activity does not increase, to judge by the relatively small number of artefacts present on such sites. An exception may be Langeland, where Skaarup (1985) argues that actual villages were established at the beginning of the middle Neolithic. This accumulating evidence is, however, hard to contain within a model of shifting settlement (except on a very local scale), while doubts have been expressed concerning its applicability for the early Neolithic as a whole (Thorpe 1996, 119–120).

It is also difficult to see what social mechanisms ensured that enclosures arose to fulfil a specific social function, then disappeared once that need was met elsewhere. The enclosures certainly did appear at a specific moment, and their importance was undoubtedly in part due to their monumental character compared with the low-key settlement remains. However, at Sarup and Toftum the picture is of highly ephemeral sites, undergoing extremely rapid change, and therefore unlike the fixed burial mounds constructed in vast numbers at this time. They seem to represent sites of conspicuous consumption, which rapidly exhausted a particular location. Rather than achieving harmony through labouring towards a common goal, it may instead have been the display of effort and the destruction of specially chosen items in sight of representatives from other rival communities which was the main motivation. Tensions between communities could well have been exacerbated by enclosure building, rather than resolving them.

This alternative view is supported by the discovery at Hygind of a skull with slash marks from the enclosure ditch, although this may not have been the direct result of conflict, but rather a sacrifice. In Gammellung Mose adjacent to the Troldebjerg enclosure on Langeland four skull fragments (from two women and two children) and some thigh bones were discovered (at least five individuals being represented altogether), one of the women having been killed by a blow to the head. Also in the bog were bones from domesticated cattle (two of these slaughtered by blows to the head) and pigs, a goat, and a dog, pottery and amber beads (Skaarup 1985, 71–72). This appears to be a typical sacrificial bog offering.

Other bog offerings seem to be less closely connected to enclosures. Koch argues (1998, 139–143) that with the exception of Troldebjerg, and a few possible enclosure sites, bog offerings are primarily associated with small specialized hunting and fishing sites on islets and headlands. Hunting, however, becomes a more ceremonial activity through time, as Koch herself notes (1998, 148). What these sites share with many causewayed enclosures is a liminal location, with most enclosures situated close to wetlands and in many cases surrounded by them.

A broader relationship is clear from Koch's analysis of the pottery offerings from the eastern Danish islands (1998, 149) – they are most common from the end of the early Neolithic and the beginning of the middle Neolithic. Moreover, she also argues that the period of the enclosures sees the production of separate functional and ritual funnel beakers, with some of the ritual type occurring at Sarup II (1998, 99–113). The time of the enclosures also corresponds with Klassen's (1997) Import Phase 3 for metalwork, in which imported axes were destroyed or embellished, while some were never intended to be functional as they could not be mounted on a shaft.

In the case of Sarup, where intensive survey work has been carried out (Andersen 1997, 89–100), this suggests that there were far more funerary monuments around the enclosures than settlements, perhaps five times as many, with no settlements apparent in the immediate vicinity of the enclosures. The recent discovery of a possible palisade enclosure near the known enclosures strengthens this tie, as it is in a dense area of megaliths (Nielsen 1997). The proximity of megalithic graves to Sarup, together with the presence of human bones on the site, has naturally encouraged theories that enclosures were places of temporary burial and the deliberate deposits parts of funerary rituals, during which deceased individuals entered the world of the dead and became suitable for interment with the ancestors in megalithic tombs. However, this may be just one part of a whole series of negotiations between the living, the dead, ancestors and the other worlds of human and animal spirits – all taking place in a special sacred place set aside from the profane world. In this light, animal bones at enclosures may derive from rituals which paralleled those undertaken for human remains. Similarly, the Toftum and Lønt enclosures have clusters of megalithic tombs near to them, which could increase dramatically if similar large programmes of intensive survey were carried out there. The crucial point, however, is that we can not separate enclosures as a field of study from their contemporary landscapes, for although they may have been arenas of social action set apart from the rest of the world the actors who temporarily entered them came from and returned to that other world.

THE AFTERLIFE OF ENCLOSURES

A number of enclosures had a final phase of activity after the earthworks had decayed, during which the area came to be occupied by a substantial open settlement. Troldebjerg (Winther 1935; 1938), covering some 2.5ha, with 50,000 middle Neolithic sherds and 24,000 animal bones and some 25 houses, seems to fit in this category. However, as noted above, Eriksen and Madsen (1984) have argued that the settlement debris is contemporary with a palisade, so there would here still be some form of enclosure operating at the time of the supposed settlement. Moreover, Andersen (1997, 333) notes that the pottery assemblage contains an unusually high number of decorated ceramic bowls and a relative lack of beakers, so we may be dealing here with selective deposition of certain classes of material.

Other large middle Neolithic sites including Blandebjerg, also on Langeland, Trelleborg, Sigersted, Markildegård, and Bundsø appear to have succeeded enclosures, but have been less intensively investigated. Once again, Sarup provides the best evidence for a site of this type. Around 3150 BC (MN A II) the Sarup III settlement developed on the site of Sarup II, but covered a larger area *c.* 4ha (Andersen 1997, 101–115). The occupation consisted of pits, postholes (some possibly forming structures) and culture layers in the ditches of both the earlier enclosures. The material from this phase closely resembles that from other settlements, with cattle now over half of the animal bone assemblage, a standard ratio of flint tools to waste and no evidence of special deposits in the ditch fills. However, the old enclosure ditches were recut, sometimes several times, and there was a dramatic variation in the volume of material, with partial excavation of segments producing between a single and 5083 objects. It may therefore be that the entire deposit in some ditches was placed there in one operation, either relating to a belief in the fertilizing quality of the waste (perhaps sometimes brought from contemporary settlements elsewhere) or to its having become spiritually polluted (Andersen 1997, 302). An alternative, given the low numbers of finds from the relatively rare contemporary settlements, even those preserved below barrow mounds, and that Sarup was the only large site in the area at the time, is that the removal and subsequent deposition of material may have a political meaning relating to the centralization of authority.

It is also clear, however, that offering pits continued to be dug in this phase and filled with pots, axes of flint and stone, flint chisels and blades, and animal bones. As with the material in the ditches, the pottery for deposition does not appear to be carefully chosen vessels of specific form, even though great care was seemingly taken in its deposition. Perhaps ritual acts of offering and disposal were carried out at Sarup on behalf of a wider community. Sarup III is certainly not confined, as Hodder once argued (1988, 71), to "practical activity".

Sarup IV (around 3000 BC MN A III/IV) continues along the same lines, covering a similar area (Andersen 1997, 118–124). Obvious ritual deposits are few in number, only two pits containing pottery, yet recutting of the Sarup I and II ditches also occurred in this phase. The volume of finds and the number of pits and postholes is far smaller than from Sarup III, although the character of the material is similar. Either the duration of activity was shorter, or the nature of activity on the site became less intense, perhaps deriving from occasional visits to this powerful place, although it did cover the same area. Settlements of this phase from the Sarup area appear to be far smaller, and are possibly specialized sites.

This suggested tendency towards occasional activity is clearer in Sarup V (around 2850 BC), interpreted as a seasonal or short term site related to hunting or pastoralism (Andersen 1997, 126–128). Pits, postholes, and culture layers are rare, with the old enclosure ditches probably not being recut and only a single offering pit containing an axe. By this time Sarup was also no longer the largest site in the area.

Other settlements succeeding enclosures, including Blandebjerg, had offering pits, while Bundsø, in the MN A III phase, produced a series of human skulls, some apparently reused as cups (Andersen 1997, 126). Unfortunately, the lack of recent work on these sites as a whole means that it is not yet possible to say how significant the occupation of earlier enclosed spaces may have been, and how far this group of sites differs from other dense and substantial groups of finds. They are certainly not the only substantial middle Neolithic sites, and indeed, two exist on Langeland at Klintebakke and Spodsbjerg in addition to the Troldebjerg and Blandebjerg sites which succeeded enclosures.

The character of these large sites as a group is not really established, as Whittle has noted (1996, 230), allowing him to argue that they may be more like points of aggregation than central settlements. At least at Sarup, however, it seems clear that we are dealing with permanent settlement. That this is probably a more general development is suggested by the evidence of microwear analysis on flint sickles (Jensen 1994, 156–159). This suggests that a considerable degree of agricultural intensification occurred at this time, at least in cereal production, further suggesting increasing permanency of fields which is matched by a greater longevity for settlements (Davidsen 1978, 160).

Given a greater investment in fields, increased longevity of settlements and a vastly increased variation in site size, the importance of occupying places in the landscape of high perceived value must have been a factor in site location. The sites of previous enclosures presumably retained a considerable ritual significance, rendering them peculiarly powerful places in the landscape, ideal for reuse as major middle Neolithic settlements.

ACKNOWLEDGEMENTS

I wish to thank those Danish colleagues who have generously shared their knowledge of Scandinavian archaeology over many years, in particular my friends at Moesgård and in the Thy Archaeological Project. I also wish to thank Philip Marter for, as ever, producing the desired illustrations at short notice.

BIBLIOGRAPHY

Andersen, N H, 1982, A Neolithic causewayed camp at Trelleborg near Slagelse, West Zealand. *Journal of Danish Archaeology*, 1, 31–33

Andersen, N H, 1988a, The Neolithic causewayed enclosures at Sarup, on southwest Funen, Denmark. In C Burgess, P Topping, C Mordant and M Maddison (eds), *Enclosures and defences in the Neolithic of western Europe* (= British Archaeological Reports International Series 403). Oxford. British Archaeological Reports. 337–363

Andersen, N H, 1988b, Sarup: two Neolithic enclosures in southwest Funen. *Journal of Danish Archaeology*, 7, 93–144

Andersen, N H, 1988c, *Sarup. Befæstede kultpladser fra bondestenalderen*, Århus. Jysk Arkæologisk Selskab

Andersen, N H, 1993, Causewayed camps of the Funnel Beaker Culture. In S Hvass and B Storgaard (eds), *Digging into the past*. Århus. Jutland Archaeological Society. 100–103

Andersen, N H, 1997, *Sarup volume 1. The Sarup enclosures*. Århus. Jutland Archaeological Society

Birkedahl, P, 1994, Stenaldertræf på Lokes Hede. In *5000 år under Motorvejen*. København. Vejdirektorat og Rigsantikvarens Arkæologiske Sekretariat

Davidsen, K, 1978, *The final TRB culture in Denmark*. København. Arkæologiske Studier

Eriksen, P, and Madsen, T, 1984, Hanstedgård. A settlement site from the Funnel Beaker Culture. *Journal of Danish Archaeology*, 3, 63–82

Evans, C, 1988, Acts of enclosure: a consideration of concentrically – organised causewayed enclosures. In C Burgess, P Topping, C Mordant and M Maddison (eds), *Enclosures and defences in the Neolithic of western Europe* (= British Archaeological Reports International Series 403). Oxford. British Archaeological Reports. 85–96

Hingst, H, 1970, Eine jungsteinzeitliche Siedlung in Büdelsdorf. *Heimatkundliches Jahrbuch für den Kreis Rendsburg*, 20, 55–69

Hodder, I, 1988, Material culture texts and social change: a theoretical discussion and some archaeological examples. *Proceedings of the Prehistoric Society*, 54, 67–75

Jensen, H J, 1994, *Flint tools and plant working: hidden traces of stone age technology*. Århus. Aarhus University Press

Jørgensen, G, 1976, Et kornfund fra Sarup. Bidrag til belysning af tragtbægerkulturens agerbrug. *Kuml*, 47–64

Klassen, L, 1997, Die Kupferfunde der Nordgruppe der Trichterbecherkultur. *Archäologische Informationen*, 20/1, 189–193

Koch, E, 1998, *Neolithic bog pots from Zealand, Møn, Lolland and Falster*. Copenhagen. Det Kongelige Nordiske Oldskrtiftselskab

Larsen, K, 1957, Stenalderhuse på Knardrup Galgebakke. *Kuml*, 24–43

Madsen, B, and Fiedel, R, 1987, Pottery manufacture at a Neolithic causewayed enclosure near Hevringholm, East Jutland. *Journal of Danish Archaeology*, 6, 78–86

Madsen, T, 1977, Toftum ved Horsens. Et "befæstet" anlæg tilhørende tragtbægerkulture. *Kuml*, 161–184

Madsen, T, 1988, Causewayed enclosures in south Scandinavia. In C Burgess, P Topping, C Mordant and M Maddison (eds), *Enclosures and defences in the Neolithic of western Europe* (= British Archaeological Reports International Series 403). Oxford. British Archaeological Reports. 301–336

Midgley, M, 1992, *TRB Culture*. Edinburgh. Edinburgh University Press

Nielsen, P O, 1996, Neolithic. *Arkæologiske udgravninger i Danmark*, 96–100

Nielsen, P O, 1997, Neolithic. *Arkæologiske udgravninger i Danmark*, 72–76

Skaarup, J, 1985, *Yngre Stenalder på øerne syd for Fyn*. Rudkøbing. Meddelelser fra Langelands Museum

Skaarup, J, 1990, Burials, votive offerings and social structure in early Neolithic farmer society of Denmark. In D Jankowska (ed), *Die Trichterbecherkultur: Neue Forschungen und Hypothesen*. Poznán. Institut Prahistorii Uniwersyteta im. Adam Mickiewicza. 73–91

Sylvest, B, and Sylvest, I, 1960, Arupgårdfundet. En oskenkrukke indenholdene kobbersmykker og ravperler. *Kuml*, 9–25

Thorpe, I J, 1984, Ritual, power and ideology: a reconstruction of earlier Neolithic rituals in Wessex. In R Bradley and J Gardiner (eds), *Neolithic studies: a review of some current research* (= British Archaeological Reports British Series 133). Oxford. British Archaeological Reports. 41–60

Thorpe, I J, 1996, *The origins of agriculture in Europe*. London. Routledge

Thrane, H, 1989, Danish plough-marks from the Neolithic and Bronze Age. *Journal of Danish Archaeology*, 8, 111–125

Westphal, J, 1996, Liselund. *Arkæologiske udgravninger i Danmark*, 169

Whittle, A, 1996, *Europe in the Neolithic. The creation of new worlds*. Cambridge. Cambridge University Press

Winther, J, 1935, *Troldebjerg, en bymæssig bebyggelse fra Danmarks yngre stenalder*. Rudkøbing. Meddelelser fra Langelands Museum

Winther, J, 1938, *Troldebjerg. En bymæssig Bebyggelse fra Danmarks Yngre Stenalder. Tillæg.* Rudkøbing. Meddelelser fra Langelands Museum